The Ffestiniog Railway Paintings of Edward Pag

Philip J. Hawkins

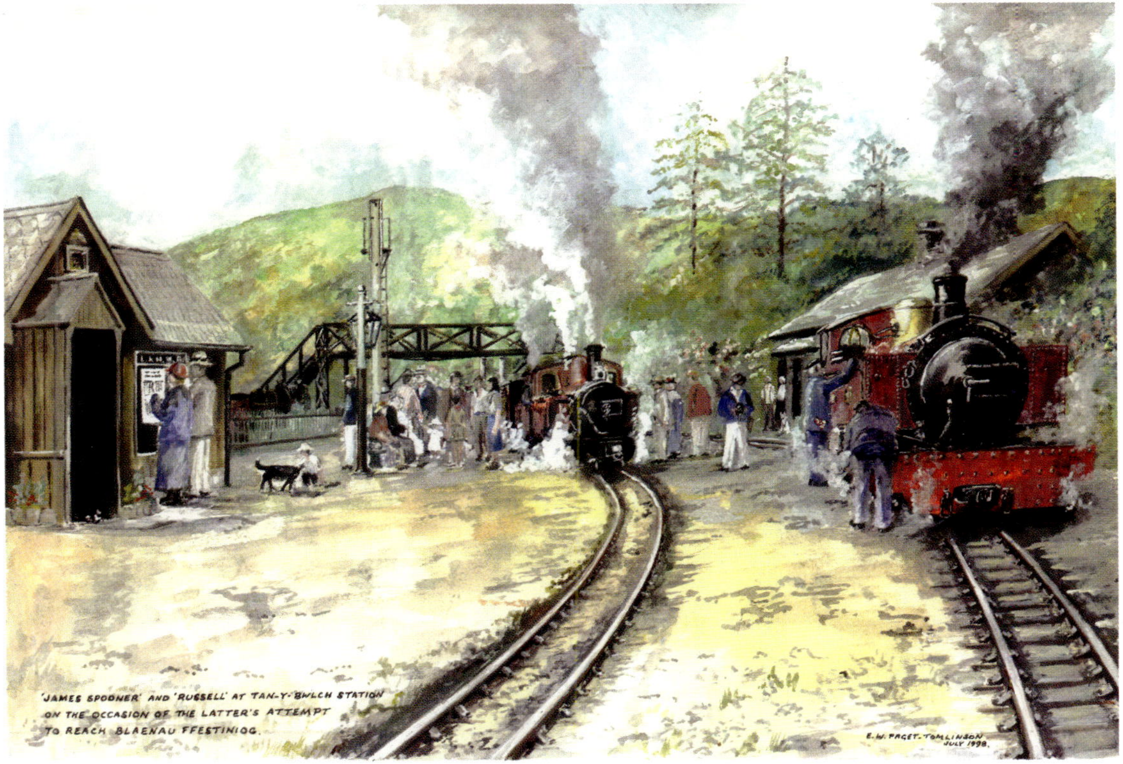

Published by

LANDMARK
Publishing Ltd

Ashbourne Hall, Cokayne Ave, Ashbourne, Derbyshire, DE6 1EJ England
Tel: (01335) 347349 Fax: (01335) 347303
e-mail: landmark@clara.net

1st Edition

13 ISBN: 978-1-84306-334-6

British Library Cataloguing in Publication Data: a catalogue record for this book is available from the British Library.

Print: Gutenberg Press Ltd, Malta

Design by: Michelle Hunt

Front Cover: Little Giant in the Woodyard Sidings, Portmadoc in 1890

Back cover Main: Boston Lodge Works in 1925

Back cover Top: Up Quarrymen's Train near Tanygrisiau in 1891 **Left: Back cover Bottom Left:** Prince at Quarry Lane Crossing in 1910

Page 1: James Spooner and Russell at Tan-y-Bwlch

The Ffestiniog Railway Paintings of Edward Paget-Tomlinson

Philip J. Hawkins

"Criticism is gladly accepted, for truth emerges from close examination"

Edward Paget-Tomlinson

Landmark Publishing

Foreword

At the time of Edward's first contact with Philip Hawkins, he had been looking for a change from the rather formal merchant shipping portraits and factual depiction of canal boat liveries that formed a large part of his output. Cooperation with the Ffestiniog Railway enabled him to do the sort of historical research into our industrial past that he enjoyed so much.

Railways were always a part of his leisure activities. On holiday in this country he would always seek out the preserved railway wherever we were. The Ravenglass and Eskdale near to his childhood home was a particular favourite. On holiday in Europe we always travelled by train and the children were used to their father spending hours on railway stations photographing locomotives. He approached the history and landscape of the Ffestiniog with great enthusiasm. The enjoyment of the historical scenes he researched was always heightened by the challenge of finding a place for his sheepdog Paddy somewhere in the picture.

Edward was very proud that money from the sale of his prints had helped to pay for the replica platform shelter at Minffordd Station. He got enormous pleasure out of the open days, chatting to fellow enthusiasts and staying with Philip and Sue (where you could look out of the window and watch the trains passing). There is no doubt that he would have been very pleased indeed that this tribute to him has stemmed from his involvement in the Ffestiniog Railway.

Pam Paget-Tomlinson

About The Author

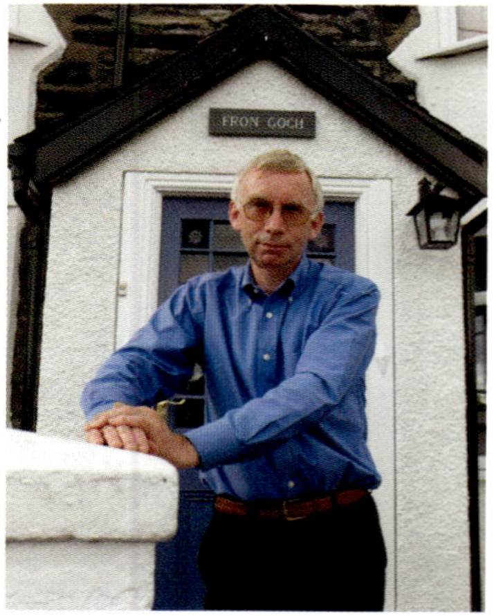

Philip Hawkins has been an active supporter of the Ffestiniog Railway for nearly 50 years, mainly volunteering on the Permanent Way and also serving as Chairman of the Ffestiniog Railway Society for four years from 2002 to 2006. A Librarian by profession, he worked and lived mainly in London, but after early retirement moved to a house beside the Ffestiniog Railway in Penrhyndeudraeth. He is committed to the Welsh community and sits as a Justice of the Peace on the Gwynedd Bench.

Contents

Foreword by Pam Paget-Tomlinson 04

Introduction 06

The Life and Work of Edward Paget-Tomlinson. 10

A Brief History of the Festiniog Railway – Adrian Gray. 15

Railway map 26

The Heritage Paintings Project 28

The Paintings 33

Pen and Ink Drawings. 108

Epilogue. 127

Introduction

This book is a tribute to a remarkable man. Edward Paget-Tomlinson possessed talents, skills and qualities that were individually praiseworthy, but in combination produced an artist and gentleman of the highest order. Thus in compiling this book and describing Edward's work for the Ffestiniog Railway over the period from early 1997 until his untimely death in November 2003, the artist and his unique qualities are ever present.

The Heritage Paintings Project came about by chance, but quickly led to a close friendship between Edward and myself. This in itself is a precious memory, but the fact that his Ffestiniog paintings have given pleasure to so many, whilst also financially assisting heritage work on the Railway, is what surely mattered most to Edward.

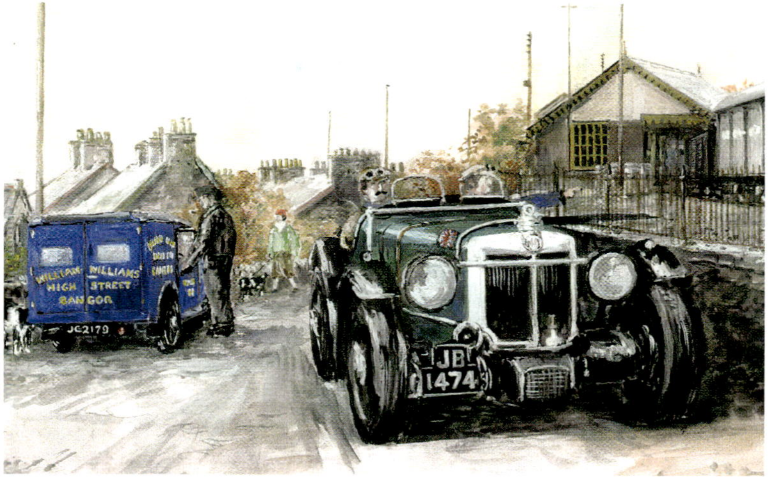

When, late in 1996, I came across a collection of paintings by Edward in a bookshop in the Forest of Dean, I little knew the impact it would have not only on myself, but also on the artist. From the chance purchase of one of those paintings grew the Ffestiniog Railway Heritage Paintings Project, which produced the 37 paintings and 18 pen and ink drawings contained in this book. That this total over a six-year period was just one small part of Edward's output is evidence of an artist with quite remarkable talent and capacity. As many reading this book will know, Edward Paget-Tomlinson already had a long-established and impressive reputation in the field of canals and maritime art.

Despite his love of canals and inland waterways, Edward was also a railway enthusiast, but apart from his book on The Montreaux-Oberland Bernois Railway, he had not delved deeply into the subject with his painting.

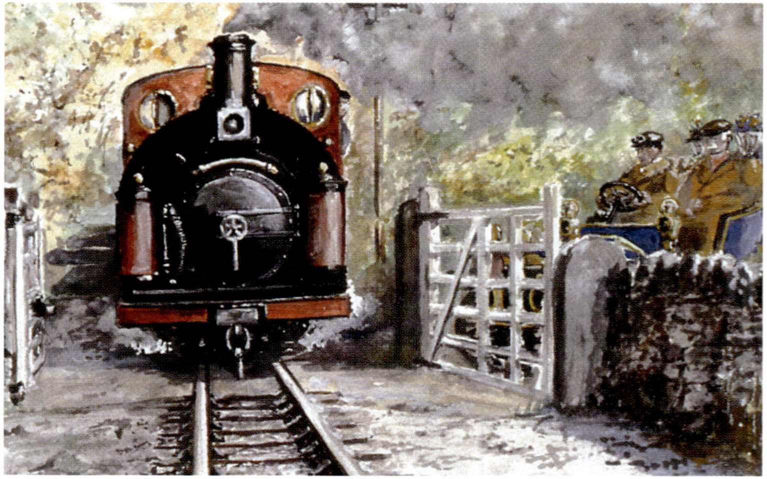

His work with the Ffestiniog Railway opened the door to an entirely new field. Thus in this book is found a quite separate manifestation of Edward's talent as an artist to that for which he is best known. It was Edward's intention that the paintings for this project should show the working railway, rather than just being portraits of trains.

Edward was always modest about his work and more than willing to accept criticism with good humour. In studying these paintings and drawings, those who know the railways well will perhaps pick up on the accuracy of details. There are points in several paintings that can be the subject of lively debate, but in nearly every case if there is fault, it is the author's as researcher rather than the artist's.

The Ffestiniog Railway is a remarkable organisation, continuing the operation after 175 years of a unique and deeply historic railway. It has always been a busy railway and even in its present form it has a sense of purpose, direction and innovation not always found on heritage railways, where simple preservation is more often the priority. It now operates virtually a year-round service, with a paid staff of over 60 and hundreds of dedicated volunteers and is, as it always has been, a vital part of the economy and commercial life of this part of Snowdonia. Since being saved from dereliction in the 1950s, the Ffestiniog has attracted a band of supporters who share a love of the railway and it has touched many lives. This is well demonstrated by the comments of those who commissioned paintings. It was also something that Edward recognised and respected, and it was the reason he devoted so much time and effort to the project, with the purpose not only of producing historic images of the Ffestiniog Railway, but also to raise funds for heritage work.

The output from Edward's studio was always remarkable and the Ffestiniog paintings took their turn with many other transport paintings and drawings, together with his work as a writer. Indeed, Edward had

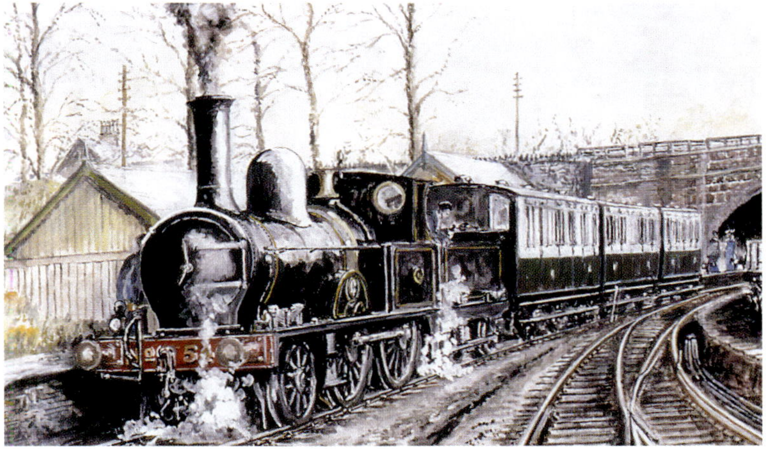

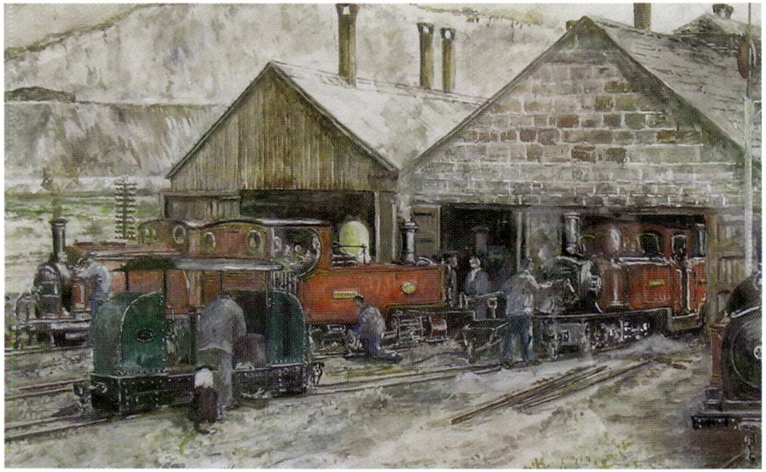

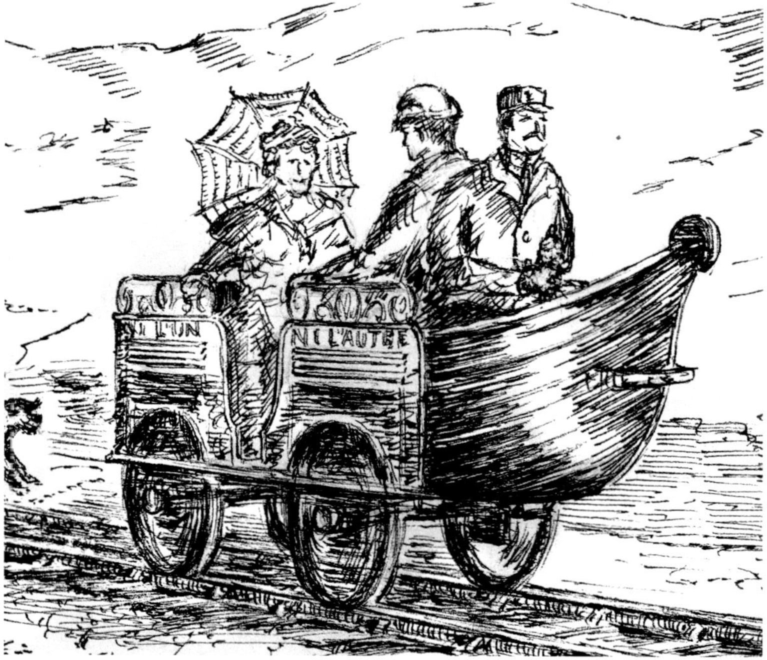

intended to write a book at the end of the project on the Ffestiniog Railway's history, illustrated with his own paintings and sketches. As the author of numerous books and magazine articles on canals, waterways and transport subjects, he knew just what he intended. Sadly this was not to be and at the time of Edward's untimely death in November 2003, as the project was drawing to its planned conclusion, the idea was still only at the concept stage. This volume thus fulfils Edward's wish, albeit in a somewhat different form.

Welsh and English Place Names

Place names used in this book are those in current use and in only two cases is any explanation necessary. The first is the occasional use of a single "F" in Ffestiniog. The Festiniog Railway Company's Act of Parliament dating from 1832 used the single letter and it is thus retained when referring to the Company itself. Similarly, the Festiniog Railway Trust and Festiniog Railway Heritage Group use the historic single "F". However, at all other times the Ffestiniog Railway is referred to with a double "Ff", as expected in an area where Welsh is emphatically the first language.

The other case is Portmadoc/Porthmadog. From its inception as a town in the early 1800s it was known as Portmadoc and only became Porthmadog in the 1970s at a time when many anglicised names reverted to Welsh spelling. The convention adopted by Edward in the titles of paintings was to use the Portmadoc version, since this was historically correct. Thus in the text of the book, both English and Welsh versions will be found, depending on the historical context.

The Role of the Societies

The Ffestiniog Railway is operated by The Festiniog Railway Company, established by Act of Parliament on 23 May 1832 and now the world's oldest independent railway. The Festiniog Railway Trust holds a majority shareholding in the company and has overall responsibility for policy and operational matters.

The Ffestiniog Railway Society plays an active role in the operation of the Railway in many ways and assists with fundraising and volunteering.

For further information contact:

The Ffestiniog Railway Society, Harbour Station, Porthmadog,

Gwynedd, LL49 9NF

Email – secretary@ffestiniograilway.org.uk

Website –www.ffestiniograilway.org.uk

At the time of writing, the Ffestiniog Railway Company is rebuilding the Welsh Highland Railway and estimates that in 2009 it will once more connect with the Ffestiniog Railway at Porthmadog Harbour Station. The section from Caernarfon to Rhyd Ddu is already open.

For further information contact:

Cymdeithas Rheillffordd Eryri, Ffridd Isaf, Rhyd Ddu, Caernarfon, Gwynedd, LL54 6TN

Email – whrs.member@virgin.net

Website –www.bangor.ac.uk/ml/whr/whrsoc

For information about train services contact:

Ffestiniog & Welsh Highland Railways, Harbour Station, Porthmadog, Gwynedd, LL49 9NF

Phone – 01766 516000

Email – enquiries@festrail.co.uk

Website – www.festrail.co.uk

Acknowledgements

Thanks go to all those who purchased both original paintings and framed copies, who in doing so made the Project the pleasure and success it has been in raising funds for the Ffestiniog Railway.

I would also like to give special thanks to:

Paul Davies for editing and proofreading my drafts.

Adrian Gray for writing the chapter on the history of the Railway.

John Alexander for assistance with maritime information.

John Dobson and Stuart Baker for assisting in copying original paintings for reproduction in the book.

Patricia and Geoffrey Layzell Ward for their advice and support.

Sue Davis for ensuring that I had the time and space to write the book in the midst of our busy lives in the Vale of Ffestiniog.

P.J.H.

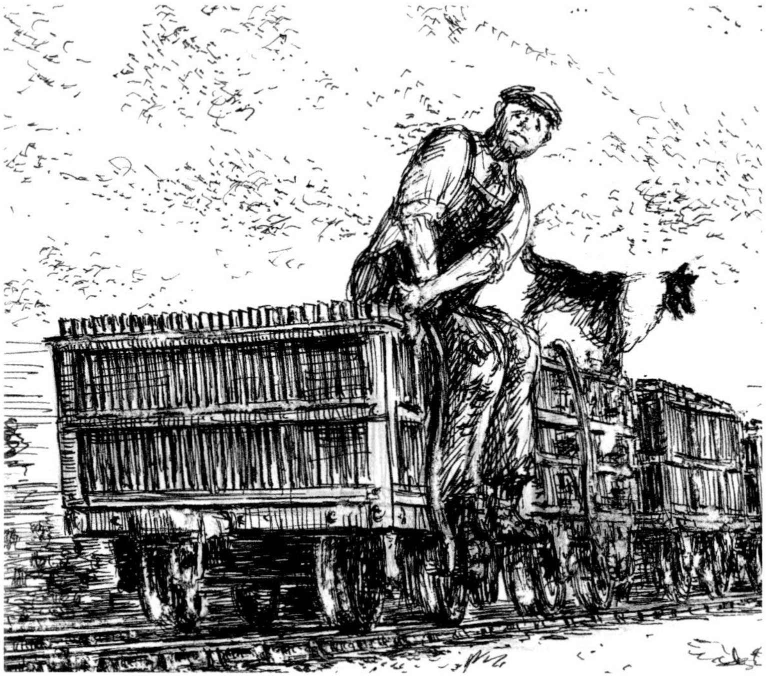

The Life and Work of Edward Paget-Tomlinson

Edward Paget-Tomlinson was born in London in 1932. His father was a doctor and his mother was a member of the Wordie family, carters and railway carriers in Scotland. Edward's family moved from London to Lincolnshire, then Yorkshire and eventually to Ulverston, in Cumbria.

Edward began drawing and painting from the age of eight on a range of subjects from fighter aircraft to boats, but by his own admission trains were his paramount interest at first. However, during journeys between home in Ulverston and boarding school in Sherborne, Dorset between 1941 and 1945 Edward had his first sight of working boats on various canals passed by the railway. He also read L.T.C. Rolt's book Narrow Boat in 1944 and became fascinated by canals and inland waterways.

Edward left Sherborne School in 1950 and did his National Service in the Royal Artillery, recalling much later that this included troop and equipment trains to the gunnery ranges near Trawsfynydd, not far from the Ffestiniog Railway, by then closed and derelict. After National Service, Edward went to Trinity Hall, Cambridge, reading history. Throughout this time his knowledge of transport and industrial history widened, but with canals, waterways and maritime subjects predominant. Such was his interest that after graduating he worked at the National Maritime Museum at Greenwich as a museum apprentice, and then moved to the Liverpool City Museum as a temporary assistant looking after the shipping collection. Edward remained there for twelve years, eventually becoming Keeper of Shipping. Here he met and married Pam, who worked at the museum with the ceramics and fine furniture collections. They have a son, John, and a daughter, Lucy.

At Liverpool, Edward also had responsibility for other forms of transport and was instrumental in securing early locomotive drawings from the Vulcan Foundry, Newton-le-Willows, including those for the Ffestiniog and North Wales Narrow Gauge Single Fairlies. He also built up the Museum's collection

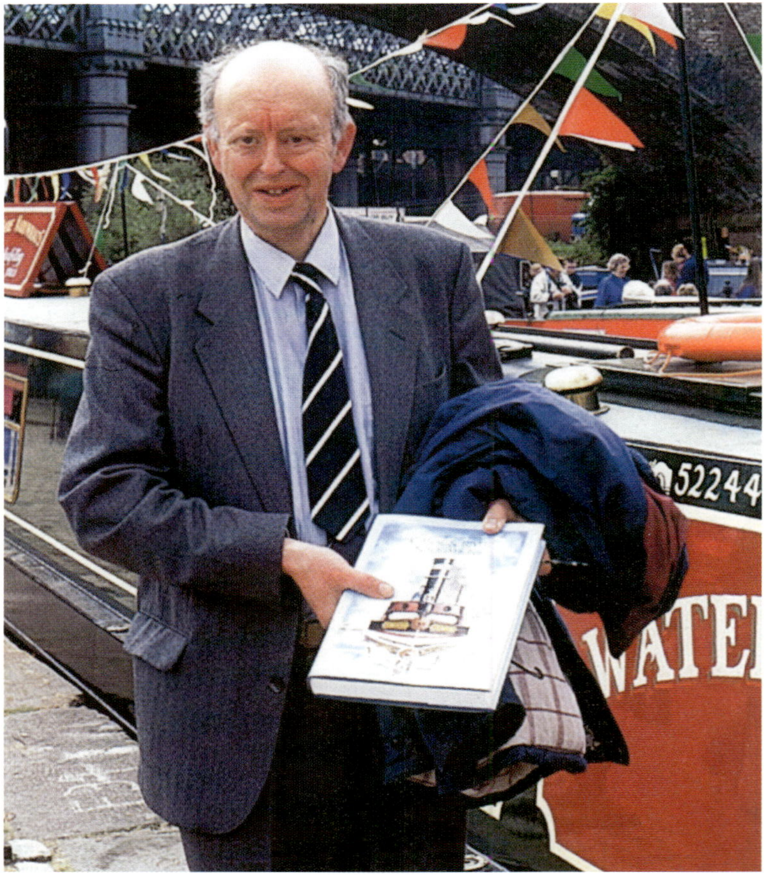

Edward Paget-Tomlinson. Photo: Waterways World

of road vehicles and was instrumental in preserving a 12-ton Burrell Road Locomotive from Robert Bridson & Son of Neston on the Wirral. The Burrell was kept in working order and was rallied by Edward and a friend for a number of years. Later, after his departure from Liverpool, the engine was dismantled for boiler work and remained in bits in the museum store for a number of years. Edward maintained a distant watch on his former charge and was indirectly responsible for an approach to the Ffestiniog Railway many years later, which led to Boston Lodge Works being commissioned to return the engine to full working order, including a high-quality repaint, completed in 2005.

During his time at Liverpool, Edward became increasingly involved in the world of canal and river transport. In 1969 he left the Museum to concentrate on researching and writing a comprehensive encyclopaedia of the inland waterways of the United Kingdom. The Complete Book of Canal and River Navigations was finally published in 1978. An enlarged and improved second edition appeared in 1993, retitled the Illustrated History of Canal and River Navigations, which has become the "bible" for all those working in this field. After a long time out of print, the book was reissued in 2006 by Landmark Publishing.

Whilst writing this book, Edward became a leading member of a group wanting to start a Boat Museum. He also acquired an old Thos. Clayton tar boat, Gifford, which eventually became one of the first boats at the Ellesmere Port Boat Museum in 1976, the culmination of the group's planning and effort. Edward also became a regular contributor to Waterways World magazine, particularly

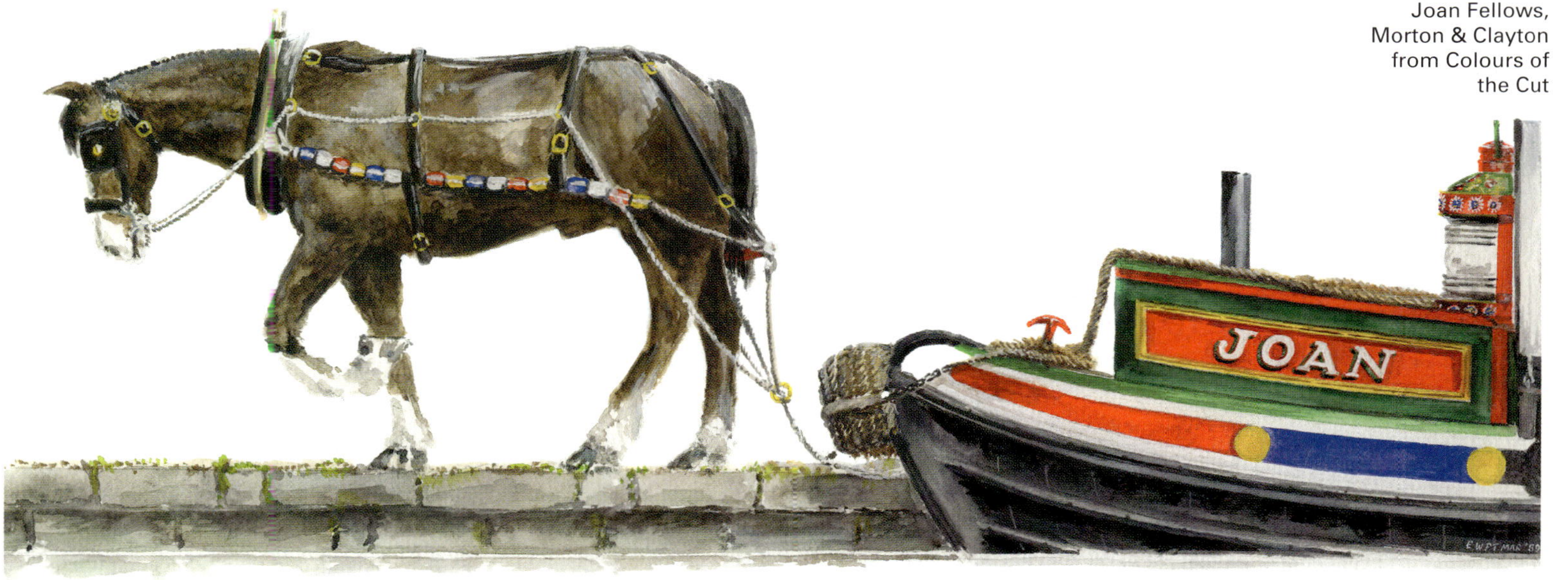

Joan Fellows, Morton & Clayton from Colours of the Cut

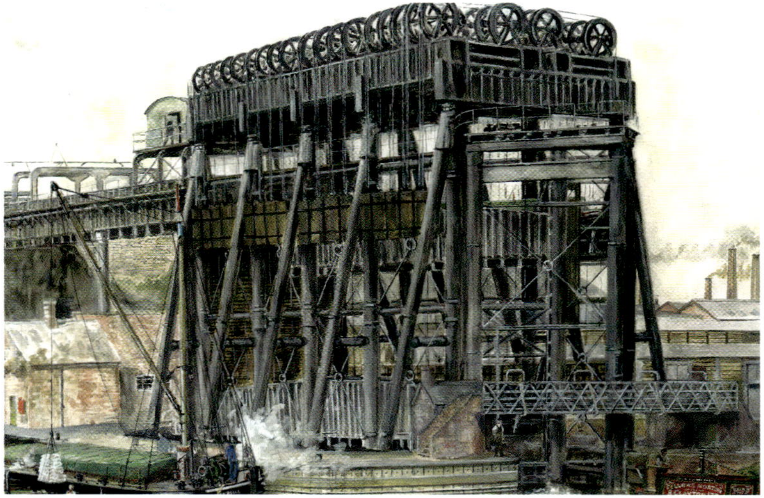

Edward's painting of the Anderton Lift, Cheshire

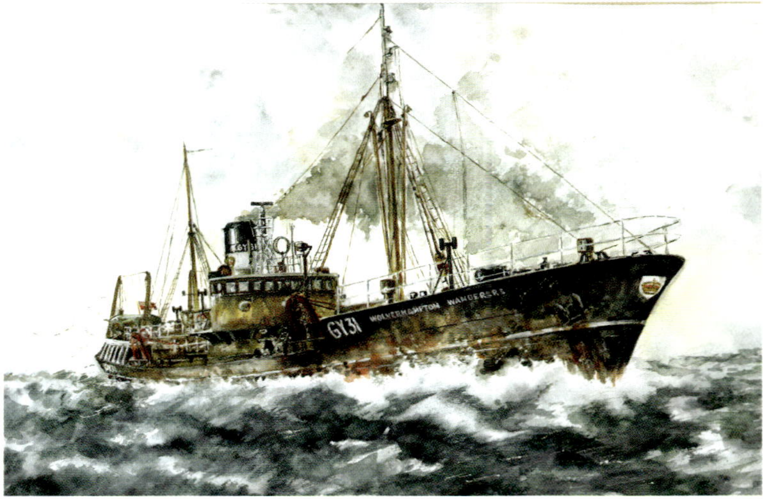

Edward's painting of a trawler

with his renowned series "Colours of the Cut". There followed a similar series, "Shipping Company Colours", for Ships Monthly. Landmark Publishing has recently issued collections of both series in book form.

From 1975 to 1978 Edward was Keeper and then Consultant at Hull Museum, with responsibility for the marine collection and the establishment of the Maritime Museum in the former dock office. During these years Edward was a weekly commuter to Hull from Ulverston, but he left Hull in 1978 after successfully opening the new museum.

A change of career then found Edward running a second-hand bookshop in Ulverston, which he described later as socially but not commercially successful. However, he further developed his artistic skills, working on paintings in the shop.

Following a move to Dorset and finally Somerset his hobby as a transport artist and writer became more and more a full-time job He concentrated mainly on marine and waterways subjects, but horses, traction engines, motor lorries and railways all emerged from his studio at Easton, near Wells. Several more books followed, including one on The Montreux-Oberland Bernois Railway, which he wrote and illustrated. His output was prodigious, and the 37 paintings and 18 pen and ink drawings for the Ffestiniog Railway in a period of five years were matched by literally hundreds of illustrations and paintings on other subjects produced in these productive years in Somerset. Edward also started selling his paintings through three shops, Books Afloat in Weymouth, another in Douglas on the Isle of Man and The Archive Bookshop at Lydney in the Forest of Dean. It was at the latter that the Ffestiniog connection started.

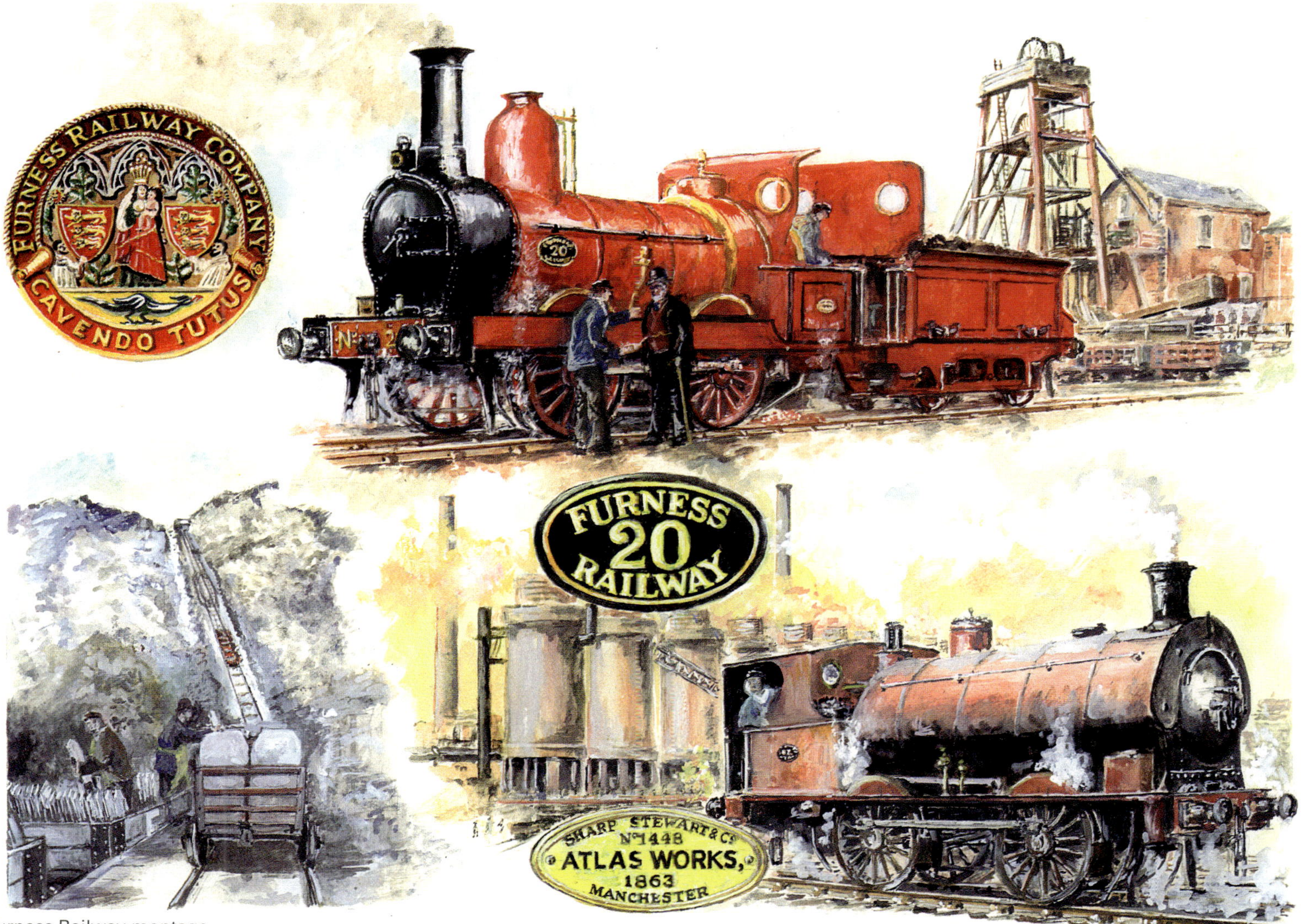

Furness Railway montage

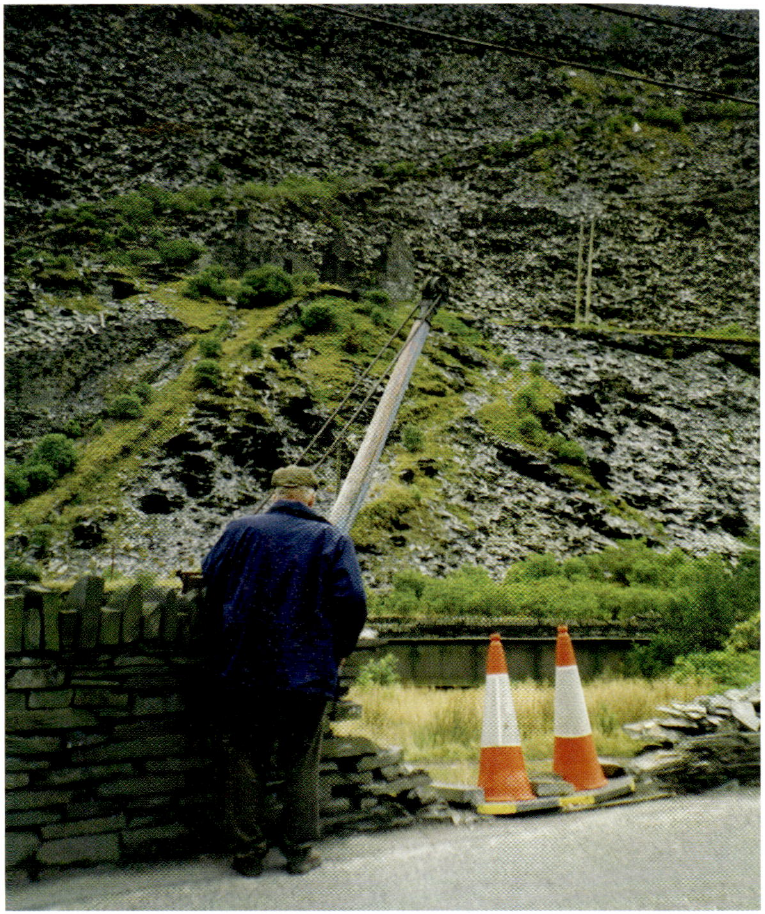

Edward in Blaenau Ffestiniog inspecting location for painting 34

Edward died in November 2003 at the age of 71 following an operation, working at undiminished rate to the last and completing a Ffestiniog pen and ink drawing shortly before going into hospital.

Such was the breadth of Edward's interests and talent that there are several quite separate and distinct strands to his work. These include the side views of canal boats and merchant vessels, paintings of canals and inland waterways, road vehicle and railway scenes, book illustrations and illustrated maps, in addition to extensive writing. Edward's work with the Ffestiniog Railway was, therefore, just one facet of a quite remarkable talent, always enriched by a combination of modesty, charm and patience. It was aptly described in one of numerous obituaries in the canal and inland waterways world: "He was a generous and unassuming man, like many who just happen to be the very best in their field."

Books by Edward Paget-Tomlinson

History of the Bibby Line, 1969, Bibby Line Ltd, Liverpool

Bibby Line 175 Years of Achievement, 1982, Bibby Line Ltd, Liverpool

Canal and River Navigations, 1978, Waine Research Publications

Britain's Canal and River Craft, 1979, Moorland Publishing; revised edition 2005, Landmark Publishing

The Montreux-Oberland Bernois Railway, 1985, MOB Chemin de fer, Montreux

The Railway Carriers, 1990, Terence Dalton & The Wordie Property Company

The Illustrated History of Canal & River Navigations, 1993, Sheffield Academic Press; reprinted 2006 by Landmark Publishing

Waterways in the Making, 1996, The Landscape Press

Colours of the Cut, 2004, Landmark Publishing

Shipping Company Colours, 2006, Landmark Publishing

A Brief History of the Festiniog Railway

Adrian Gray, Hon. Archivist, FR Company

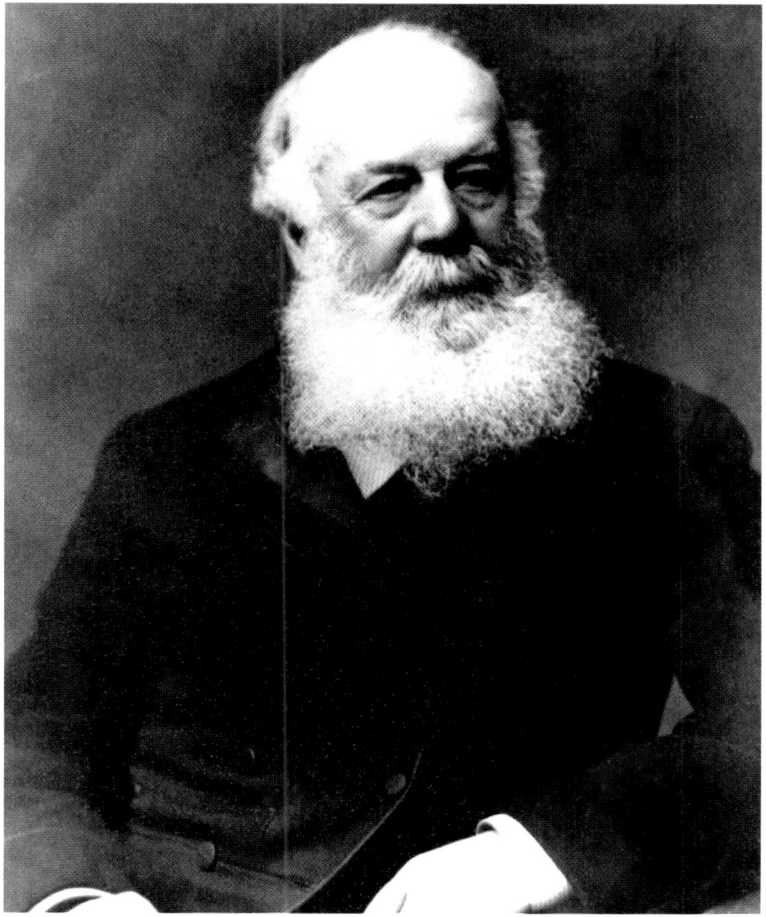

The story of the Festiniog Railway begins in the reign of King William IV, rises to a bright zenith as Victoria's reign matures and enjoys a comfortable prosperity during the Edwardian period. This is shattered, along with so much else, by the effects of the Great War, after which begins a steady decline, culminating in closure immediately after the second world conflict.

Fortunately the legacy of the Victorian fame and prosperity, together with memories of the railway in the period between the wars, ensured that the railway retained sufficient allure to provoke interest in its preservation after World War II. The venture succeeded and the FR flourishes today as one of Britain's premier heritage railways and having regained some of its former reputation for excellence and innovation.

Let us return to the beginning and the latter part of the eighteenth century. Good quality slate had already been discovered in the hills to the north-west of the village of Ffestiniog, near the headwaters of the Afon Dwyryd, by the time W.A. Madocks, an inveterate 'improver' and MP for Boston, in Lincolnshire, bought an estate on the western shore of the Traeth Mawr, the tidal estuary of the Afon Glaslyn, with the aim of improving its poor agricultural ground. By building an embankment Madocks was able to exclude the tidal waters from an area of salt marsh on the edge of the estuary and reclaim it for rough grazing.

Encouraged by this modest success, Madocks conceived his grand plan, to build an embankment, a dam, across the mouth of the Traeth Mawr to exclude the sea so the land could be reclaimed for improvement. The scheme began in 1807 and the Cob, as the embankment became known,

Charles Easton Spooner, 1818-1889, Engineer & Secretary to the FR Co., whose energy drove through the introduction of steam locomotives and the successful transformation of the Festiniog Railway from a mineral tramway to a public railway during the mid-19th century

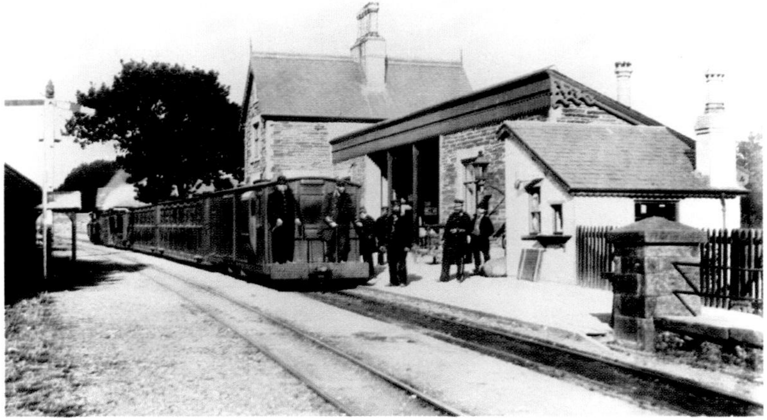

An Up train at Minffordd in 1887. The inspiration for one of the paintings is clear

was finally completed in 1811. At its western end sluice gates allowed the Afon Glaslyn to flow out and this scoured a channel that enabled the establishment of a harbour, authorised by an Act of Parliament in 1821, deep enough for ocean-going vessels. Inevitably this, and the town that grew up around it, became known as Port Madock (later Portmadoc and now Porthmadog).

During the same period the slate quarries and mines at Blaenau Ffestiniog were being developed, with their products being sent ever further afield once a punitive duty on sea-borne carriage of slate had been repealed. Overland transport was impractical, so the route from the quarries involved pack animals or carts, over rough tracks, to the shores of the tidal Dwyryd and thence by small flat-bottomed boats to ocean-going ships lying at an unsheltered anchorage in the mouth of the combined estuaries of the Dwyryd and Glaslyn. The vagaries of weather and tides made this an unsatisfactory and sometimes dangerous arrangement. The harbour at Portmadoc was a welcome improvement for the final transhipment, but the earlier stages of the journey for finished slates were still slow and expensive.

Madocks had aspired to a "railroad" to connect the quarries with his harbour since 1820 but the building of the Cob had bankrupted him. Several schemes were proposed but it was not until 1829, when quarry proprietor Samuel Holland fell in with a young Dubliner, Henry Archer, that the prospect of a railway became a reality. Archer was looking for a scheme to invest in and Holland persuaded him of the benefits of a railroad to carry slates from his, and other, quarries to the harbour at Portmadoc. Archer pursued the idea energetically, raising the money required in Dublin, starting the process to obtain the Act of Parliament required for the powers to build a railway and engaging James Spooner, a surveyor trained by the Ordnance Survey, to plan a route for the proposed line.

The gauge chosen was "two feet", the same as already in use in the quarries, and from the outset it was planned to exploit the 700ft difference in altitude between the quarries at Ffestiniog and the harbour at Portmadoc so that loaded trucks would run down under gravity. The narrow gauge allowed Spooner to plan a sinuous course, following the contours along the valley of the Dwyryd and falling at a steady rate along its thirteen-mile route.

The Festiniog Railway Company received its Act of Parliament in May 1832 and construction started in early 1833 with Archer as Managing Director, Spooner as Engineer and a contractor engaged to do the work. As so often happened the early estimates did not match the actual costs and, in the end, the contractor was dismissed and work was completed under Spooner's direction. The line opened in 1836, but not quite as Spooner had planned it. To maintain the gradient through a shoulder of Moelwyn Bach, Spooner had planned a tunnel, but to save money the line was opened with a pair of inclines to carry the line over the obstruction. Archer approved of these but Spooner did not, recognising that they would be expensive to work and a bottleneck as traffic developed; he pressed for the tunnel to be built. The Board supported Spooner, Archer resigned, and Spooner became Manager. The tunnel was opened in 1842 and, following initial resistance from some quarry proprietors, the Festiniog Railway began to prosper. Loaded wagons rolled effortlessly down to the harbour under gravity and were returned empty up the line in trains of about a dozen at a time, by horses.

For the next twenty years James Spooner, assisted by his sons, who had trained as civil or mechanical engineers, pursued a policy of steady improvements in all aspects of the railway. The rather cheaply built formation was improved by strengthening embankments and easing curves and the early forms of permanent way were upgraded, cast iron giving way to wrought iron and later to rolled rails, in line with contemporary practice elsewhere.

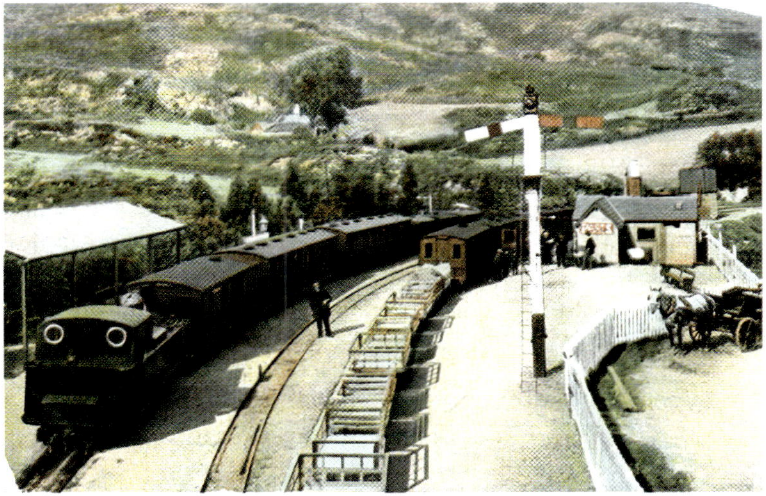

Single Fairlie Taliesin brings a train for Portmadoc into Tan-y-Bwlch about 1890. The Up train is typical 'tail' of empty slate wagons behind the carriages. The wooden building, on the right, is the original station of 1873 and is still standing today

James Spooner was an astute manager; it was his decision that the railway should provide the quarries with the wagons required to send their traffic over the line and to balance their inclines, an arrangement that kept them in thrall to the railway and gave the FR a virtual monopoly of their traffic for nearly a century. These wagons were built both by contractors and in the railway's own workshops at Boston Lodge, at the opposite end of the Cob to Portmadoc, established in a quarry from which stone for the embankment had been obtained. The improvements that Spooner made were driven both by the need to keep the railway fit for slate traffic that increased at an extraordinary rate and because he hoped to introduce steam locomotives, in order to convert his mineral tramway into a public, passenger-carrying railway. By the time he died in 1856 the FR was almost ready to fulfil his ambition.

Charles Easton Spooner, James's second son, was appointed to succeed his father and energetically pursued the same policy of improvement. By the 1860s slate traffic had grown to such an extent that the horse and gravity working was at the limit of its capacity; the horses could not haul long enough trains to return sufficient wagons to the quarries and the provision of extra passing loops, to enable more trains to be run, would have been an expensive and inadequate solution.

The answer was clearly steam locomotives, but very few had been built to run on gauges as narrow as that used by the FR. Invitations to tender designs were, however, answered by almost all the established firms, though some designs were quite extraordinary, even by contemporary standards. Eventually a contract for the construction of three small four-coupled tank engines was made with George England & Co. of London, one of the few firms not to have responded in the first instance! The decision was heavily influenced by the appointment of Charles Holland, nephew of the railway's principal customer, Samuel Holland, as a consultant in the process of designing and acquiring locomotives and by Charles Holland being otherwise employed in London at the same time.

England's design, influenced by Holland, was simple and robust and the first pair of locomotives, named Mountaineer and The Princess, were delivered to Portmadoc in July 1863. They proved disappointing, as the boilers had no domes; England had wanted to fit them but had been overruled by Holland. After negotiating the construction of a fourth locomotive, England sent his men to fit domes to the first pair and delivered the second pair, named The Prince and Palmerston, with domes, in early 1864, and they were set to work without problems.

With the locomotives in use the railway was ready for the next stage of the Spooners' plan to transform the line, the establishment of a public passenger service. However, there were some obstacles to be overcome, not the least of which was the prevailing legislation that forbade the building of any railway for public passenger services to a gauge less than standard (4ft 8½in). (The argument at the time was between the merits of Brunel's broad gauge and Stephenson's narrow (standard) gauge.) Nonetheless, the FR applied for approval to carry passengers and the Board of Trade sent Captain Henry Tyler to inspect the line. Tyler's report was generally favourable. The narrow cuttings made him recommend that carriage doors be locked, a practice that continues to this day and, almost as a footnote, he suggested that bogie carriages might suit a line with so many sharp curves. Most significant, however, was Tyler's elegant solution to the question of gauge. Recognising that the FR had been built long before the restrictive

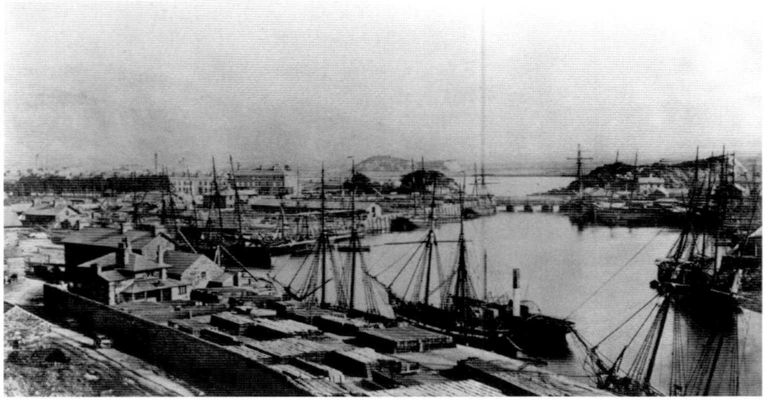

A busy scene at Portmadoc Harbour about 1880 with several ships loading slate from well-stocked wharves

legislation, he was able to decide that it did not apply, so he could recommend approval for passenger traffic!

The FR began its public passenger service in 1865, though the quarry proprietors were not enthusiastic. They believed that passenger trains would reduce the line's capacity for their slate and they had a point. Within four years the FR was applying for an Act of Parliament to authorise doubling of the line to increase capacity in the face of still greater slate traffic. As before, this would have been an extremely expensive undertaking but the existing locomotives were at the limit of their capabilities when returning empty wagons to Blaenau Ffestiniog; loaded trains were not a problem as they still ran under gravity.

Fortunately a solution was at hand, in the form of Robert Francis Fairlie and his patent, double-boiler, double-bogie, locomotive. Looking for all the world like a pair of small locomotives joined back to back, but with the wheels and cylinders mounted in swivelling bogies, the Fairlie double engine had the advantage of delivering a great deal of power while still being able to work around sharp curves; precisely what the FR required.

The aptly named Little Wonder was built at George England's factory and put to work on the FR in 1869, with immediate benefits. Slate traffic continued to grow and the railway was able to pay dividends of 7½ per cent per half year, a return quite unheard of on railway stocks and one which gave the railway the capital to improve itself still further, even to the extent that one contemporary observer described it as being "like a main line in miniature".

These results caused the FR to feature regularly in the contemporary technical press, with its example being held up as being the one to follow wherever railways had to be built in difficult terrain or on limited budgets; precisely the conditions that applied in many of Britain's rapidly developing colonies at the time and in other countries just getting to grips with the railway age. Captain Tyler had made these points, as part of his report, in 1865, and subsequently in addresses to technical institutions.

In 1870 Spooner and Fairlie arranged a series of trials, pitting the Little Wonder against other FR locomotives and attended by the technical press and by delegates from colonial and foreign powers, including Scandinavia and Russia. The trials provided an emphatic demonstration of the value of an articulated locomotive on a line such as the FR and the manner in which a narrow-gauge railway was able to carry substantial traffic across difficult terrain while being built at relatively low cost. The reports of these trials, fanned by Tyler, Fairlie and Spooner, eloquent advocates of their parts in the enterprise, established the Festiniog Railway Company's fame.

Fairlie and Spooner promoted the double engine and the narrow gauge respectively, publishing books and articles arguing their points of view on railway development while Tyler promoted colonial development. The FR was, genuinely, at the forefront of some developments. Following the success of the bogie double engine, in 1872 the FR was amongst the first railways in the world to put iron-framed bogie carriages into service, as Captain Tyler had suggested in his report of 1865.

Such was the enthusiasm for the narrow gauge in the 1870s that a grand scheme was developed to serve much of North Wales with a network of 2ft gauge lines built on the pattern of the FR. Charles Easton Spooner was heavily involved and his eldest son, Charles Edwin, served as engineer during construction. Fairlie also had a hand in the scheme, persuading the promoters to sign an agreement to use only locomotives built to his Patent; they bought two Single Fairlies. Known as the North Wales Narrow Gauge Railways, the only parts of the scheme to be completed were a line from Dinas, near Caernarfon, to quarries near Bryngwyn on the slopes of Moel Tryfan and a line, joining this one, which reached other quarries

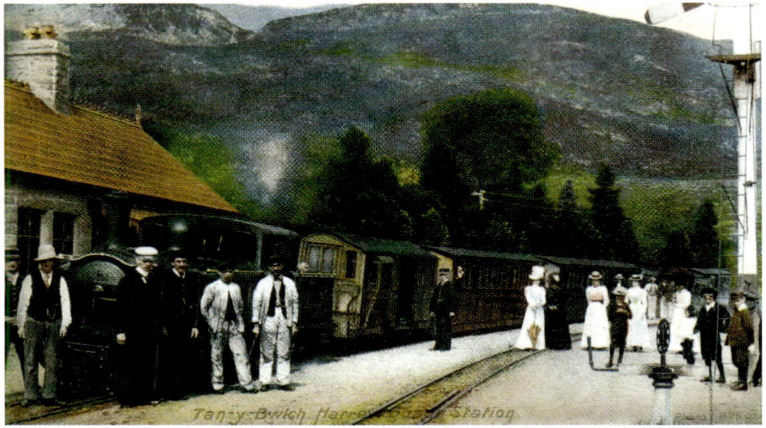

Double-Fairlie locomotive on Down train at Tan-y-Bwlch in Edwardian days

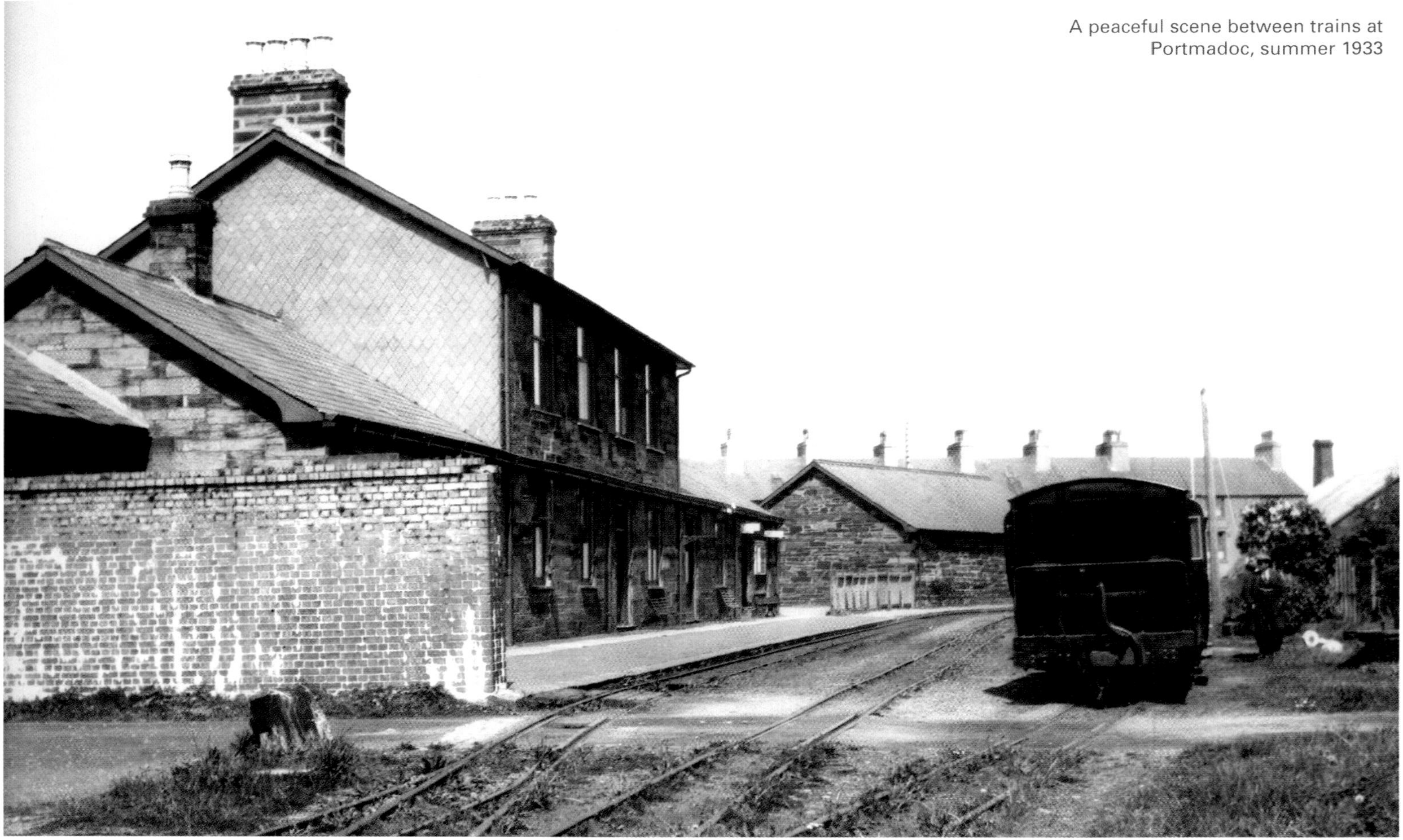

A peaceful scene between trains at Portmadoc, summer 1933

Redundant carriages and surplus wagons amidst the growing weeds at Portmadoc in August 1945, just before the railway closed to traffic

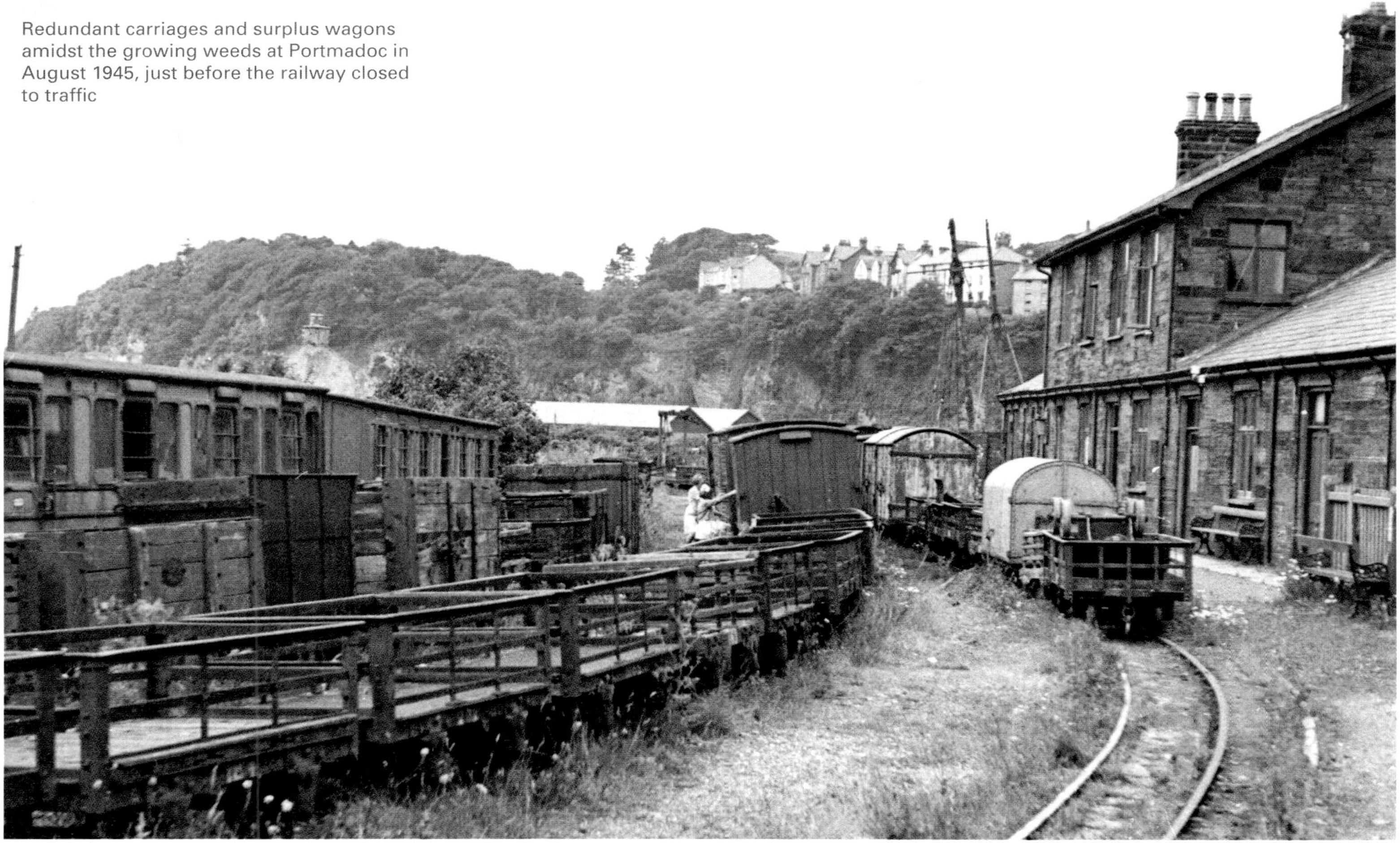

and a remote hamlet at Rhyd Ddu, under the western slopes of Snowdon. The quarries operated sporadically and the line spent much of its life in the hands of receivers. By the time of the First World War it was all but derelict, running only occasional goods services. This railway will feature again in the history of the FR.

In the late 1870s the FR faced its first threat from the standard-gauge railways. The London & North Western Railway approached Blaenau from the east, via a long tunnel from the Conwy valley, and the Great Western approached from the west via a branch from Bala that would eventually absorb and convert the narrow-gauge Festiniog & Blaenau Railway, an independent line between the two villages that actually functioned as a branch of the FR, in spite of having been built to compete with it. The LNWR hoped to take some of the lucrative slate traffic but was undermined by the FR's practice of providing wagons directly into the quarries and reductions in rates that kept the narrow gauge competitive. The GWR's route to the inland markets was long, so their influence was reduced. Another line, the Cambrian Railways, had initially threatened a branch to Blaenau from their line along the coast but a more cooperative relationship with the FR was developed and an extensive exchange yard for the transfer of slate and incoming goods was laid out at Minffordd.

The FR continued to prosper under Spooner's management, assisted by his son George Percival, who had trained as a mechanical engineer. Another Double Fairlie, James Spooner, was acquired in 1872, followed by a Single Fairlie, Taliesin, in 1876, together with several more passenger carriages. In 1878 the decision was taken to construct a third double engine, to Percy's design, in the railway's own workshops at Boston Lodge, using parts obtained from outside; Merddin Emrys emerged in 1879 and was followed by Livingston Thompson in 1886, though Percy had left just after Merddin Emrys was finished.

Charles Easton Spooner died in 1889 and, from then on, the FR was never quite the same. His successors had to cope with a gradual decline in the slate trade, though there was a small boom around the turn of the century when a prolonged strike and lockout at Penrhyn Quarry, near Bangor and then the largest in the world, severely restricted the supplies of Welsh slate.

During the Edwardian period the slow decline of slate traffic was, to an extent, offset by the rising practice of tourism. The benefits of a journey over the line to enjoy some of the best scenery in North Wales, to take the "Toy Train thru' Faeryland" as one leaflet put it, were enjoyed by many and the railway benefited.

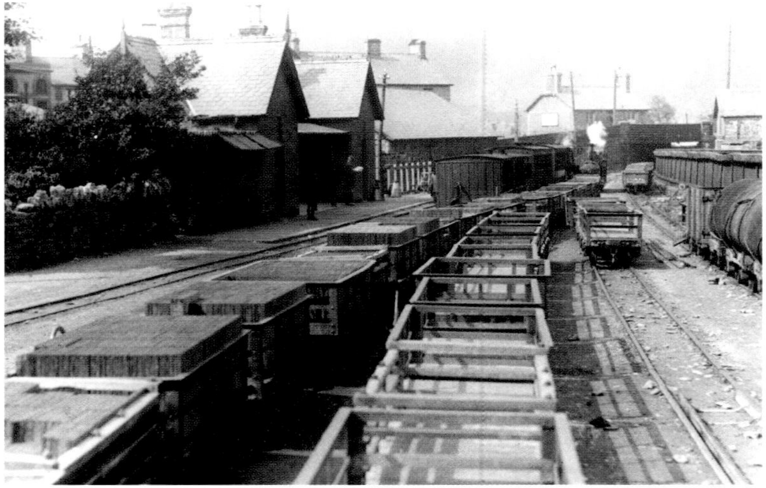

Duffws in the 1930s with an England locomotive collecting a train of loaded slate wagons. The empties in the centre will shortly go up an incline into the quarries

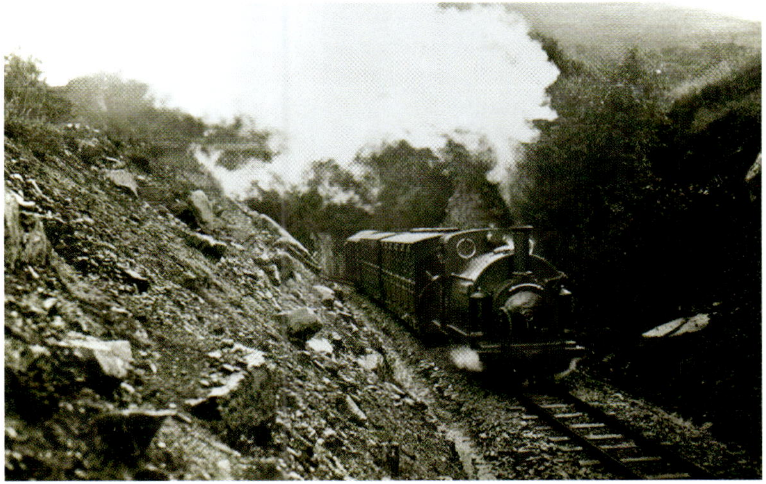

The smaller Festiniog locomotives often worked over the WHR. Palmerston and a train of FR carriages are heading south to Portmadoc

The outbreak of war in August 1914 saw all railways taken under government control. Parts of Boston Lodge were devoted to the manufacture of artillery shells and, though the trains still ran, maintenance was cut to a minimum. At the quarries large numbers of men either volunteered or were conscripted to join the Forces, many never to return. As a consequence the industry never recovered its former strength after the war. The railway, too, had been left in a poorer state than at the outset, as a result of the reduced maintenance and government control of income.

After the Great War the FR relied even more upon the summer tourist traffic for revenue, though slate traffic continued. In the 1920s, as part of a scheme to relieve unemployment in the area, a new railway, to be known as the Welsh Highland (WHR), was built to connect the former NWNGR at Rhyd Ddu with the FR at Portmadoc. This new line ran through some spectacular scenery around Beddgelert and should have been a great success with tourists. Unfortunately the rise of motor transport took some potential traffic and a chronic lack of resources made services infrequent and unreliable, in spite of the FR working some of the trains. As the post-war slump deepened into Depression both railways struggled with ageing stock and insufficient revenue to afford the repairs required.

The FR took a lease on the WHR, but still failed to make it pay; the drain came close to bankrupting the FR, until it could repudiate the lease in 1936, when the WHR was closed. The FR continued until the outbreak of the second war in 1939, when passenger services were suspended. Slate traffic, once again greatly reduced by the loss of men from the quarries, was carried throughout the war with trains running three days a week, or as required, until the beginning of the quarries' annual holiday in August 1946 when, literally overnight, the Railway closed, one hundred and ten years after it had opened.

Attempts to revive the Railway began soon after it closed, but none succeeded until 1954 when Alan Pegler, bankrolled by his father and supported by the recently established Ffestiniog Railway Society, obtained control of majority shareholdings in the Company. The Company was woefully short of money and relied upon volunteers from the Society for labour and donations of materials. Work to restore the line began at Harbour Station and Boston Lodge and a brief summer season of trains between the two ends of the Cob was run during July and August 1955. For the 1956 season they ran as far as Minffordd and in 1957, following the installation of a loop, the terminus was Penrhyn. Between Penrhyn and Tan-y-Bwlch a great deal of vegetation had to be cleared from the course of the line, but this was achieved in time for train services to be extended to Tan-y-Bwlch for 1958. Prince had been the first steam locomotive restored, in 1955, followed by Double Fairlie Taliesin (ex-Livingston Thompson), in 1956.

Bogie carriages were also restored as swiftly as possible but in the manner of the early slate traffic, passenger numbers increased at a greater rate than vehicles to accommodate them and the strain was already being felt.

There was also a substantial obstacle to be overcome if the railway was to regain its upper terminus in Blaenau Ffestiniog, as the new owners always intended. Unfortunately, just as the new administration had taken control of the railway, a section of line above the Moelwyn tunnel, as far as the station at Tanygrisiau, a village on the outskirts of Blaenau, had been compulsorily purchased for the construction of a power station and the route to Blaenau Ffestiniog had been blocked. After much deliberation the company decided to stick to their original intention to return to Blaenau, but were faced with the question of how to get around the large lake that had been put in their way, and how to obtain compensation for the severance of the line.

While those answers were sought, the line from Portmadoc to Tan-y-Bwlch was improved and more locomotives and rolling stock were restored. Traffic continued to grow as more and more families took their holidays in North Wales. The railway was the subject of a live television broadcast by the BBC in July 1960 – shades of the Spooner/Fairlie publicity of the 1870s – and this generated huge traffic during that and the following season. Fortunately Merddin Emrys was finally returned to traffic in 1961, relieving the strain on Taliesin, which had required a great deal of attention to keep it running.

The two double engines began to show signs of their age early in 1962 and the railway was fortunate to be able to obtain Linda, a large 0-4-0 saddle tank locomotive, from the nearby Penrhyn Quarry railway to ease the strain. Her sister, Blanche, was acquired the following year and both have since given sterling service.

Several schemes to avoid the flooded line above the tunnel had been proposed over the years and, in 1963, a proposal to build a spiral around the station at Dduallt, a unique feature for a UK railway, was considered by the Board and approved. Work was to be done, as far as possible, by volunteers and it was not to detract from volunteer efforts on the section of the line already open.

At the same time the Board considered the prospects of reopening the section of line between Tan-y-Bwlch and Dduallt and commencing a programme of building brand new carriages and both were approved.

The first sod was turned on the Deviation, as the new line between Dduallt and Tanygrisiau became known, in January 1965, and later in the year No. 24, the first new carriage, was put into service; it was later renumbered 100, to celebrate the FR's centenary of passenger traffic.

Dduallt became the new upper terminus when services were restored in April 1968, but only after a national outbreak of foot and mouth disease had made opening very uncertain by severely curtailing volunteer work. The station, an idyllic and isolated spot, was now the centre, almost literally, of the civil engineering work for the spiral that allowed the railway to get through the same shoulder of Moelwyn that necessitated the former tunnel with sufficient height to emerge above the level of the new power station lake. A new tunnel was driven by a team of Cornish miners and, following delays to deal with loose rock, the railway was opened to a temporary station at Llyn Ystradau alongside the power station lake in June 1977. The Deviation was formally completed in June 1978, when a new station on a slightly altered alignment was opened at Tanygrisiau. The old alignment was regained just beyond the Blaenau end of the station.

The Deviation had involved countless hours of volunteers' work over more than a dozen years. In the early days it operated on a shoestring but after the tunnel was complete it benefited enormously from a variety of grants and job creation schemes.

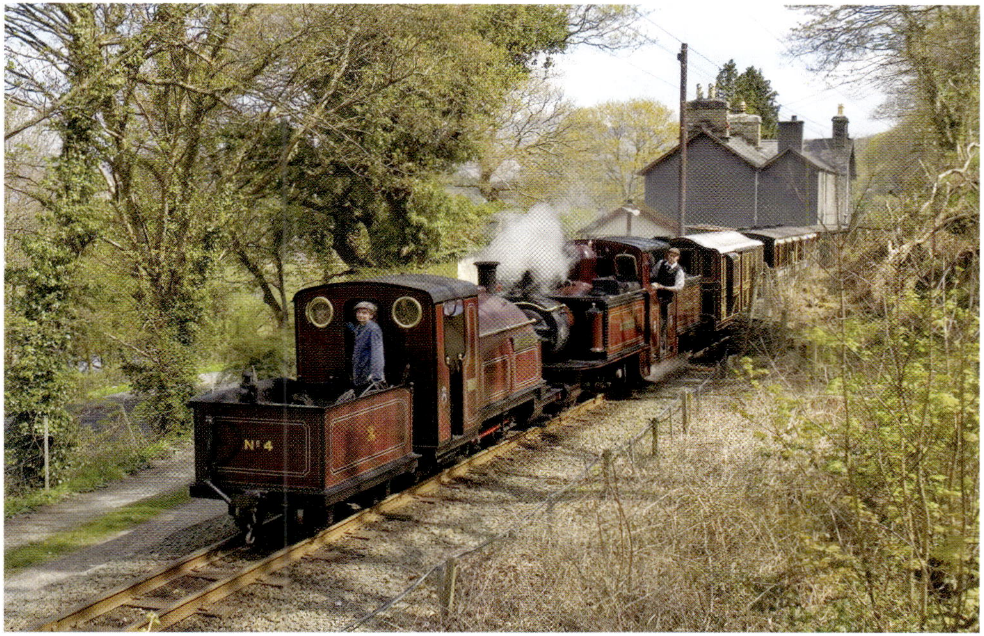

Palmerston and Merddin Emrys with 1870s train at Boston Lodge Halt during a Vintage Weekend in 2006
Photo: Martin Cowgill Collection

It took another four years to refurbish the section of old line from Tanygrisiau to a new station in Blaenau Ffestiniog (all the old sites were inaccessible or had been built over). The limitation was money as the Company had spent a great deal on the Deviation, in spite of receiving compensation from the Electricity Authority that had built the power station.

Completion of the railway back to Blaenau Ffestiniog was marked with a ceremony on 25 May 1982, one hundred and fifty years from the Original Act of Parliament receiving Royal approval and just less than thirty years since restoration had begun.

While the line was being rebuilt the FR had built itself a brand new Double Fairlie, Earl of Merioneth, in 1979, rebuilt its original locomotives Prince and Merddin Emrys several times, acquired Linda, Blanche and an ex-WD, American-built, 2-6-2 tank engine that was named Mountaineer, converted its steam locomotives from burning coal to oil, acquired several large diesel tractors and adapted them for passenger services and built a large fleet of modern, corridor carriages to carry its ever-expanding passenger traffic.

All these developments, together with the remarkable achievement of the Deviation, had kept the Ffestiniog Railway in the technical and public press in a manner very reminiscent of its Victorian heyday.

Since 1982 the FR has continued to develop. Another new Fairlie, David Lloyd George, entered traffic in 1992; a replica of the Single Fairlie, Taliesin, was completed in 1999; the derelict remains of Palmerston, the fourth England engine of 1864, were restored; and a large, bogie diesel locomotive, Vale of Ffestiniog, has been put to work. Having given many years of service all the surviving carriages, some dating from the 1860s and 1870s, have been extensively, and expensively, restored.

Since 1989 the FR has been involved with rebuilding the long-closed Welsh Highland Railway, extending it along the track of a former standard-gauge line to a station alongside the castle in Caernarfon.

Edward's Unfinished Historical Ffestiniog Railway Map

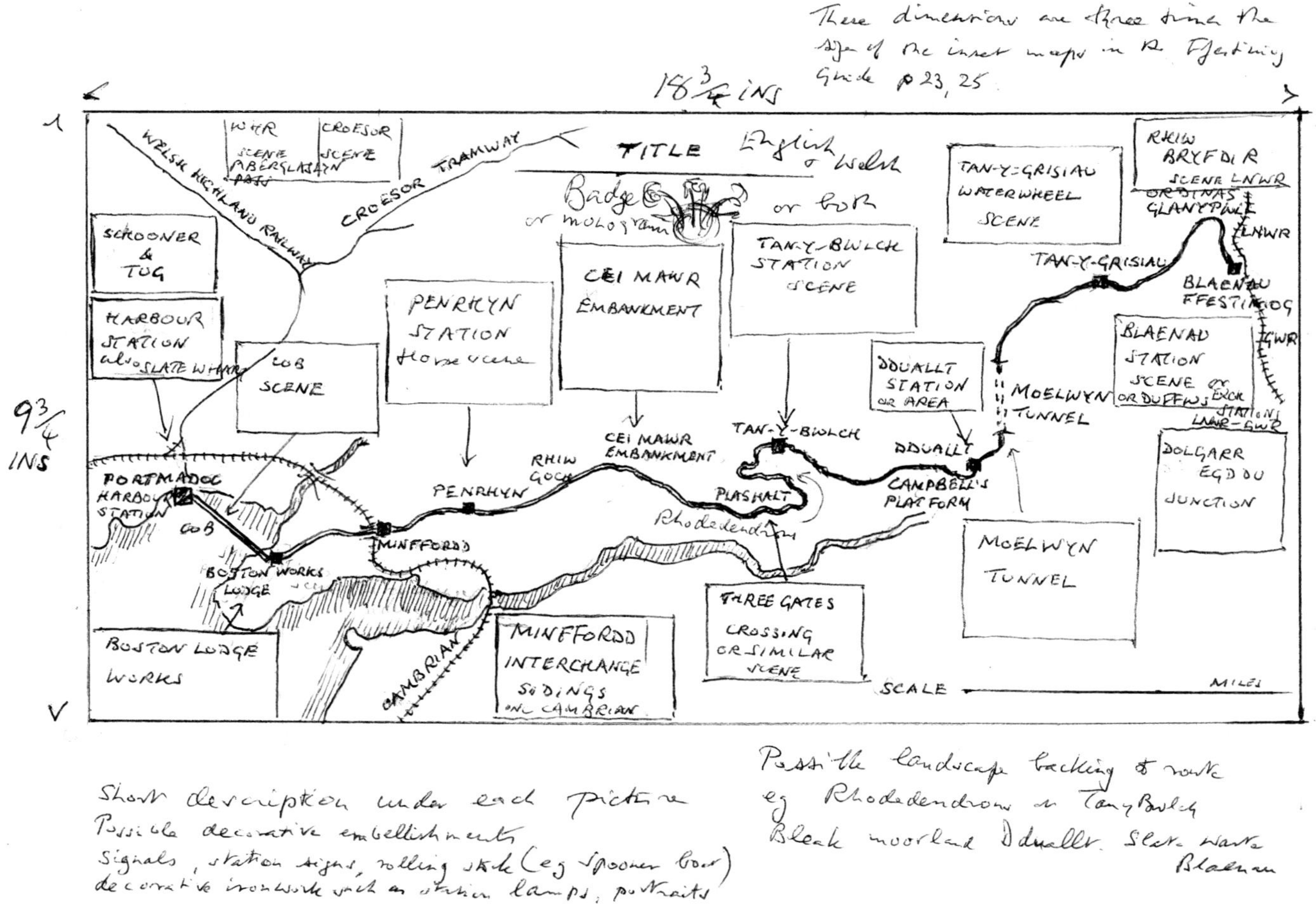

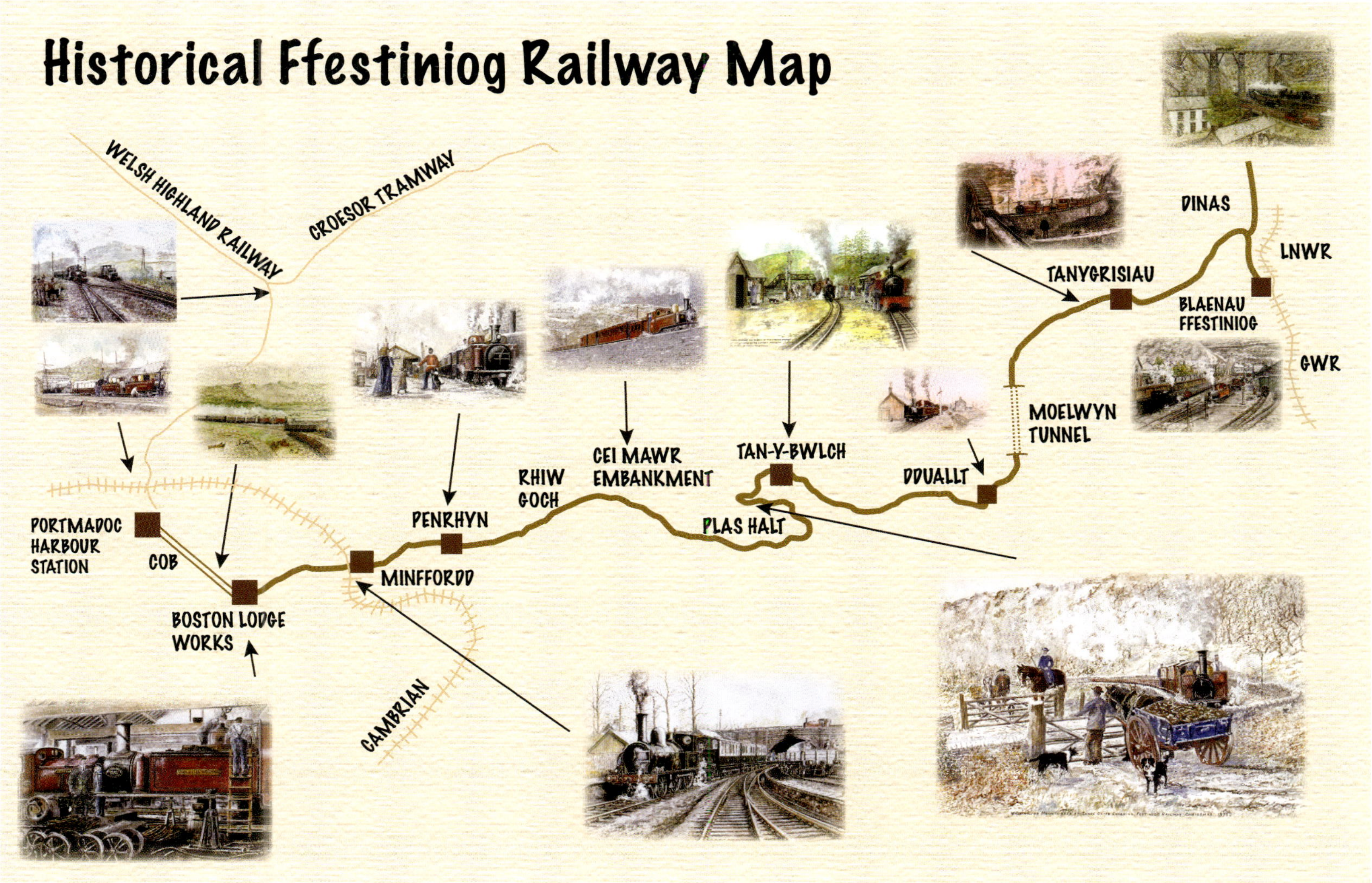

Example of how the finished map may have looked

The Heritage Paintings Project

The Heritage Paintings Project started by the chance purchase of one of Edward Paget-Tomlinson's paintings, then grew by stages to become a significant part of Edward's work in later years and also a source of pleasure for the numerous people who either commissioned paintings or purchased copies.

The starting point is a personal one. For some years until 1994, I was Director of Leisure Services for Camden Council in London. Soon after being appointed, my department had the curious experience of literally digging up a steamroller in one of its parks, not a mile from Euston Road and all the bustle of central London. The Aveling and Porter 10-ton had been retired from service in 1950 by St Pancras Borough Council and was later placed on the Cumberland Market Playground, then being created to mark the Queen's Coronation. Brightly painted, it remained a popular piece of play equipment until general decrepitude and a more safety-conscious age made it redundant once more. In the 1960s, rather than scrap the steamroller it was decided that, covered in cobblestones and earth, it would make a perfect mound on which to mount a children's slide. There it remained until its rediscovery by a contractor's JCB clearing the site in readiness for yet another refurbishment of the park. The years under the ground had left the roller remarkably unscathed, the cobbles having entombed rather than buried it. After careful restoration by a traction engine enthusiast it became a familiar sight at vintage vehicle rallies, now bearing the name Cumberland after its old home. By chance it is now in the keeping of another steam enthusiast who lives not 30 miles from the Ffestiniog Railway and is now to be seen out and about in North Wales.

At the end of 1996 I took early retirement from Camden and to mark the occasion spent a weekend in the Forest of Dean. There at Lydney in the Archive Bookshop I came across a number of paintings by Edward Paget-Tomlinson, including one of an Aveling and Porter steamroller at nearby Tintern. I purchased it and picked up a leaflet about Edward and his work as a transport artist who accepted commissions.

The thought occurred of commissioning a painting of Cumberland in a scene recorded in local papers of an incident during the Blitz when the engine was used to provide warm water to save the life of a man trapped under rubble in a bombed building near Camden Town Tube station. In a discussion over the telephone, Edward quickly became intrigued by the story and the painting was soon completed. We had enjoyed creating the scene from photographic evidence and contemporary accounts and we explored the idea of a painting of the Ffestiniog Railway, with which I have been involved as a volunteer for over 45 years. As Edward also declared a long-term interest in the Ffestiniog Railway, an historic painting of the railway appealed to us both. We developed a plan to make copies of the painting to sell to raise funds for heritage work on the railway, a cause close to Edward's heart.

We then hit a problem. Edward, with a lifelong interest in, and a good knowledge of, railways, declared a wariness of painting such a well-known subject as the Ffestiniog Railway. He suspected that some railway enthusiasts are rivet counters and that he would be picked up on detail. However, upon reflection, he decided to take the risk. In fact, as the project developed, the idea that the paintings would inevitably provoke discussion about historical accuracy became a positive feature and all part of the fun.

From the start we agreed some basic rules. The paintings would be of pre-preservation views of the Ffestiniog and Welsh Highland railways not captured on photographs. This particularly appealed to Edward, because it added to the visual images of the railways and with his usual skill with words he described the project as "pictures beyond camera reach". It was agreed that a maximum of forty original paintings would be produced and

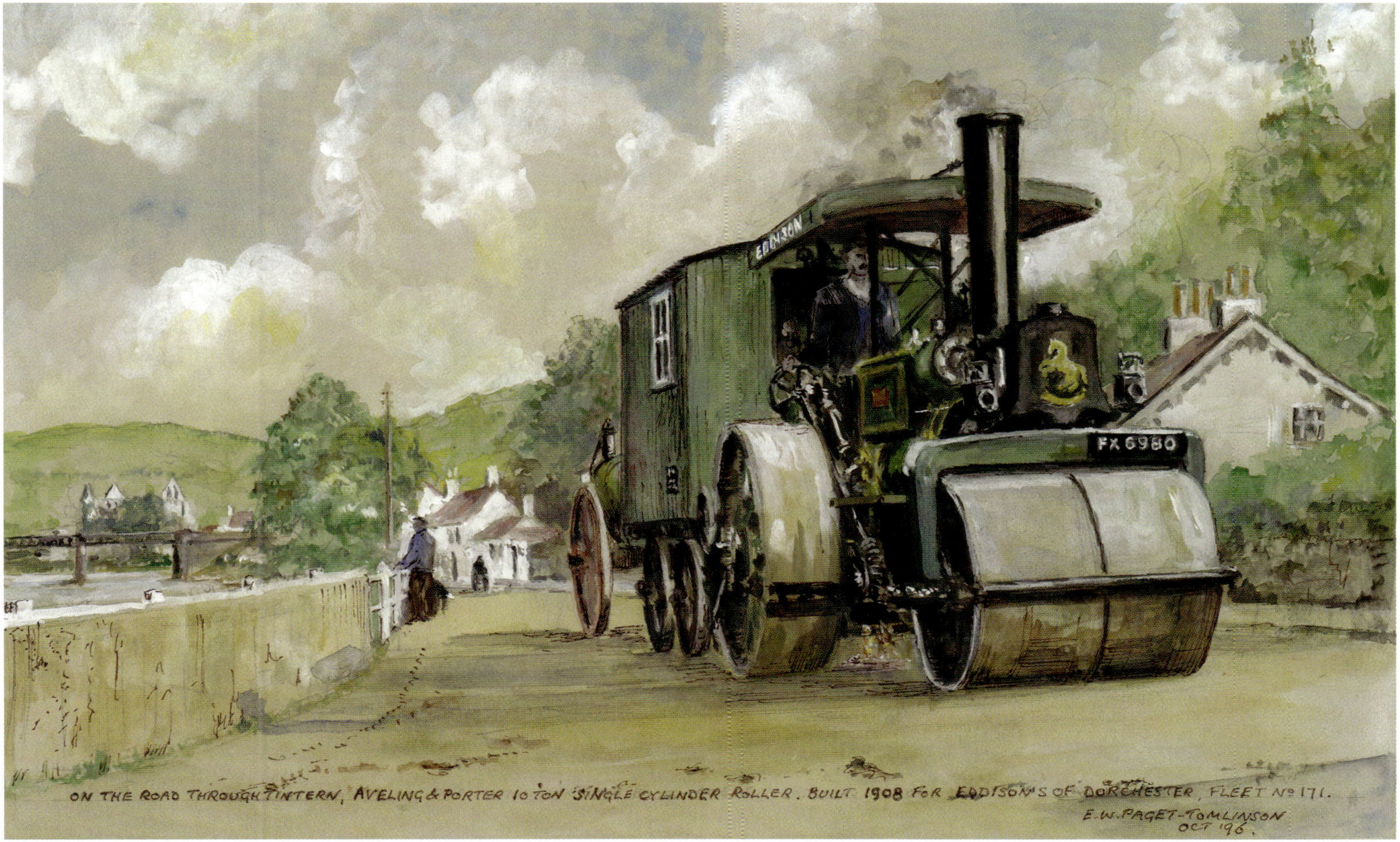
EDDISON
FX 6980
ON THE ROAD THROUGH TINTERN, AVELING & PORTER 10 TON SINGLE CYLINDER ROLLER. BUILT 1908 FOR EDDISON'S OF DORCHESTER, FLEET No 171.
E.W. PAGET-TOMLINSON
OCT '96.

that print runs of copies would be strictly limited, soon defined as editions of twenty-five numbered copies. They would be sold framed, but with the price kept as modest as possible to make them easy to sell as an impulse purchase at special events on the railway. The project was run under the auspices of the London Area Group of the Ffestiniog Railway Society, of which I am a member, although now living alongside the railway in Penrhyndeudraeth. The funds raised by the project have been carefully targeted by the Group at heritage work on the railway in line with Edward's wishes.

My choice for the first painting was easy. I have always thought the Double Fairlie James Spooner in original condition to be one of the most elegant FR locomotives and the Curly Roofed Vans to be intriguing. Locating the two together in the original Harbour Station, before the present stone buildings were erected, which is little recorded in early photographs, had the added advantage of giving Edward the comfort of including the complex masts and rigging of a couple of topsail schooners. Ships appear in several of the paintings and Edward always said that he would defend their accuracy against all criticism, in contrast to his caution over the railway details. The painting was finished in February 1997 and the first dozen or so copies sold easily from the Festiniog Railway Heritage Group stand at a gala on the railway that May.

Our thoughts then turned to the subject of the next painting. Following the gala sales, the Heritage Group had expressed an interest in using one of Edward's paintings on a Christmas card. Thus the next painting was aimed at this market. A winter view was required and once more I chose a locomotive I very much admire, Single Fairlie Taliesin in a pleasing location, Cei Mawr embankment, which had been little photographed in early days. I next commissioned a third painting, The Princess at Cornhill, and copies of all three paintings then sold well at the railway's Vintage Weekend in the autumn of 1997. The Heritage Group Christmas card was also a success and the project was really finding its feet.

So far I had commissioned the original paintings and was happy to do so for a while longer. Not only was I the owner of some very nice paintings, but it was also a good way to assist the railway with raising funds. However, at the Vintage Weekend, David Gordon, a Director of the FR Society, asked about commissioning a painting of Merddin Emrys, his favourite locomotive. David did not have any particular location in mind, so I suggested a view on the Welsh Highland Railway. Photographs of Double Fairlies on this railway are very rare, since they were only used intermittently for a couple of years after it opened in 1923, before proving quite unsuitable for its switchback route.

This added a new dimension, since I became the link between the commissioner and the artist. Thus I was suggesting aspects, checking sources and trying to ensure historical accuracy, whilst also ensuring that the paintings met commissioners' requirements but that Edward had the freedom to produce paintings that satisfied him artistically. Through this process, Edward and I developed a close working relationship and friendship, which grew with the project.

After the painting of Merddin Emrys in Aberglaslyn Pass, for a while we reverted to me as the commissioner. The Heritage Group again wanted a painting for their 1998 Christmas card and the view of the Dinas terminus in Blaenau Ffestiniog is widely regarded as the most pleasing of those used on the cards. The project was written up in the Summer 1998 Ffestiniog Railway Magazine and the proposition that commissions were welcome was encouraged. From then on there was always a waiting list of those wanting to commission paintings of special or favourite aspects of the Ffestiniog and Welsh Highland Railways. The original list of possible topics thus became modified by personal preference, although by the end of the project most of the intended views had been achieved. On the other hand, some subjects were on the limit of the project's rules, but in fact these always sold. Curiously, the most popular view of all, the "Missing Link" (Painting 29),

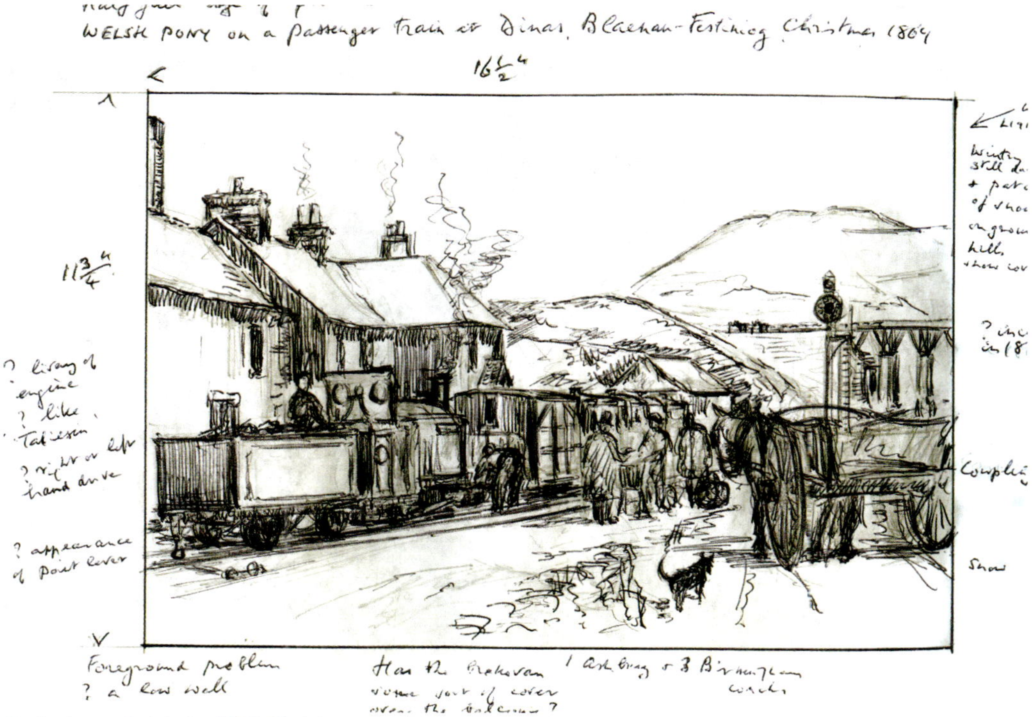

Preliminary sketch for 1998 Christmas card

showing a Portmadoc, Beddgelert and South Snowdon Railway electric train crossing the bridge at Beddgelert, was indeed of a scene beyond the reach of the camera, since the line never existed in this form.

Working with Edward was always fun and creating the paintings together became a routine we both thoroughly enjoyed. With a less modest artist, the process might have been fraught. Since I was gathering as much historic data as I could and then interpreting for Edward before he started work, his first draft needed to balance the wishes of the commissioner, historic accuracy and his own artistic views. There was scope for disagreement, but it never happened in any serious way. Whether it was the overall concept or a number of details not to the commissioner's satisfaction, Edward was always willing to make changes without demur and cheerfully made the requested changes. Often his response would be "Yes, I wondered about that myself."

The routine became well established. From photographs, maps and notes, Edward would produce rough sketches until a version was agreed. He then started work on the painting itself and he would send a copy for comment and correction. Again this was viewed as a draft until all necessary changes were made and only when all parties were satisfied would Edward put his signature to it. The painting then came to me and I arranged for the copies to be run off. The originals are all approximately 42cm x 29cm (approximately A3) and the main print run of copies was A4 size. In each case a couple of A3 and A5 copies were also made.

The whole basis of the project was to raise funds for heritage work on the Ffestiniog Railway, but without the need for a large investment of capital. This was achieved by the small print runs, by carrying out the framing work ourselves and by selling direct to Society members. Prices were kept reasonable, the intention being that they could be a readily accessible impulse purchase. Most sales were made from a sales stand located on the platform at Porthmadog Harbour Station during gala weekends and other special events. Edward came to Wales on a number of occasions to man the stand and he greatly enjoyed the chance to chat to people about his work. His modesty made him many friends and a number of commissions came directly from such conversations.

The temptation to expand the project in light of its popularity was resisted, in the main because as a volunteer venture it was important that it should not become too onerous. Thus the limited edition framed copies were always the mainstay, with the Heritage Group eventually using five paintings on Christmas cards and the first painting also appearing on a mouse mat.

There was always an underlying element of fun in the paintings. There are figures in odd garb, caricatures of well-known personalities, visual jokes, but perhaps most of all the animals that appear in nearly every painting. Edward confessed to being nervous when painting human figures and sometimes he felt he hadn't got them quite right. Such worries never occurred with animals. Whether as a main feature of a painting, or with a few brush strokes as an incidental detail, his animals are always spot on. Horses were a particular favourite of Edward's and they appear whenever he could reasonably justify their inclusion. However, the most consistent appearance was by Edward's beloved Border collie, Paddy. Paddy appeared in the very first painting, furtively approaching the engine and clearly up to no good. Having been left out of the second painting, Paddy then appeared in virtually every painting whenever Edward could find him a role. The only paintings from which he was banned were the two maritime views, Edward explaining that Paddy was frightened of water. Other animals were also featured. When Edward and Pam acquired another collie, Meg, she then also started making regular appearances. Commissioners' own animals could also be included and any animal – dog, cat or horse – seen in a painting will have a story.

By the time of his death in November 2003, Edward had completed thirty-seven of the planned forty paintings. They vary greatly in style, composition and mood, reflecting various factors: the original idea and expectations of the client; the author's interpretation of these and the results of his research into the subject; finally and most important, Edward's interpretation of the subject and his need for a degree of artistic licence. Thus while the paintings make an attractive collection, they were not painted primarily with publication in a book in mind, but as individual works to give pleasure as originals and as framed copies. The final three paintings planned are described in the Epilogue, thus bringing to a conclusion a project that has given great pleasure to all concerned. The publication of this book not only offers the opportunity to share that pleasure with others, but also to provide a permanent record of a less well-known aspect of Edward Paget-Tomlinson's artistic work.

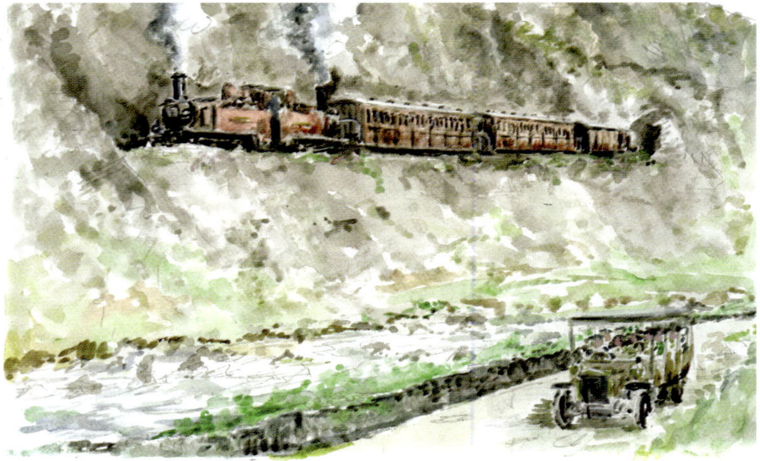

Preliminary sketch for painting 4

The Paintings

1. James Spooner at Portmadoc Harbour Station in 1875
2. Taliesin on Cei Mawr in about 1920
3. The Princess at Cornhill in about 1890
4. Merddin Emrys in the Aberglaslyn Pass in 1923
5. Little Giant in the Woodyard Sidings, Portmadoc in 1890
6. Welsh Pony at Dinas, Christmas 1869
7. James Spooner and Russell at Tan-y-Bwlch
8. Prince at Quarry Lane Crossing in 1910
9. Palmerston on Britannia Bridge in 1878
10. Moel Tryfan and Prince at Duffws in 1926
11. Little Wonder at Penrhyn, Christmas 1881
12. Two Baldwins at Croesor Junction in the summer of 1929
13. Boston Lodge Works in 1925
14. Taliesin at Duffws in 1887
15. Two Palmerstons at Minffordd Stations in 1889
16. Up Quarrymen's Train Leaving Portmadoc Harbour Station in 1903
17. Kerr Stuart Diesel Locomotive No. 4415 at Boston Lodge in 1929
18. Lottie's Crossing in 1963
19. Dolgarreg Ddu Junction, Blaenau Ffestiniog in 1880
20. Steam Tug Wave of Life Leaving Portmadoc Harbour in about 1890
21. 590 and Palmerston at Tryfan Junction in 1923
22. Merddin Emrys at Tan-y-Bwlch in 1946
23. Five Fairlies at Porthmadog
24. Mountaineer Approaching Three Gates Crossing in 1875
25. Welsh Pony and K3 MG at Penrhyn in 1934
26. Prince on a P.W. Train at Minffordd in 1892
27. Up Quarrymen's Train Near Tanygrisiau in 1891
28. Merddin Emrys at Dduallt in 1895
29. Portmadoc, Beddgelert & South Snowdon Railway in 1910
30. The Topsail Schooner C.E. Spooner off Harlech
31. Taliesin and Gravity Train at Minffordd in 1902
32. Little Wonder passing Boston Lodge Works in 1881
33. Crossing the High Street, Portmadoc, April 1923
34. The Welsh Slate Company's Viaduct at Rhiwbryfdir in 1887
35. Beddgelert at Bryngwyn in 1892
36. Spooner's Boat at Portmadoc Harbour Station in 1871
37. The New Arrivals at Boston Lodge in 1923

Painting 1: James Spooner at Portmadoc Harbour Station in 1875

The Ffestiniog Railway's passenger terminus in Porthmadog is the Harbour Station. It is now a bustling centre of tourist activity, but in the early days it was a more modest affair, dovetailed into a convenient bit of land on the edge of the port. Surrounded by slate wharves and shipyards and with a foundry and Custom House as a backdrop, it has never been a quiet place. The first station building was a single-storey wooden affair, remnants of which can still be seen at Penrhyndeudraeth. This building is seen to the right of the painting, while to the left is the original goods shed. A topsail schooner is tied up at the Holland's Wharf and the rigging of other slate-carrying ships can also be seen. The year is 1875, almost the height of the ship-based slate trade, when contemporary photographs show upwards of twenty vessels in the inner harbour, all loading slate for worldwide trade. In the background rises Moel-y-Gest and beneath it the elegant terraces on Y Garth.

James Spooner is in original condition in all its full Victorian finery as built in 1872 by the Avonside Engine Company and is attached to one of the passenger brake vans in the short-lived dark brown and ivory livery. The roof, now referred to as curly roof, but more correctly turtle roof, was designed to give the guard standing on the rear balcony a view along the train without the risk of decapitation on the line's tight cuttings and tunnels. The train crew are wearing the uniforms seen in early photographs, the driver and fireman in light-coloured jackets and the guard in frock coat with a sash. Paddy, Edward's dog, makes his first of many appearances in the paintings, lurking suspiciously near the tempting engine wheels.

Client's comments

With a free choice of any location and train, this painting pulled together a number of Ffestiniog features that I particularly like. There is a photograph of James Spooner basking in sunshine at this location when nearly new. Its condition and general design exude the confidence and style that was the FR in the high noon of the Spooner era. The fittings, bells and whistles, and the elegant proportions are a delight. The Curly Roof Vans have always been an intriguing Ffestiniog rolling stock quirk from a lost age and when the painting was commissioned few would seriously have thought that Boston Lodge Works would soon build a beautiful replica. The vans had accommodation for the guard, luggage and a separate dog compartment, all required when the Ffestiniog was providing a miniature main-line service. Several photographs exist of complete trains at this time, but photography was in its infancy and precious glass plates were not usually wasted on chance scenes. Thus the painting catches a brief moment during shunting, which must have happened but was never captured by the camera. The original station building has also always rather intrigued me, since it was replaced so soon after the railway opened for passenger traffic, yet has somehow survived for all those years at its new home at Penrhyndeudraeth. Finally the choice of Porthmadog gave the chance to have a taste of Edward's prowess at painting shipping subjects, with the topsail schooners in the background and the rowing boat in the foreground being a reminder of just how closely the railway and harbour coexisted.

P.J.H.

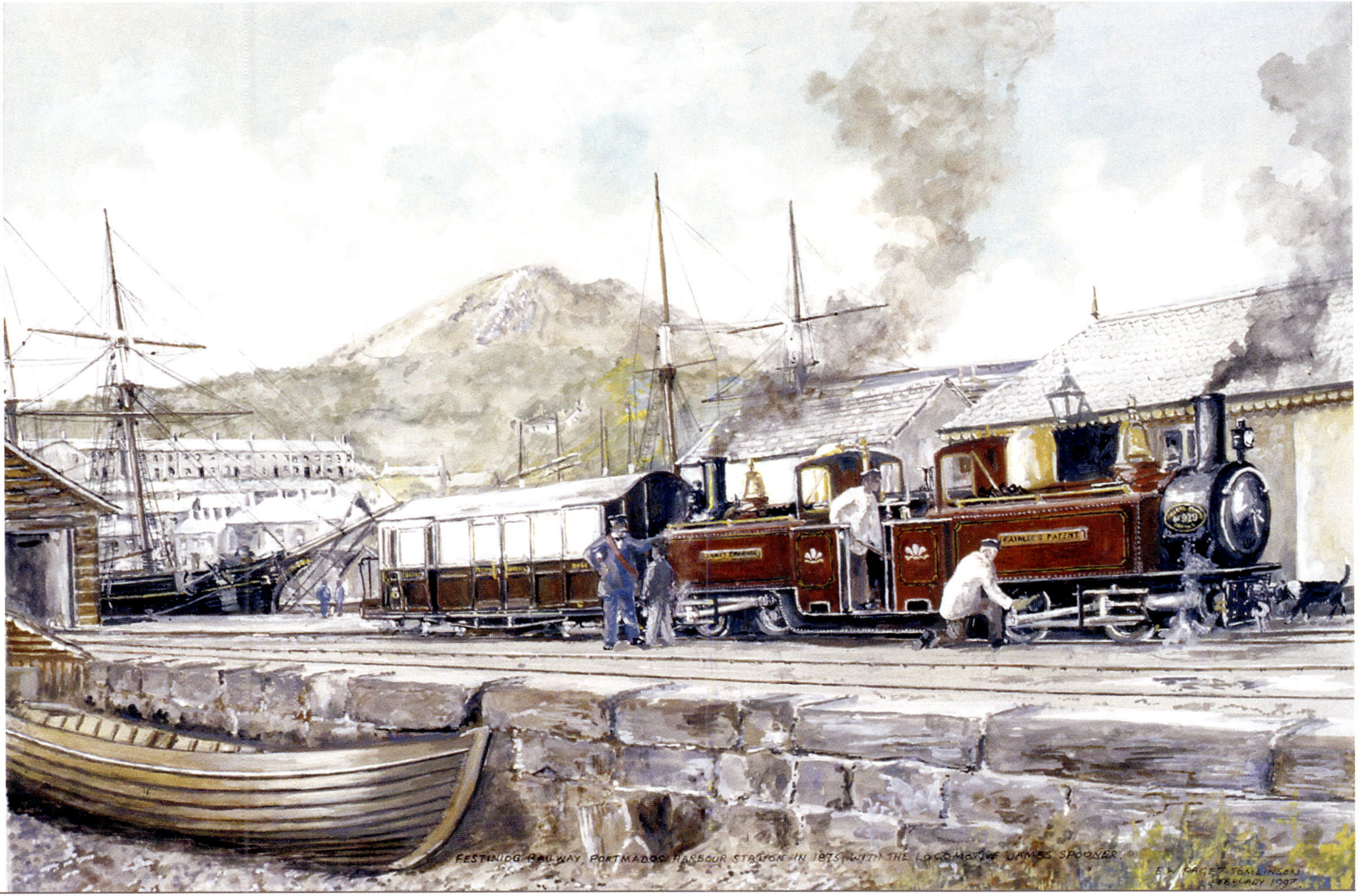
FESTINIOG RAILWAY, PORTMADOC HARBOUR STATION IN 1875, WITH THE LOCOMOTIVE JAMES SPOONER.
FAIRLIE'S PATENT
E.W. PAGET-TOMLINSON
FEBRUARY 1997.

Painting 2: Taliesin on Cei Mawr in about 1920

The success of selling copies of the James Spooner painting at Harbour Station led to the idea of producing a suitable view for a Festiniog Railway Heritage Group Christmas card. Again there was full scope for the choice of location and train, but something with a winter feel was required.

Client's comments

The location was easy. Cei Mawr is a 60-foot high drystone embankment across a valley a mile or so above Penrhyn and a truly remarkable feat of engineering dating from the earliest horse-drawn days of the railway. Now surrounding trees lessen its impact, but look down from the train to the stream in the valley bottom way below and the sheer scale of the achievement and the setting becomes clear. Despite its grandeur, Cei Mawr, meaning Great Quay in English, appears in few historic photographs. Short winter trains prior to the cessation of the year-round passenger service in 1930, all that were required once the buses took much of the local traffic, also seem to have been little photographed over the years.

A winter train would typically be a single bogie coach, preceded by one of the small Birmingham four-wheeled coaches which were always used to lessen the strain between the pulling power of the Fairlies and the bogie stock. Behind is one of the two larger bogie luggage vans, soon to be converted into a passenger vehicle, and a long string of empty slate wagons being returned to the quarries in Blaenau Ffestiniog. The choice of locomotive was easy too. Taliesin, the railway's sole example of a Single Fairlie, is less well represented in the photographic archive than the Double version, particularly towards the end of its working life when its worn condition made it less reliable. The engine is in its final form, with full cab, in contrast to the rather more stylish half cab to be seen in Painting 14. Taliesin was reputed to be popular with footplate crews, although not powerful enough for the heaviest trains and the full summer service. Thus it was an obvious choice for the lighter winter service. The bogie coach is one of the four bowsiders built by Brown Marshalls and the Gloster Wagon Company, surely one of the most pleasing and elegant designs of narrow-gauge coach. Remarkably, all four have survived into preservation and have now been restored to pristine condition. The large van also survives, although as a passenger coach as rebuilt in the late 1920s. Sadly the original locomotive was dismantled in the 1930s, but a perfect replica was completed in 1999.

A winter sky with snow flurries completes the scene. Sadly Paddy was left out. Edward had considered including him together with a shepherd, and indeed they had appeared at the first working sketch stage, but in the end he felt that a more formal composition was appropriate for a Christmas card.

P.J.H.

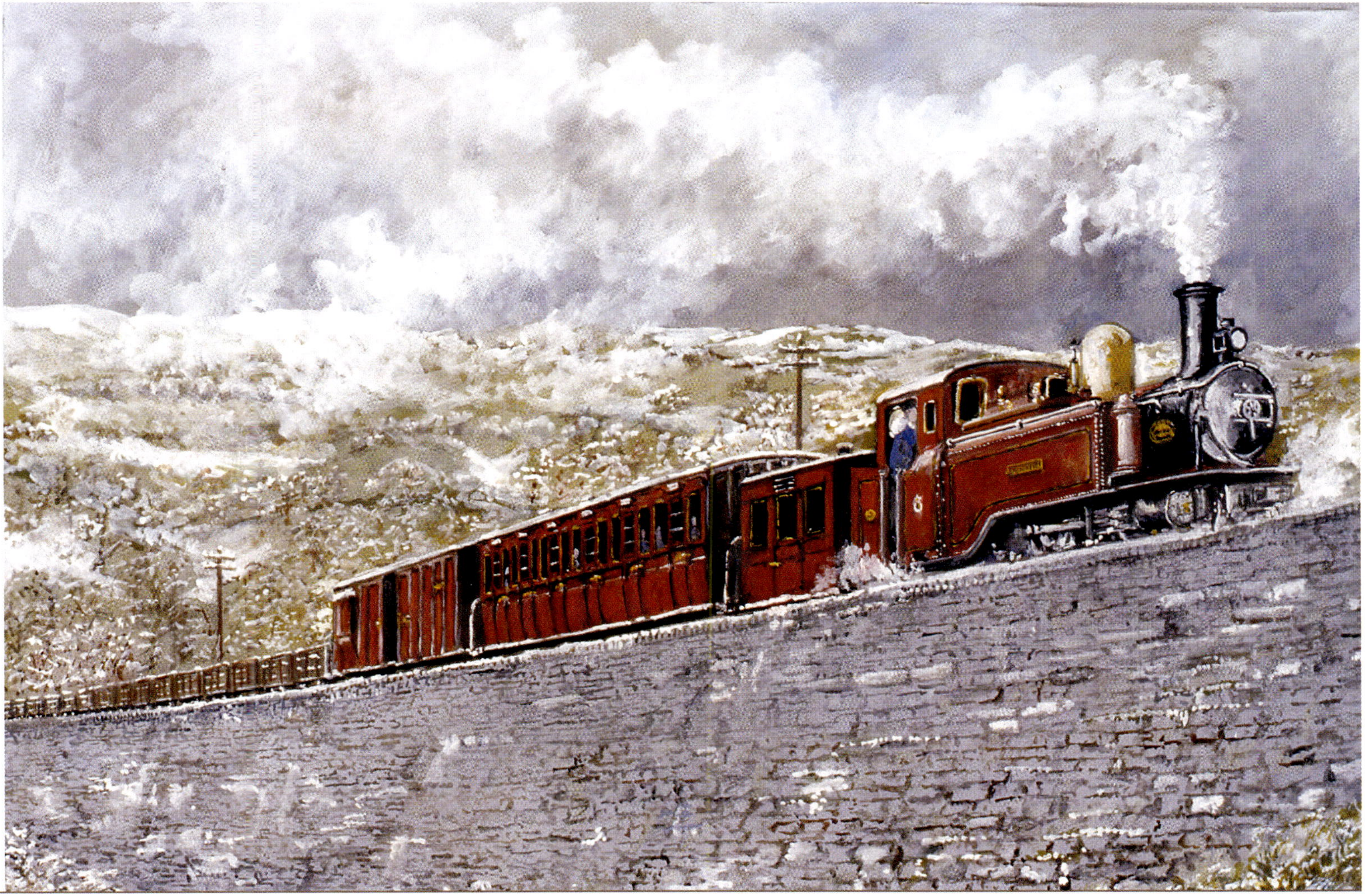

Painting 3: The Princess at Cornhill in about 1890

Beyond the Ffestiniog Railway's passenger terminus at the Harbour Station, there once extended a long network of lines serving the slate wharves, stretching almost as far as Borth-y-Gest. Here was the railway's original raison d'être and the destination for much of the slate traffic from Blaenau Ffestiniog. Indeed the railway's zero point, from which mileages were measured, was located near the spot where The Princess stands in the painting. Each of the main quarries had its own wharf, where slates were stacked ready to be loaded on the fleet of sailing ships that plied from here to many parts of the world. Slate wagons, having come down from Blaenau Ffestiniog in long gravity trains, were taken to the wharves by the Bottom Shunter, usually one of the George England engines. Final shunting was done by hand, with small turntables being used to get the wagons to the wharf side.

The painting shows The Princess performing the Bottom Shunter duties. It stands on Pen Cei in front of Cornhill, with a train of loaded slate wagons for the wharves away to the left. The date is 1890 and the engine is in near original condition, with side tanks and only a cab front sheet. The next year it was taken into Boston Lodge Works and emerged looking as it does today with the distinctive saddle tank and enclosed cab. In the foreground a schooner is being loaded by hand with slate. The loaders wear the distinctive leather aprons for protection as the slates slide down planks to the ship. Markers in the slate stack to the right help keep the tally.

Client's comments

The Pen Cei area of Porthmadog is now a tranquil spot, with just a pub and café serving mainly the tourist trade. Cars park on the cobbled triangle of land between the steep slope of Y Garth, with its attractive terraces of houses, and the harbour, now used mainly by yachts. There is no trace of the railway or all the numerous trades that were plied in this busy port area. The buildings have all found new uses and the Maritime Museum now occupies the one remaining slate shed. In the heyday of the slate trade, Cornhill, the three-storey building behind The Princess's tender, was the centre of commercial maritime life, housing Casson's Bank, the navigation school, the steam tug company, shipbrokers and other businesses. Now it contains flats and a clinic.

Despite the importance of the railway to the slate trade, hardly any of the numerous historic photographs of the harbour show it at work. The ever-present Bottom Shunter seems to have eluded photographers and the railway always seems to be incidental, yet without it Porthmadog could not have prospered. It intrigued me that such an important spot in the days of the slate trade could be so changed and I wanted a painting to recreate some of the bustle of those years and to show the Ffestiniog Railway within this industrial townscape. Having discussed this with the artist, he suggested placing the engine in the middle distance and using the foreground to depict the slate-loading activity.

P.J.H.

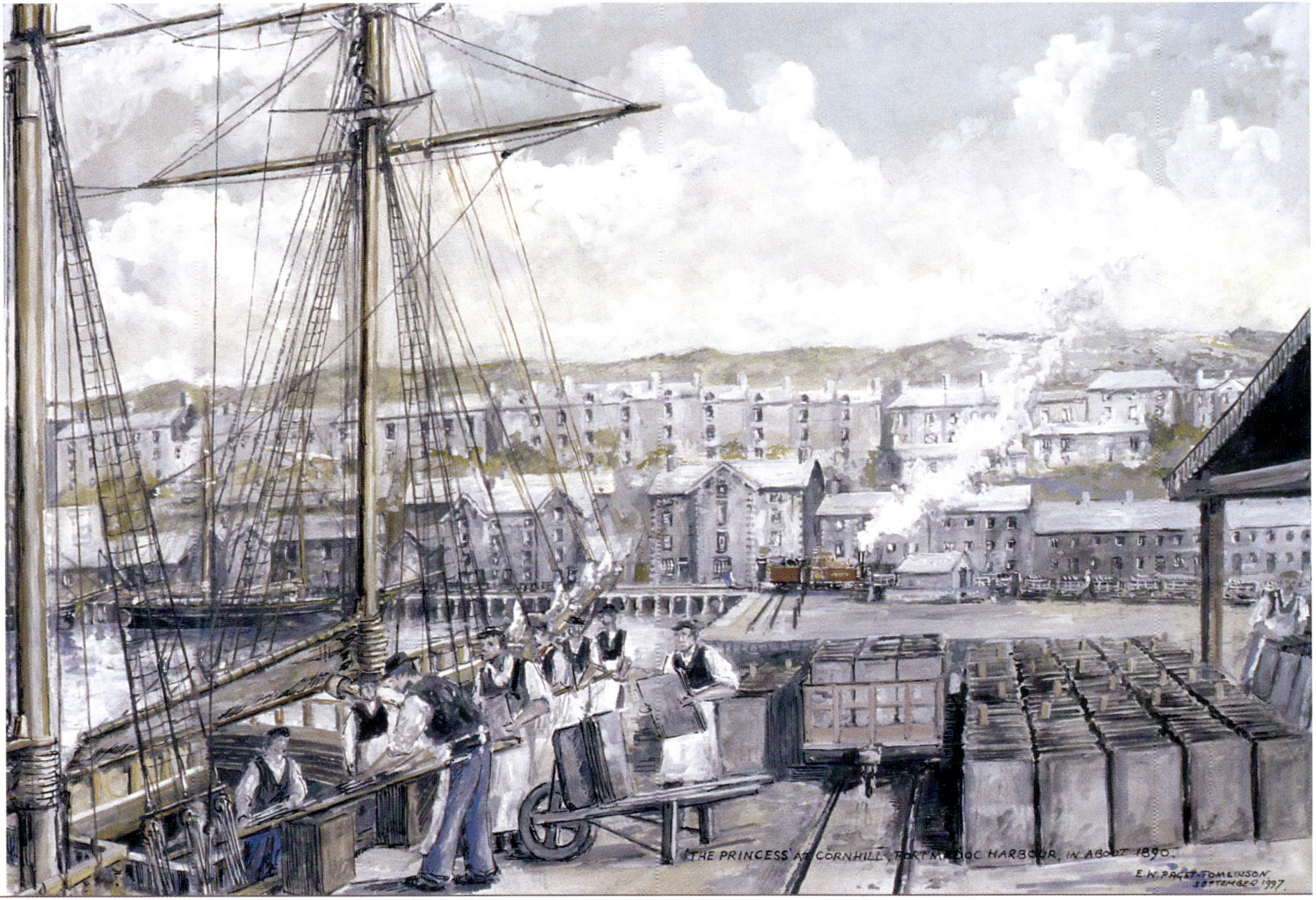
'THE PRINCESS' AT CORNHILL, PORTMADOC HARBOUR, IN ABOUT 1890.
E.W. PAGET-TOMLINSON
SEPTEMBER 1997.

Painting 4: Merddin Emrys in the Aberglaslyn Pass in 1923

The commission for a painting of Merddin Emrys without a specific location gave the opportunity to produce a study of that most elusive of workings for a Double Fairlie, the Welsh Highland Railway. Only two or three photographs exist showing Double Fairlies on the WHR up to 1925 and thereafter none, since their power proved uneconomic for the new line. The location chosen is perhaps the most evocative and romantic on the WHR, the Aberglaslyn Pass. A classic photograph taken in 1923 shows an Austin 7 at this spot. Replicating this would have been too obvious, but Edward fancied a charabanc and careful research came up with a suitable vehicle working in the area at the time. The train formation of Ffestiniog stock, comprising two bowsiders and a curly roof van, but unusually without the usual obligatory Birmingham four-wheeler, is one used for a series of press photographs taken at the time of the opening. Paddy and his master watch the train go by.

Client's comments

The double engine is to me iconic of the Ffestiniog Railway. Although but one of the Railway's engineering achievements during its long history, it is certainly the one that makes an immediate impression on the casual visitor, as it did to me on my first visit to the Ffestiniog in 1967. Perhaps it was Merddin Emrys that inspired me to volunteer on the Railway over the next forty years!

Merddin Emrys is the oldest of the four surviving double engines on the Ffestiniog Railway and also has the distinction of being the first locomotive to be built in the Railway's workshops at Boston Lodge. Built in 1879, it was satisfying that its latest rebuild and restoration was completed in time for its 125th birthday. Not only is Merddin Emrys of enormous historic importance but also it is vital to the commercial success of the Railway in the present age – only the double engines have the power to pull the long trains of high summer. I think this is an interesting tribute to the robustness of Robert Fairlie's invention.

So my commission had to be of Merddin Emrys, a locomotive that has given me so much pleasure and inspired me over the years. But at which location should the painting be?

The Railway's archives have numerous photographs of Merddin Emrys, starting with the "building team" in front of the completed engine outside Boston Lodge in 1879 and the new locomotive hauling a quarrymen's train in the same year. But so far as I am aware, no photographs exist of Merddin Emrys on the Welsh Highland Railway. The physical connection between the Ffestiniog and the Welsh Highland was made in June 1923. In the euphoria of the early days, double engines were used from time to time to haul heavy trains on the Welsh Highland. But the Welsh Highland never achieved the traffic expectations of its creators and by 1925, usage of double engines ceased, as smaller engines were more economic on smaller trains. Receivership of the Welsh Highland followed in 1927 and passenger trains ceased in 1936. Thus Merddin Emrys venturing to the Aberglaslyn Pass and beyond would only have happened in 1923, 1924 or 1925 and it would not have happened very often even in those years. No wonder it was not photographed!

The revival of the Welsh Highland dream means that – on present projections – it will be possible for Merddin Emrys to once again traverse the Aberglaslyn Pass from Summer 2009. Whether it will or not depends on detailed traffic planning yet to be published. And on whether or not – second time around – the promoter's dreams end in success or bankruptcy. **David Gordon**

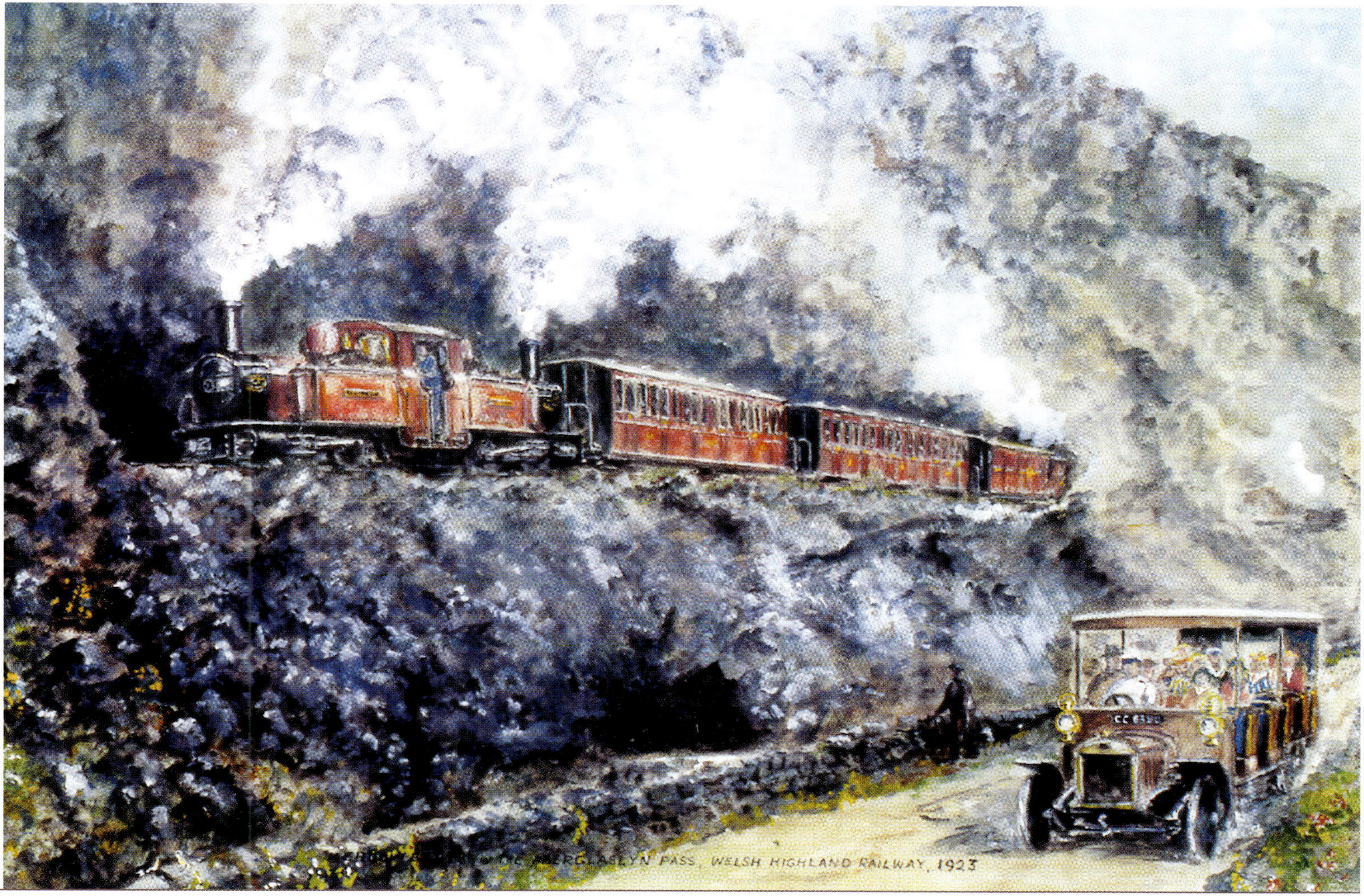
PASS, WELSH HIGHLAND RAILWAY, 1923

Painting 5: Little Giant in the Woodyard Sidings, Portmadoc in 1890

Little Giant, hauling a bolster wagon loaded with timber from the woodyard, stands on the line that curved round from Porthmadog High Street and then ran behind the slate wharves towards Pen Cei and Cornhill. To the right is the woodyard itself, with its distinctive crane and sawmill. The horse is hitched to a pair of huge wheels, beneath which is suspended timber for the keel of a ship. There were three shipyards in Porthmadog, which built over 150 ships between the early 1800s and 1913, so this must have been a common sight around the harbour. All of this area has changed beyond recognition and is where Y Ganolfan, craft shops and a café now stand.

Little Giant would not have been the railway's first choice for Bottom Shunter, since it and Welsh Pony, the last two England engines, were slightly larger than their four predecessors. In the tight confines of the wharves the smaller engines were preferred and indeed Palmerston had its cab reduced in length in later years to ease its passage through some of the tighter curves. Little Giant passed through Boston Lodge works in 1890 to have new frames fitted and therefore is in almost ex-works condition in the painting.

Client's comments

Research for the earlier painting of The Princess at Cornhill reminded me just how much traffic was carried over the network of lines beyond Harbour Station and Britannia Bridge. Particularly intriguing was the woodyard, with its own sidings, which was an essential part of the port's shipbuilding industry. As it would almost certainly have supplied timber to the quarries, there must have been a significant amount of its products carried up the line. Just a couple of historic photographs show the woodyard and then really only as incidental to the main subject, so it required some imagination to produce the scene in the painting. One panorama of the harbour area includes the huge pair of wheels and Edward's knowledge of both shipping and haulage made them an obvious feature. They also gave the opportunity for Edward to include a horse, which he always painted and drew with extraordinary sensitivity. Paddy was again included by mutual agreement, but once more his interest in wheels is worrying. The choice of engine was again easy: Little Giant, having been scrapped in the interwar years, is one of the Ffestiniog's lost engines and therefore has a poignant appeal. Overall the painting came together remarkably well from rather disparate data and remains a particular favourite.

P.J.H.

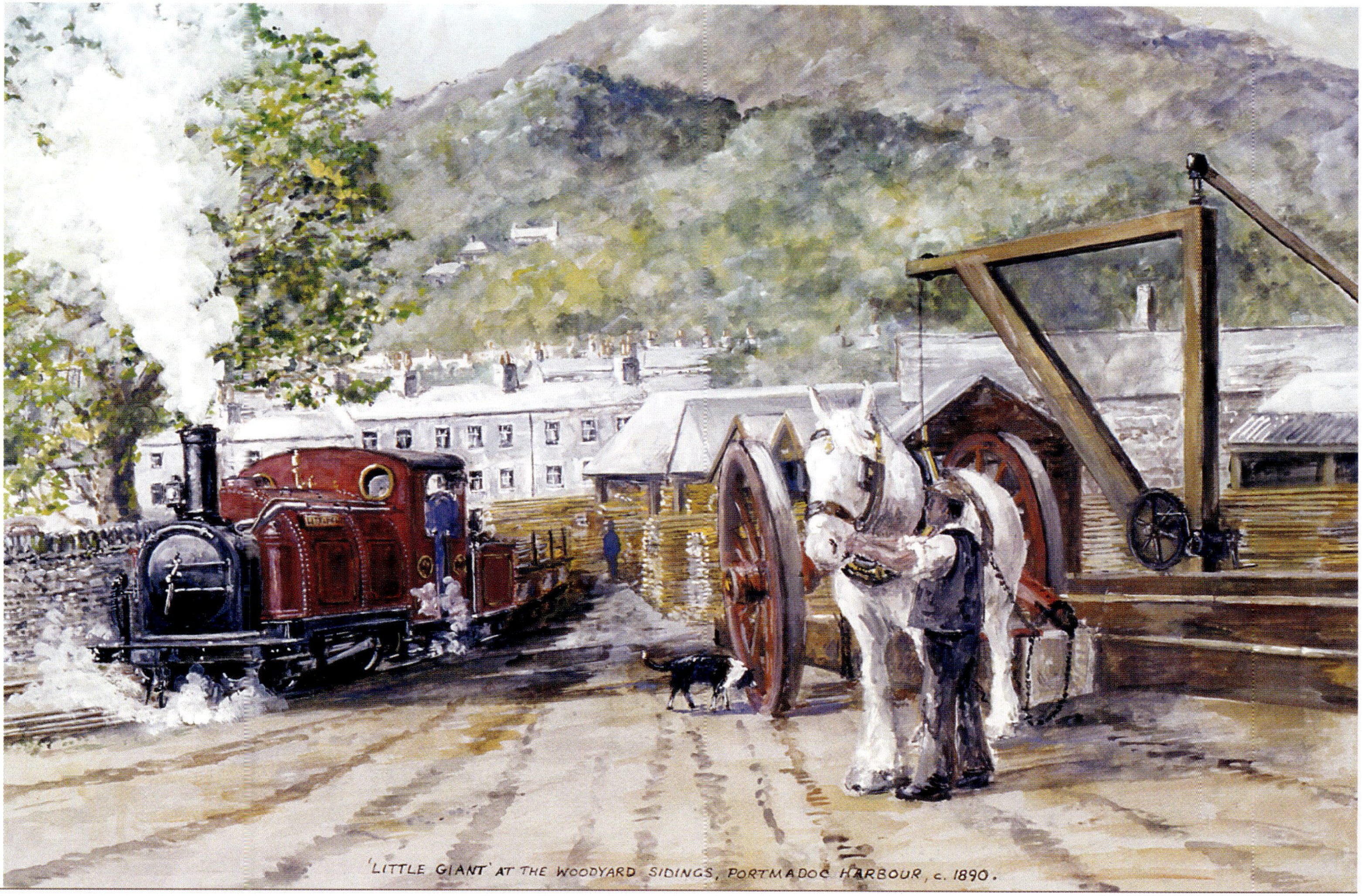
'LITTLE GIANT' AT THE WOODYARD SIDINGS, PORTMADOC HARBOUR, c. 1890.

Painting 6: Welsh Pony at Dinas, Christmas 1869

The setting for this painting is that most elusive of Ffestiniog stations, Dinas in Blaenau Ffestiniog. This was the railway's original upper passenger terminus, opened in 1865, but as the town developed, Duffws supplanted it and Dinas was closed in 1870. However, the original main line on which it stood then became a branch and a most important source of slate traffic, serving Oakeley and Llechwedd quarries. At the time the painting was done no photographs showing the passenger station in use were known and therefore the usual careful study of later photographs, maps and plans, plus an element of speculation, were used to compose the scene. Ironically, within months a remarkably clear photograph was discovered, but fortunately it confirmed that the painting is broadly right.

Dinas station building stands behind the locomotive, with the engine shed to its left. The shed remained in use for some years after the cessation of the passenger service, only later being replaced by a larger shed at Glan-y-pwll. To the right behind the coaches is the goods shed and further along still is a disc signal. In the distance a pair of horses are crossing the Welsh Slate Company's viaduct with a train of empty slate wagons being returned to the quarry.

Welsh Pony is in original condition as delivered only two years earlier. The first vehicle in the train is one of the early four-wheeled brake vans, replaced by the curly roofed vans in the early 1870s. The coaches are some of the line's original four-wheelers built by Brown, Marshalls & Co. of Birmingham. Remarkably, six of these have survived, now running in heritage trains and affectionately known as Bug Boxes.

The horse and cart have approached the station along the road from the village of Dinas to collect the trunks on the ground. Paddy watches the whole scene with interest.

Little remains to be seen at Dinas now, just heaps of stone where the buildings once stood and the empty track bed, the rails having been lifted in the early preservation days. However, were the earlier embryo plans to link the Ffestiniog Railway to the Llechwedd Slate Caverns ever to come to pass, then Dinas might yet see passenger trains again.

Client's comments

Following the success of the Taliesin on Cei Mawr scene, the Festiniog Railway Heritage group decided to commission a painting to appear on their 1998 Christmas card. It was decided to go for an unashamedly romanticised Victorian view of the railway, with snow and figures standing round a brazier. Only a robin is missing from this nostalgic confection, but Edward enjoyed painting it enormously.

P.J.H.

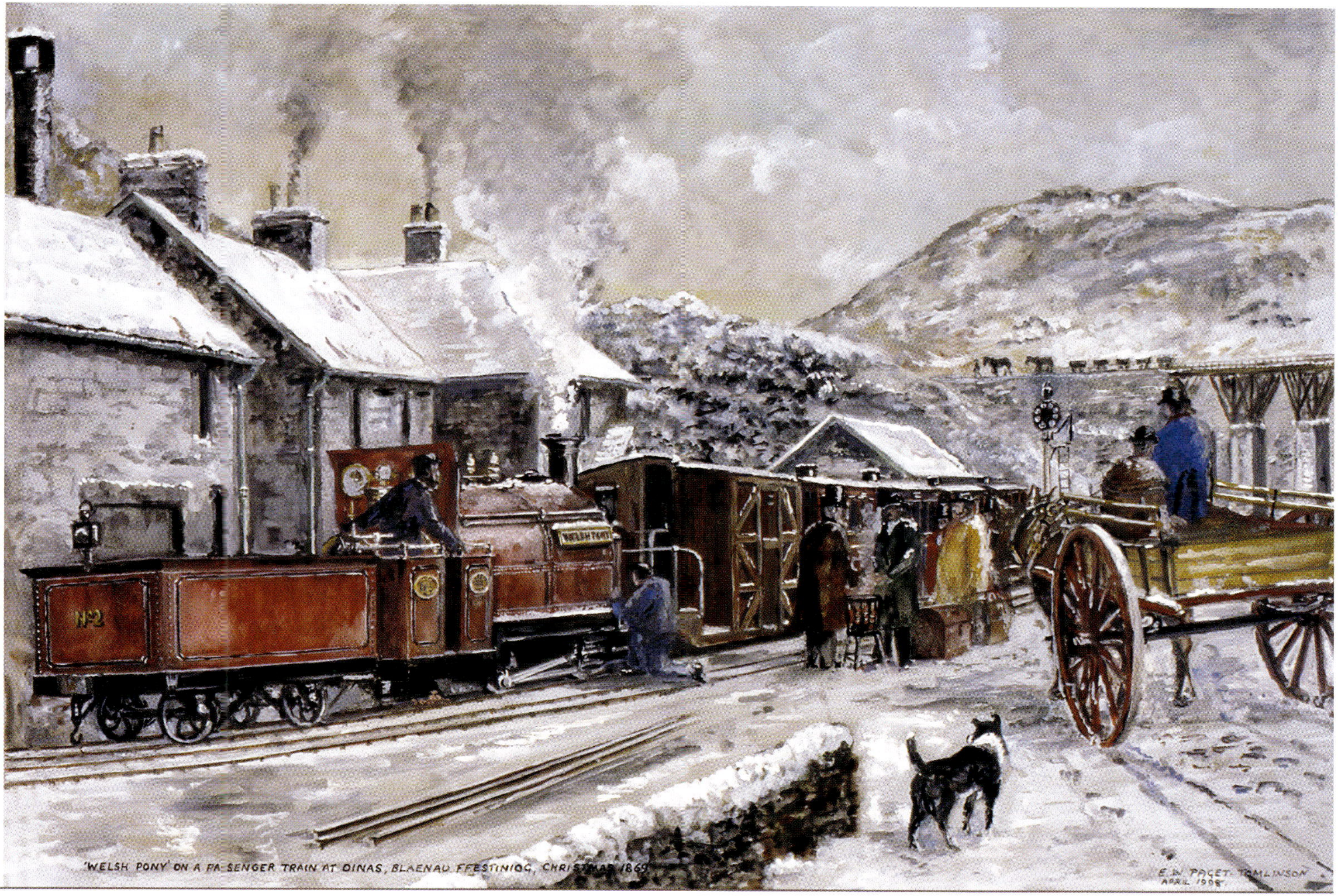

'WELSH PONY' ON A PA SENGER TRAIN AT DINAS, BLAENAU FFESTINIOG, CHRISTMAS 1869
E. W. PAGET-TOMLINSON
APRIL 1998
No2

Painting 7: James Spooner and Russell at Tan-y-Bwlch

Of all the scenes "beyond the reach of the camera", this painting is perhaps the most intriguing. Dinas Works' attempt to cut down the Welsh Highland Railway's previously elegant Hunslet Russell in order for it to fit the Ffestiniog's smaller loading gauge is generally considered to be an act of desecration. The cab, dome and chimney were reduced in height and would have fitted, but the tanks and cab side sheets were just too wide for some of the Ffestiniog's cuttings and the Moelwyn Tunnel, with rock outcrops actually scratching the engine. It is assumed that Russell made just one trip up the Ffestiniog to prove the point, with details sketchy, but it is thought that the engine actually got stuck in the Moelwyn Tunnel. Certainly no photograph was taken to record the event and thereafter Russell never ventured beyond Boston Lodge.

The painting has Russell standing on the Down line at Tan-y-Bwlch after the unsuccessful trip. The driver and fireman are inspecting the damage to the side tanks, before continuing their journey back to Boston Lodge and Dinas. A passenger photographs the scene. It is a busy day at Tan-y-Bwlch and James Spooner is pulling in with an Up train, leaking steam from its flexible joints, as Fairlies were prone to do when maintenance standards dropped in the interwar years. The old wooden footbridge carrying a footpath over the station remains, not being demolished until 1933, and the Oakeley Arms horse and cart waits behind the station building. The signal post is devoid of arms, disused since the Ffestiniog became a Light Railway, with much simplified operational arrangements to coincide with the opening of the WHR in 1923.

Client's comments

I have always been intrigued by the cutting down of Russell to fit the FR. The first narrow-gauge book I bought in 1960, Patrick Whitehouse's Narrow Gauge Album, had two similar photographs of the engine standing in Beddgelert Station in "before" and "after" condition and told the story of the unsuccessful work. The same year I saw the engine itself standing forlornly beside the Narrow Gauge Museum at Tywyn and soon after was fortunate to meet Reg Crick, the luckless Boston Lodge apprentice fitter sent to Dinas to cut down the engine. Since then I have harboured a fondness for the engine and whilst I quite understand why the WHR Ltd has since restored Russell to its original outline, I rather feel that in its shorn condition it somehow epitomised the rugged spirit of the WHR's brief interwar period of operation. Tan-y-Bwlch was the obvious location for the painting, since it is likely to have been where the train crew paused after their frightening experience in the Moelwyn Tunnel. The chance to include James Spooner, by then in its twilight years, and all the hustle and bustle of Tan-y-Bwlch, so obvious in numerous photographs of the station, made up a most pleasing scene. Edward was also intrigued by the story of Russell and took a lot of care getting the trains right, concentrating on them and the passengers to such an extent that the first draft of the painting completely omitted the station house to the left. Where it should stand, Edward had painted some trees, and while he corrected the mistake as soon as it was pointed out, the draft is in the project's file as a pleasing curiosity.

P.J.H.

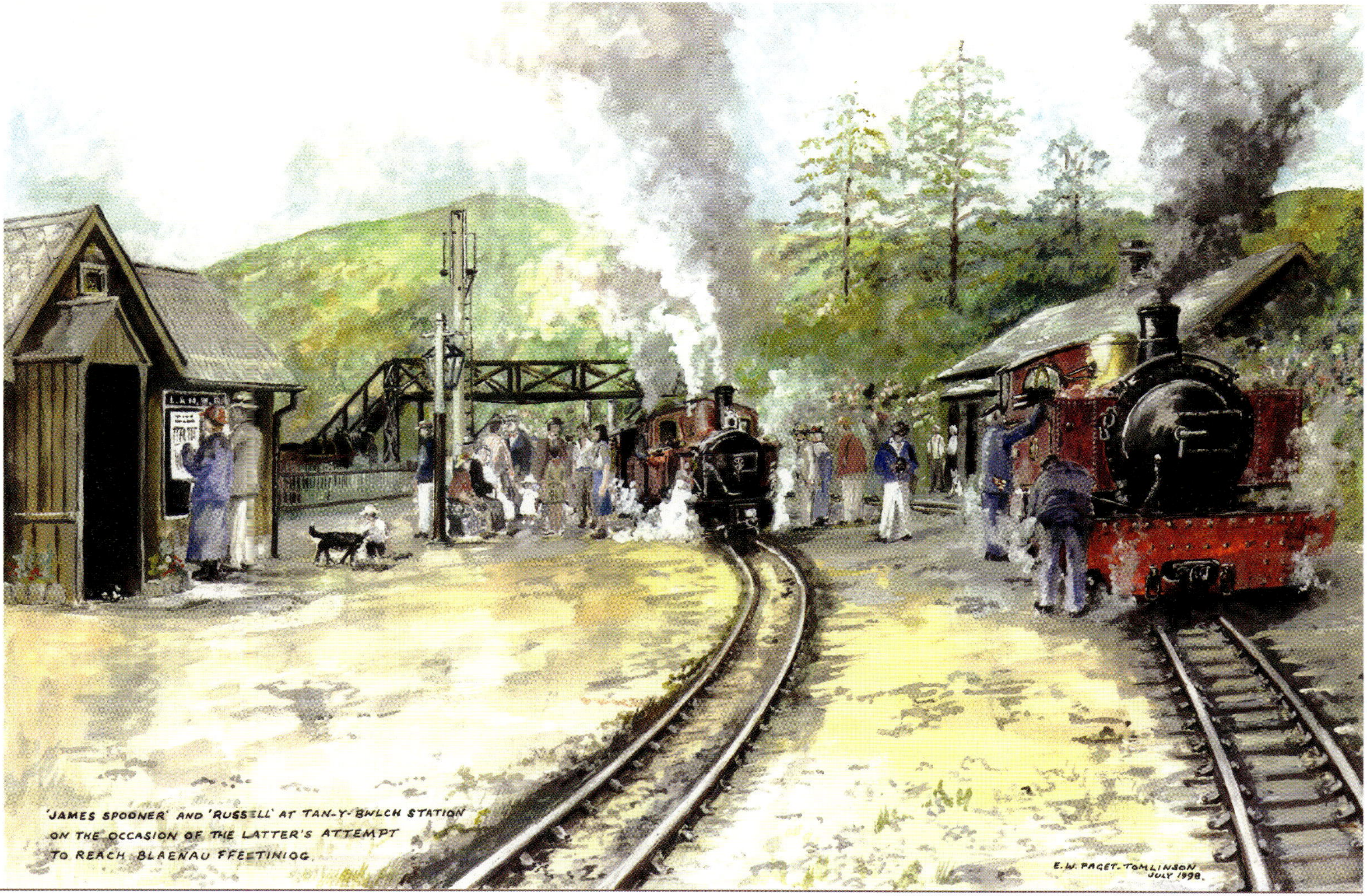
'JAMES SPOONER' AND 'RUSSELL' AT TAN-Y-BWLCH STATION
ON THE OCCASION OF THE LATTER'S ATTEMPT
TO REACH BLAENAU FFESTINIOG.
E.W. PAGET-TOMLINSON
JULY 1998.

Painting 8: Prince at Quarry Lane Crossing in 1910

The first major station on the Ffestiniog Railway, travelling up the line from the terminus at Harbour Station, Porthmadog, is at Minffordd, where the FR crosses the standard-gauge Cambrian Coast line. About a quarter of a mile below Minffordd Station there is a level crossing over a minor road, off which is a large quarry, originally owned by the Pwllheli Granite Company. Known locally as Minffordd Quarry, much of the ballast for track relaying on the FR has come from this source in recent years. It is a major feature of the landscape and is the reason for the official name of Quarry Lane Crossing for this point on the Railway. The manning (or, more usually, "womanning") of the crossing gates had been a requirement since the early days of the Railway and the company built a cottage by the side of the line, the occupancy of which was contingent on the occupiers acting as crossing keepers. In the early preservation days the crossing keeper was Lottie Edwards and to this day the crossing tends to be known as Lottie's Crossing, rather than by its official title. Lottie's door was always open to volunteers working on the railway and her kettle was always boiling for tea.

The painting presented Edward with a problem, since the location does not lend itself to a panoramic view. Faced with this, Edward decided on a head-on view and used incidental details to add interest. Having decided on an Edwardian scene, Edward introduced a period car waiting at the crossing and a lady crossing keeper as a tribute to Lottie. Paddy, waiting patiently with his master, pokes his head through the gate to watch the train, but ignores the cat sitting on the wall. The cat is the author's Brown Burmese, surely an unlikely breed to find in Wales at that time, but allowable through artistic licence.

The old crossing gates with stone posts are in their original narrow position, not liked by the Railway Inspectorate when reopening took place, and therefore now widened. In the right foreground is the capstan, which operated the protective signals above and below the crossing. Such capstans were to be found at all stations and road level crossings and a few, including the Quarry Lane example, survived into the preservation era. Sadly the Railway Company's lack of interest in heritage until recent times means that remaining examples are stored pending a museum setting. Edward, with his usual attention to detail, has captured the corbelled corner of the crossing house in which is located the front door.

Prince is on a Down train, possibly as Bottom Shunter, and is facing downhill. Prior to the 1920s England Engines were turned on turntables at Boston Lodge and Glan-y-pwll, but latterly always worked uphill.

Client's comments

Peter Wood from the FR Society's London Area Group was one of the volunteers who frequented Lottie's Crossing and it was a place of fond memories for him of early days on the railway, as it also is for many others. Peter was keen to commission a painting of the crossing, but as the rules of the project precluded the preservation era, he was happy to have an historic view. Together we worked up the initial ideas, deciding that the engine should be Prince, also the subject of many fond memories for pioneers of the line's preservation. Edward then used his usual skill to produce the painting. Sadly, Peter died in 2004 and the whereabouts of the original of the painting are now unknown.

P.J.H.

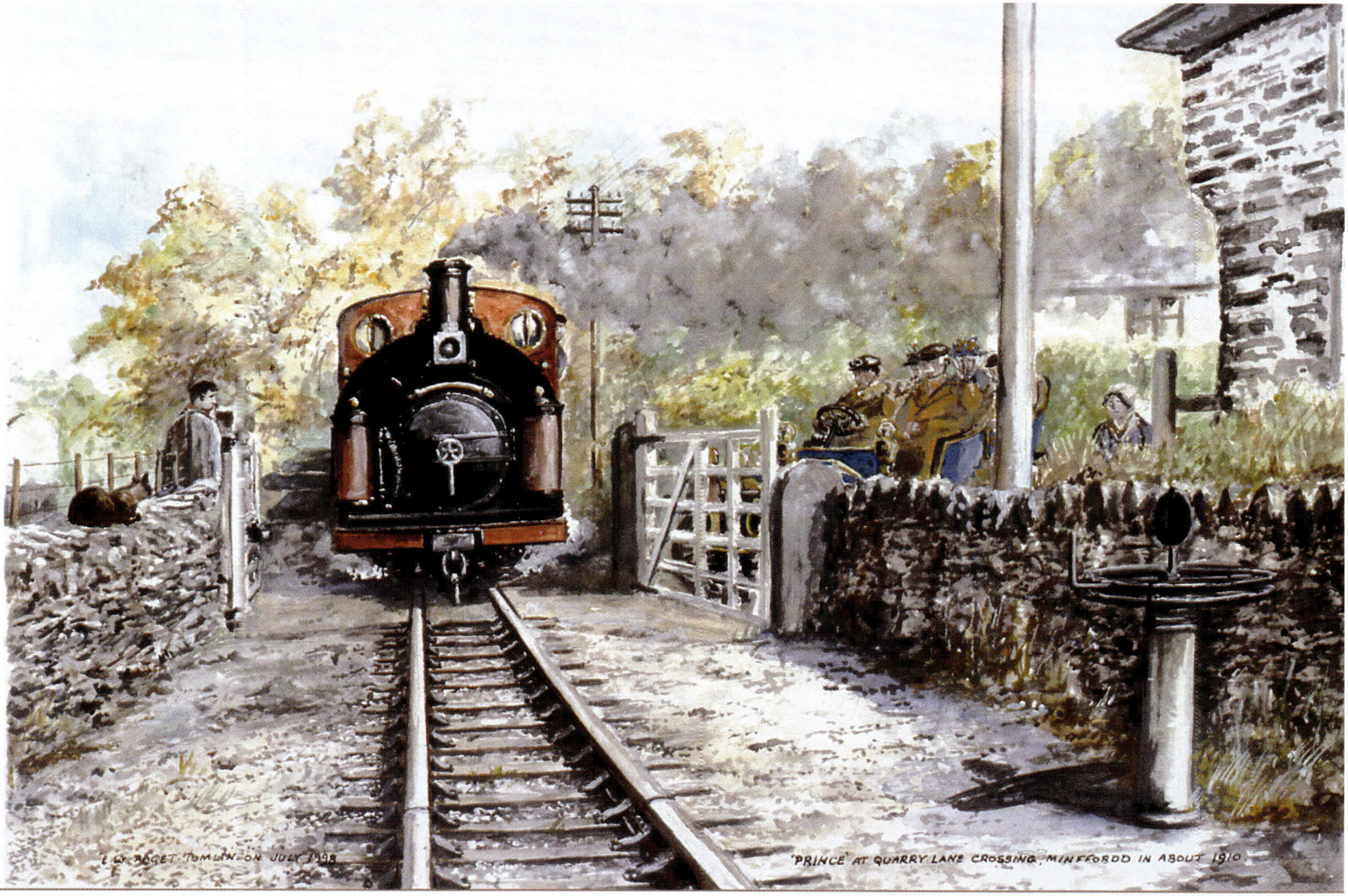
E.W. PAGET-TOMLINSON JULY 1998
'PRINCE' AT QUARRY LANE CROSSING, MINFFORDD IN ABOUT 1910

Painting 9: Palmerston on Britannia Bridge in 1878

In this view, Palmerston, in original condition, is carrying out the duties of Bottom Shunter, returning empty slate wagons to Harbour Station for attaching to the next train to Blaenau Ffestiniog. It is running over Britannia Bridge, the original location of the sluice gates that stop the tide running up the Glaslyn valley above the Cob. Beside the train, a team of horses is pulling the Woodyard's massive wheels supporting the keel timbers for the Cadwalader Jones, launched in 1878.

It was only through the recent purchase of a copy of Porthmadog Ships by Emrys Hughes and Aled Jones that the author discovered that he has inadvertently introduced an inaccurate detail into the painting by choosing the Cadwalader Jones as the ship being built. The date is correct, but she was built at Borth-y-Gest rather than Porthmadog, so the timber is going in the wrong direction! The Woodyard is away to the right of the painting, beyond where Paddy and his master are walking.

The harbour is typically full of ships, mainly Porthmadog's distinctive topsail schooners, of which the Cadwalader Jones was an example, and one of the harbour's three steam paddle tugs. Above the engine's smoke can be seen Cornhill, featured in Painting 3. The building in the left foreground, then a slate quarry office but now a private house, was not given its distinctive slate-hung walls until somewhat later than the date of the painting. On the hillside above the harbour are the houses on Y Garth. Here lived the more affluent Porthmadog residents, sea captains and those running the town's numerous businesses, in much grander houses than the terraces to be found in the streets below. Further to the left along the hillside was Bron-y-Garth, home of the Spooner family in the railway's heyday.

Client's comments

Many old photographs show panoramas of the harbour at Porthmadog in Victorian times, but very few have any direct railway interest. The inspiration for this painting is an intriguing photograph taken from a similar angle which shows not only the harbour full of shipping, but also, as a quite incidental detail, track repairs being done to the line across Britannia Bridge. By adding Palmerston and train, the railway becomes the focal point. The harbour and environs have always fascinated me, having seen great changes even in the years I have known them. Some still remains of its ambience, but somehow its vibrant past is not really celebrated by the town to the extent it deserves. This painting is thus a record of an amazing place at the height of its success. The vantage point for this and many other photographs over the years has also rather intrigued me. This is the rather underrated Ynys y Towyn, the small and easily ignored rocky hill, which was one of the larger islands in Traeth Mawr. It was used by William Madocks as the starting point for the Cob, with the original sluice gates being located between it and the shore. It was the scouring effect of the Afon Glaslyn's water surging out of the sluices that led to the building of the harbour between 1821 and 1825. Ynys y Towyn was much reduced in size through its use as a quarry for stone to build the Cob and is now once more a tranquil spot and owned by the National Trust.

P.J.H.

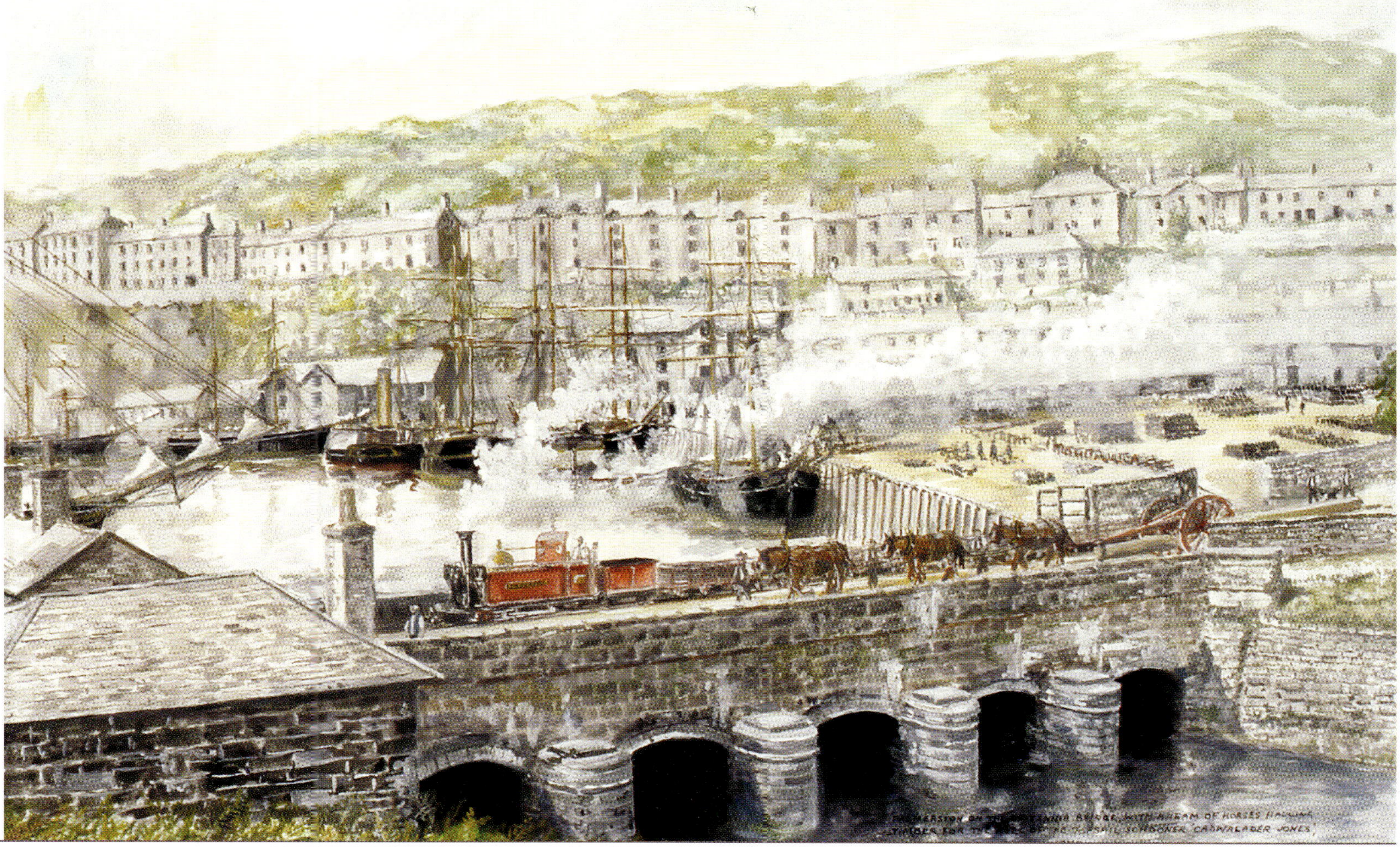

MERSTON ON BRIDGE, WITH A TEAM OF HORSES HAULING
TIMBER FOR THE OF THE TOPSAIL SCHOONER 'CADWALADER JONES'

Painting 10: Moel Tryfan and Prince at Duffws in 1926

Duffws Station in the centre of Blaenau Ffestiniog was the Railway's upper passenger terminus for many years. It was not the original terminus, which was Dinas, featured in Painting 6. The line to Duffws was at first just a branch and the station did not open until 1866, but the rapid development of this part of Blaenau as the slate industry expanded made it the focal point for passenger traffic, with Dinas ceasing to be used in 1870.

The end of the main line in the middle distance was marked by the commencement of two inclines to various quarries in the mountains above, one of which is visible. Thus it was at Duffws that empty slate wagons waited to go up to the quarries, and once loaded were collected and then run down to Minffordd and Porthmadog in gravity trains. The station building with its distinctive gable ends is visible to the right of the passenger train with the Goods Shed in front of it. Various point indicators remain in use, although the main signalling system had been abandoned in 1923. Duffws was indeed a hive of activity and interest, although it had been closed for passenger traffic from 1923 to 1925, reopening in 1926 and finally closing in 1930. Thereafter the joint station with the GWR, roughly where the present-day Network Rail station is situated, just a couple of hundred yards down the line, became the railway's upper passenger terminus.

The inclusion of Moel Tryfan in this painting is a good example of Edward's concept of "beyond the reach of camera". Unlike Russell the engine had been successfully cut down to fit the Ffestiniog's loading gauge, with chimney, dome and cab reduced in height rather unaesthetically. The engine is then known to have worked through to Blaenau on a fairly regular basis, but no photographs have yet been found of Moel Tryfan anywhere further north on the FR than Boston Lodge.

The Top Shunter in this painting is Prince, marshalling a line of loaded slate wagons ready for the next gravity train. Most of the paintings in the project have the odd detail or two that can be the subject of debate about their historical accuracy. In this painting, however, there is no doubt that the author, advising Edward on detail, made a mistake, since at this date Prince would still have been in the FR's red livery. The dark green, introduced by Colonel Stephens, appeared slowly from 1925 onwards only as engines went through Boston Lodge for major repairs.

Client's comments

This station would make a great model. It has all I want – passenger facilities, goods road for shunting, through lines, loop, loco facilities, an urban background, a bridge for a scenic break at one end and an incline at the other, with a slope that just happens to match my loft wall where it meets the original house. The year chosen is 1926, the station having just reopened, and when Single Fairlie Moel Tryfan was working through from the Welsh Highland Railway, the only engine from that line able to fit the Ffestiniog's tighter loading gauge. There is also the ever-present England shunter. The station building still exists in a sea of tarmac and the painting, as do so many in the series, illustrates a section of the railway where its purpose and lifeblood have been swept away and can never be restored. This is where the slate was gathered and started its journey down the line to the outside world. It is all hustle and bustle, beautifully captured; an unusual engine, the passenger train, slate wagons, gunpowder vans and general merchandise. The painting brings together all these elements. This isn't a pastoral landscape; this is the Ffestiniog Railway at work, a railway in decline, yet still living and hoping with the opening of the Welsh Highland Railway of a bright new future. Edward has captured all these points for me and the work is a constant inspiration to me to fulfil this vision and create the scene in model form. Thank you, Edward. **Richard Pyatt**

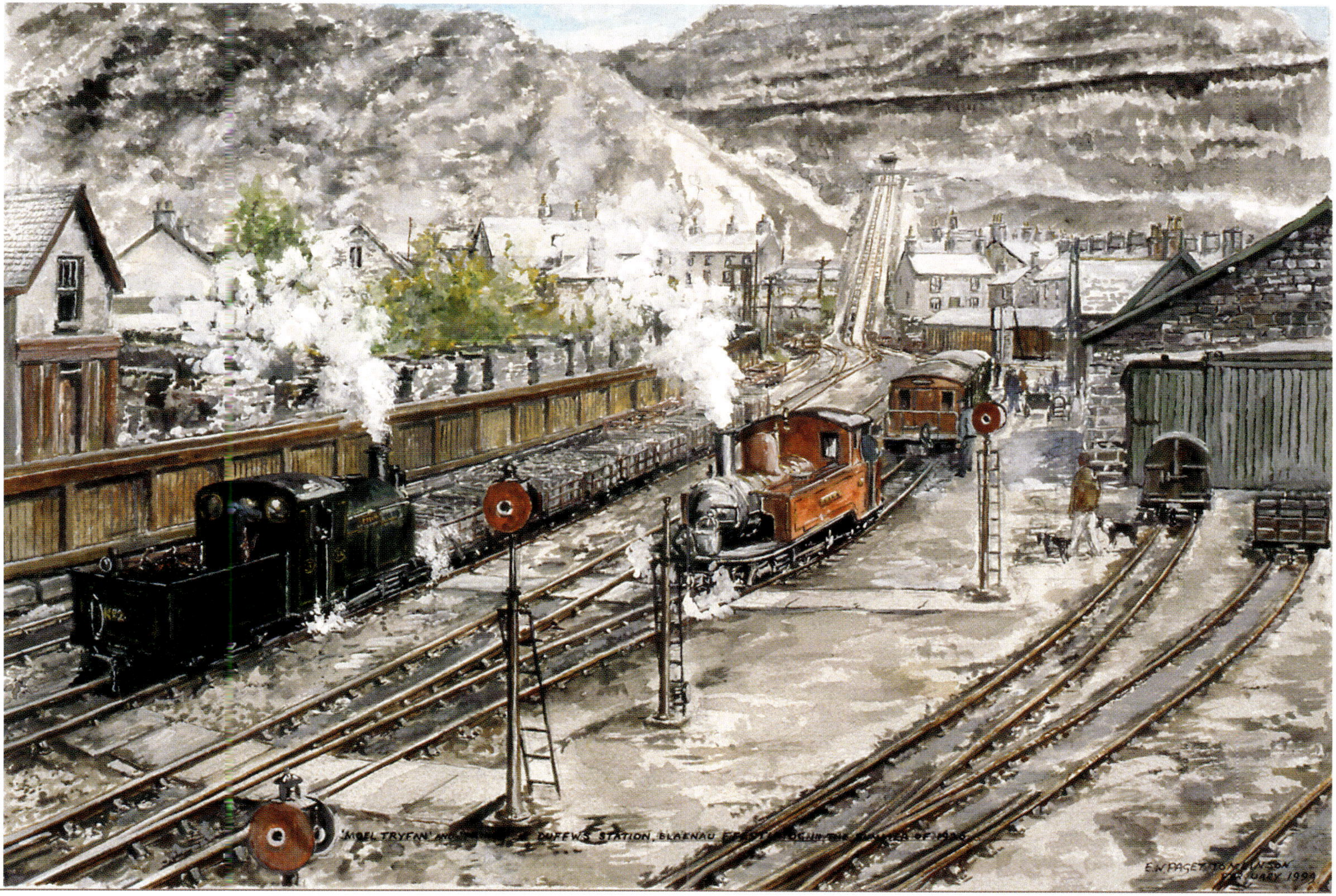
'MOEL TRYFAN'
DUFFWS STATION, BLAENAU

Painting 11: Little Wonder at Penrhyn, Christmas 1881

Following the success of the 1998 Christmas card, the Heritage Group again wanted a suitable winter scene. For 1999 Penrhyn Station was chosen, with the original Double Fairlie Little Wonder on an Up train. Penrhyn is a particularly pleasing wayside station, little changed since it opened at this location in 1879 and comprising sections of the former Harbour Station wooden building. The original Penrhyn Station and siding were nearer the level crossing over the main road, where the formation widens and the crossing keeper's hut now stands. Both stations would have been an integral part of village life, with coal, flour, beer and many other necessities arriving by train, as reflected by the clutter of barrels and the porter's barrow. Passenger traffic was also brisk, including many quarrymen travelling up to work in Blaenau. To the right are Bryn Meirig and Railway Terraces, which still stand overlooking the station. These days the station is a more peaceful spot, serving as a hostel for volunteers working on the railway, but still retaining all its charm.

Little Wonder, although only 12 years old, has only a year more in service before withdrawal. The refinement in the Double Fairlie design to be found in the 1879-built Merddin Emrys had made the pioneer engine effectively redundant. The train, comprising the usual four-wheeler followed by the pair of original Brown Marshall bogie coaches, is in the early ivory and purple livery, no doubt with a string of slate wagons behind.

A soldier returning from leave for Christmas is greeted on the platform by his wife, child and dog, which has more than a hint of the artist's own Paddy about him. Edward has also slipped in the author's springer spaniel, just discernable in front of the group of passengers under the station canopy. The draft for the painting had the soldier's wife in more workaday clothes of shawl, long skirt and apron. However, Edward must have thought the soldier's return deserved something smarter and the long and rather distinctive cape appeared in the final version, with just a hint of incongruity, as some have remarked.

Client's comments

This painting was speculative and once it had been used for the Heritage Christmas card it passed through a couple of hands before being presented to Amy Hore, who had served for many years as volunteer warden for Penrhyn Hostel. Sadly Amy has since died, but the painting remains in good hands. Although not the most popular of the paintings in terms of sales of copies, seeming to work rather better as a card, it is generally reckoned to be a most powerful portrayal of Little Wonder at work and conforms well with the "not captured by camera" criterion.

P.J.H.

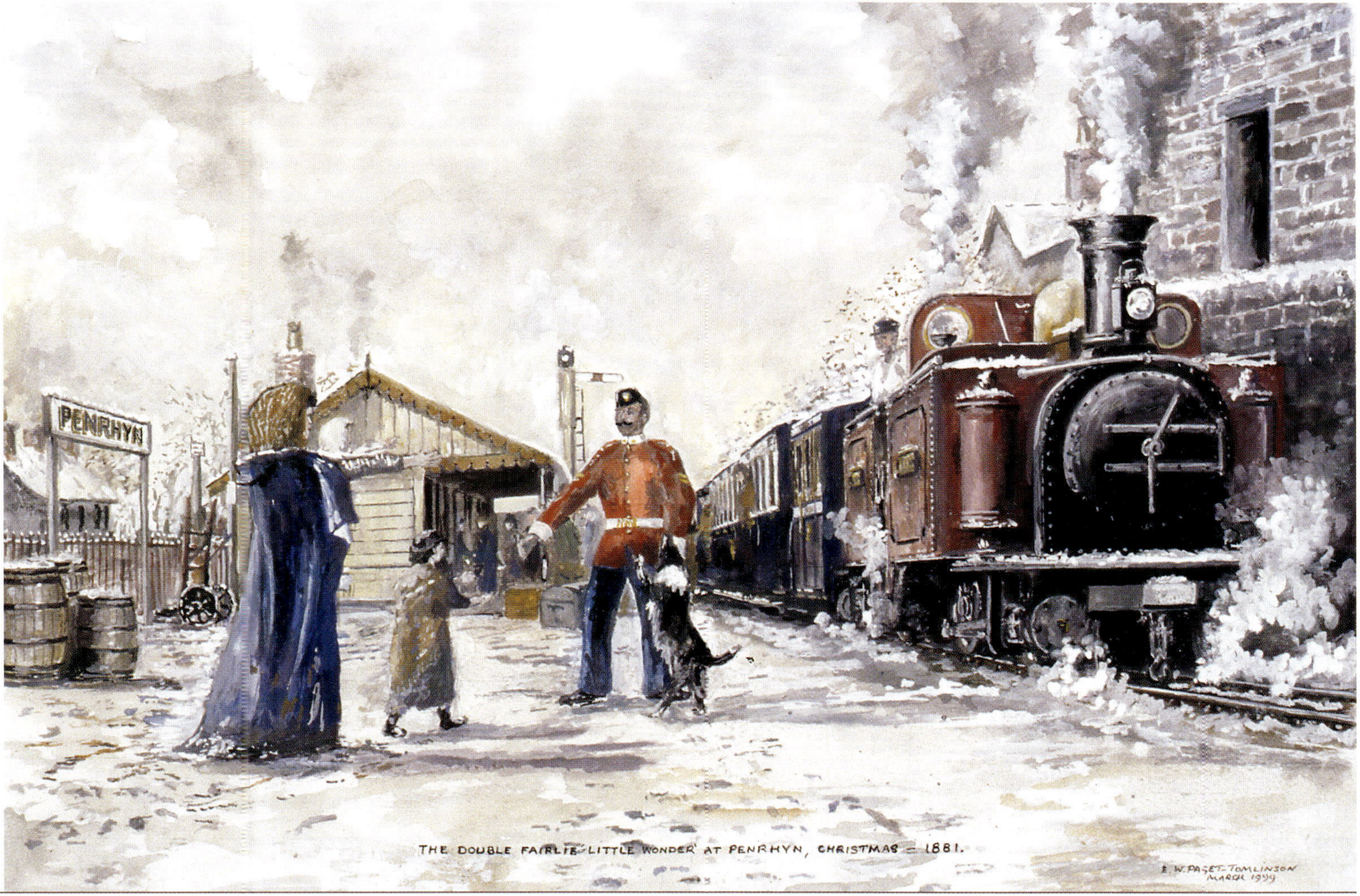
PENRHYN
THE DOUBLE FAIRLIE 'LITTLE WONDER' AT PENRHYN, CHRISTMAS – 1881.
E. W. PAGET-TOMLINSON
MARCH 1999

Painting 12: Two Baldwins at Croesor Junction in the summer of 1929

Although Welsh Highland engines had featured in two earlier paintings, all the locations used for the project had been on the Ffestiniog Railway itself. The Baldwin petrol tractor managed to elude the camera most of the time and records of actual use are sketchy. A typical Colonel Stephens purchase, it was intended to replace the England engines on shunting works. However, one of its more interesting uses was collecting wagons from the Croesor quarries and it was this working that was selected for the painting.

Croesor Junction is situated in the Glaslyn valley some three miles from Porthmadog and marks the point where the Welsh Highland Railway left the much older Croesor Tramway. Station facilities were never more than an old Ffestiniog coach body used to house the train staff, but it did just about figure in the public timetable.

Both engines were built by the Baldwin Locomotive Works, Philadelphia, for service on the temporary lines behind the trenches on the Western Front. The Welsh Highland's No. 590 is coming round the curve on a typical three-coach passenger train from Beddgelert, while the Ffestiniog's petrol tractor waits on the Croesor Tramway with a couple of loaded slate wagons collected from a mile or so further on before the first incline. By this time the quarries in the Croesor valley were almost moribund, but there was still a little traffic on the old tramway.

The two poles to the left are for the Welsh Highland phone and telegraph system, but the more substantial ones straddling the Croesor Tramway belong to the North Wales Power & Traction Company, which supplied power to a number of quarries in the area from its Cwm Dyli hydroelectric power station in Nant Gwynant. Its earlier more grandiose plans involved working what would later become the Welsh Highland with three-phase electrification, but the scheme foundered in 1906/7.

The Scout troop is not entirely fanciful, since a published photograph of Rhyd Ddu Station in 1927 includes a similar group, but without Edward's signature Border collie, so perhaps they were camping near Croesor Junction.

Client's comments

Croesor Junction. Oh what a lonely place! I don't know how many tickets were ever issued to or from this spot, but a troop of scouts would be like rush hour at this remote location. The Two American Exiles might be another title for the painting of these First World War survivors in wild Wales. The origin of the painting was what some people view as my philistine interest in internal combustion and electric traction as well as steam. So when discussions started for the painting, I originally thought of just the Baldwin petrol tractor, now well known in its modern guise as Moelwyn. It was then suggested that by including the Welsh Highland's Baldwin steam engine a more interesting picture could be produced. Whether such a combination at this location took place we will never know, but the petrol tractor was used on the trip workings for the Croesor Valley slate quarry traffic up as far as the Llanfrothen road crossing, the limit of flat-bottom rail laid by the Welsh Highland, and sometimes even as far as the bottom of the first incline over the horse tramway T-section rail.

Rodney Thorp

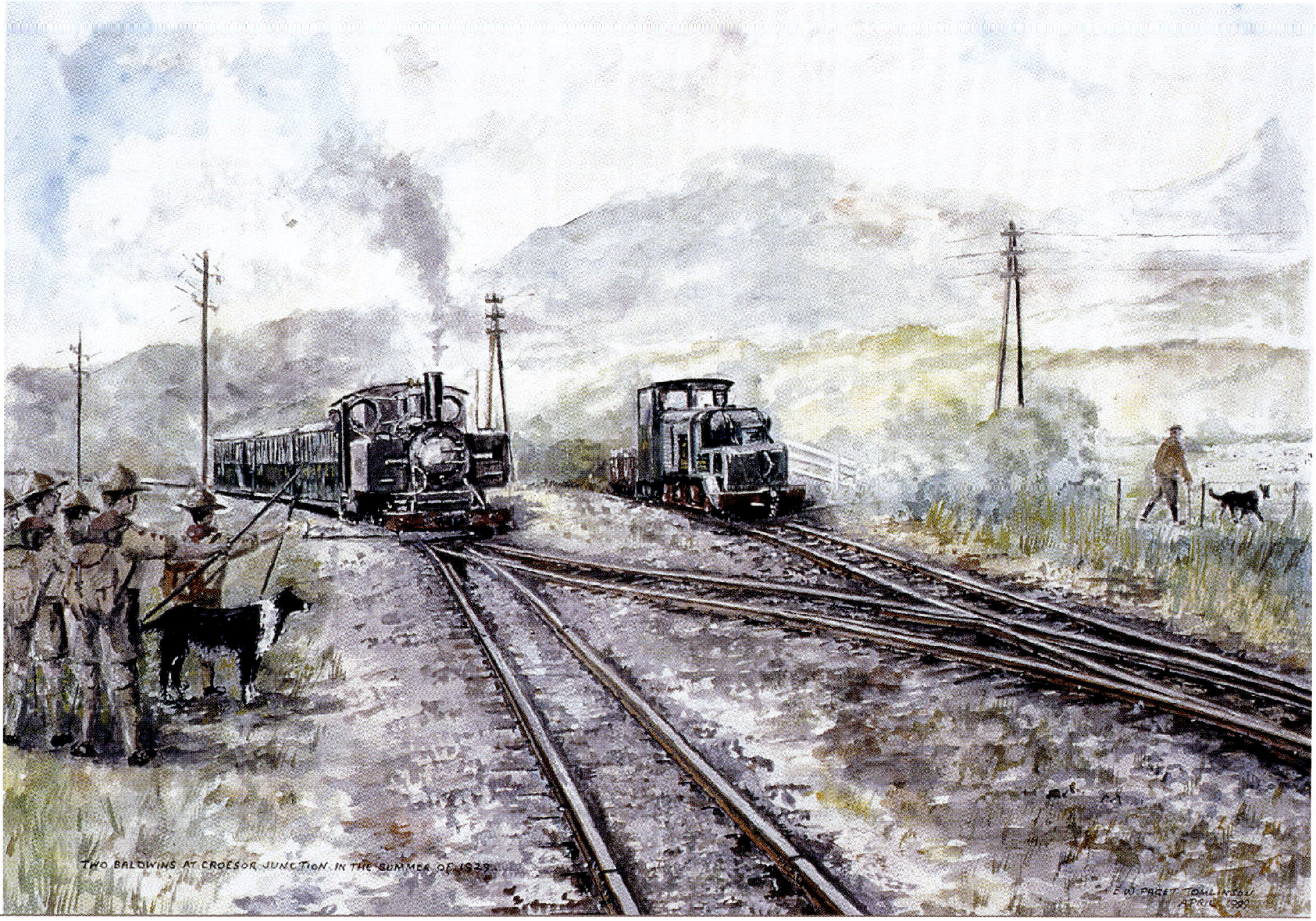
TWO BALDWINS AT CROESOR JUNCTION IN THE SUMMER OF 1929.
E W PAGET TOMLINSON
APRIL 1999

Painting 13: Boston Lodge Works in 1925

Boston Lodge Works has always been an engineering works befitting a narrow-gauge railway which was virtually a miniature main-line operation. Here by the height of the Spooner era could be found all the facilities and trades necessary to build, repair and service locomotives and rolling stock. As the railway's fortunes waned, so Boston Lodge struggled to keep the Ffestiniog running in the old style. Standards inevitably dropped and working methods and arrangements were challenged, never more so than when the Ffestiniog became a Light Railway. Economy in all things became the order of the day and with the appointment of the redoubtable Colonel H.F. Stephens as Civil Engineer and Locomotive Superintendent in 1923 and then as Chairman and Managing Director in 1925, tension and conflict between the railway's traditions and the need for economy was certain. The painting seeks, in part, to illustrate this.

The view is of the main erecting shop with Princess and Livingston Thompson receiving attention, the latter with its bottom end bogie removed. In the foreground are wagon wheels and piles of locomotive fire bars. The overhead shafting used to drive the machines in this part of the works is just visible above the men working on Livingston Thompson.

The two figures standing in conversation depict an imaginary meeting of the old and new orders on the railway. On the left is the tall figure of Colonel Stephens, whilst on the right is Dafydd Dafis, doyen of the Ffestiniog's footplate men. He came from a family who served the railway for much of its history, including sons Tom and Wil Davies, the last driver and firemen on the payroll in charge of Princess on the final slate run before closure in 1946. Dafydd, whose dapper figure with well-trimmed grey beard is seen in various old photographs, had the reputation of being a spirited driver and no doubt he knew everything about getting results from the Ffestiniog's fleet.

Colonel Stephens was running the Ffestiniog at a distance from his Light Railways office in Tonbridge, Kent, and his visits to the railway were usually adversarial. In one letter back to his office he shared his thoughts: "The FR people are quite different to our people . . . they can't help it, it's in their nature." It is easy to imagine this going through his head as he talks to the Dafydd Dafis about changes in the way the Ffestiniog locomotives should be operated and maintained. Paddy's intentions as he stands behind Colonel Stephens are open to conjecture.

Client's comments

When I first started visiting the Railway in the late fifties in London Area Group working parties, we would arrive at about 5.00 or 6.00 on Saturday morning, far too early to descend on Mrs Owen at the Commercial ("Comical") Hotel. So we would all go for a tour of Boston Lodge to see what had happened during the previous month. I was always struck by the appearance, the ancient but still functioning lathes, drills and other machines driven from the line shafting on the massive wooden trusses supporting the roof. I remember reading in the Railway Magazine in that period an enthusiastic description of Boston Lodge as one of the last remaining Victorian engineering workshops, which was still working, together with the confident prediction as to its survival as it was owned by a preservation society. Well, that did not happen; the immediate needs of the time, together with the generosity of the owners of more modern machinery, led to the disposal of most of that belt-driven machinery. So, when I had the opportunity to commission a painting, I jumped at the chance of obtaining a more permanent reminder of the old workshop which I remembered. Edward thought this sounded interesting, but then someone mentioned Colonel Stephens, which he considered more exciting, and the picture was the result. It does give a good impression of the erecting shop as I remember it, an excellent portrait of The Colonel, and it does have glimpse of the line shafting, but disappointingly for me, does not show even one of the belt-driven machines. **Geoffrey Layzell Ward**

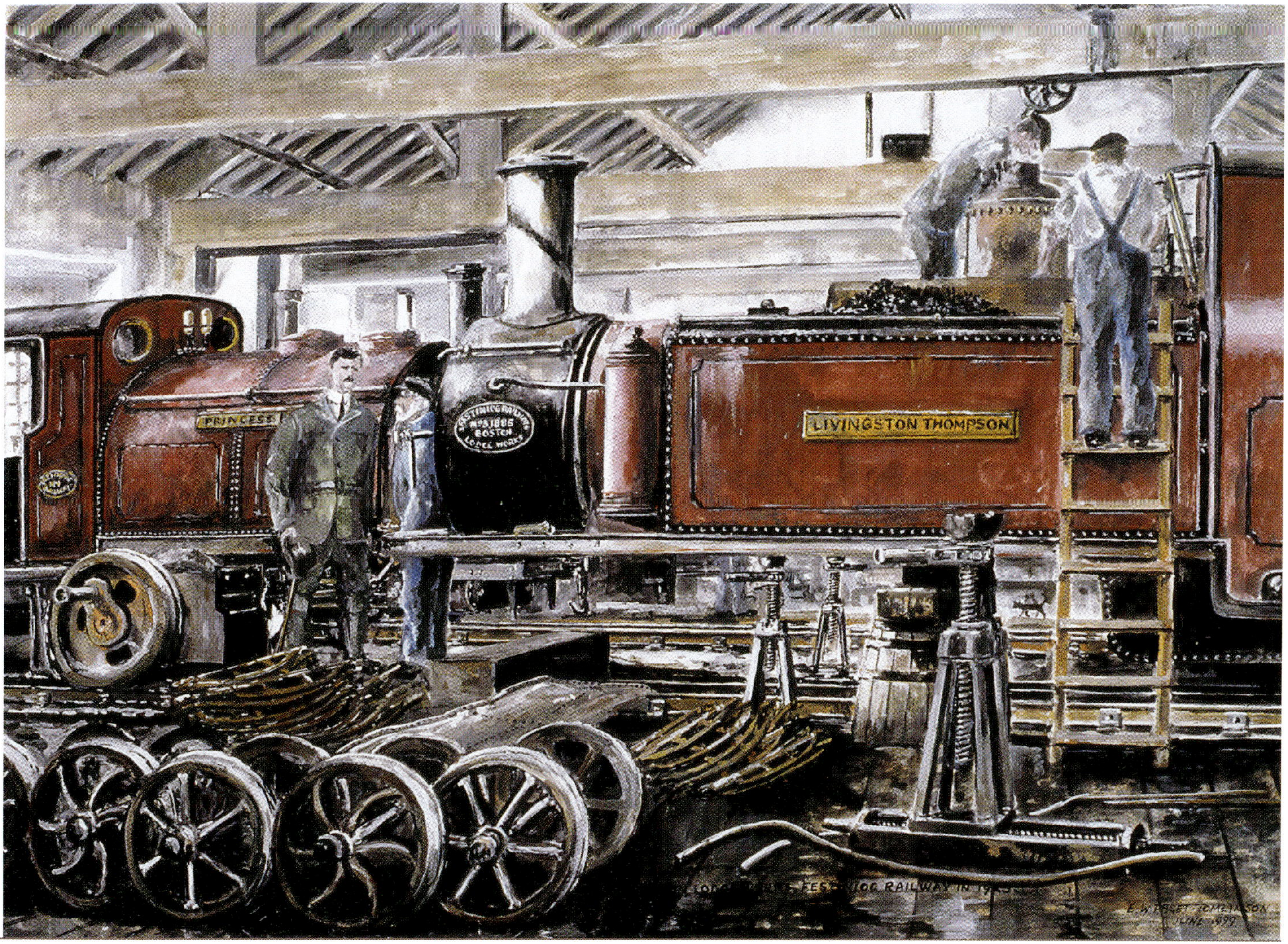
PRINCESS
LIVINGSTON THOMPSON
BOSTON
RAILWAY IN
E.W. PAGET-TOMLINSON
JUNE 1999

Painting 14: Taliesin at Duffws in 1887

Having agreed that project paintings would be beyond camera reach, the request from Peter Pardington for a variation on a well-known Victorian photograph presented a bit of a dilemma. However, the author was not against the proposal, since he considers the photograph in question to be one of the most evocative and pleasing historic views of the railway. Edward in turn displayed his usual equanimity and good nature and agreed to take on the commission.

Commercial photographer John Thomas took the view of Taliesin at Duffws in 1877. Thomas was born in Cardiganshire, but ran his business in Liverpool, where it is said he did well selling prints of Welsh clergymen to Welsh exiles. The subjects of his photographs needed to be saleable and railways clearly fitted the bill. Thus Thomas took several photographs of the Ffestiniog Railway during visits to Blaenau in the 1870s, included in a self-selected collection of his work, which came into the ownership of the National Library of Wales in 1927. The Taliesin photograph appears in several books, but perhaps most effectively as a double-page spread in Peter Johnson's Ffestiniog Railway – A View from the Past. This is a particularly high-quality reproduction and includes detail not always apparent. It was this version that Edward worked from as he changed particular features on the engine to update it to 1887 condition. It was also Edward who spotted that just visible in the photograph are two small boys peering over the wall at the photographer and with his usual artistic humour he included them in the painting, with the addition of Paddy as a companion.

Upon completing the painting, Edward admitted that it had not been the most challenging commission, but he was well pleased with the result. Others too have thought this and it has been amongst the best sellers in copy form.

Client's comments

When J.I.C. Boyd published his Narrow Gauge Rails to Portmadoc in 1949, my father bought a copy and proceeded to construct a model of Taliesin in the then unusual scale of 7mm to 1 foot on "00" gauge track using the drawing by R.E. Tustin contained in the book, together with the photograph in the yard at Boston Lodge Works taken by R.H. Bleasdale in 1887. Many years later, I commenced construction of the same locomotive, this time in live steam at 2½" to 1 foot for 5" gauge track using the same Bleasdale photograph as a reference. Whilst the picture in the works yard contains a wealth of detail for the model engineer, I have to say that the photograph taken at Duffws c.1877 is far more aesthetic although in a slightly earlier guise, having the square sand boxes, original number plate, lubricator on top of the smoke box, etc. Whilst perusing the displays at one of the Ffestiniog Galas, I mentioned the fact to Martin Cook, Chairman of the London Area Group of the FR Society, who said: "Commission a painting of it and you can have what details you like." Having established the likely cost, the painting was duly ordered with the request that the loco showed the later style of sand pots etc. In other words, the Bleasdale photo moved to Duffws. It is rare for an artist to be willing to paint an exact copy of a photograph and this one is no exception, containing as it does a few details of Edward's own choosing. I'll let the reader determine what these are.

Peter Pardington

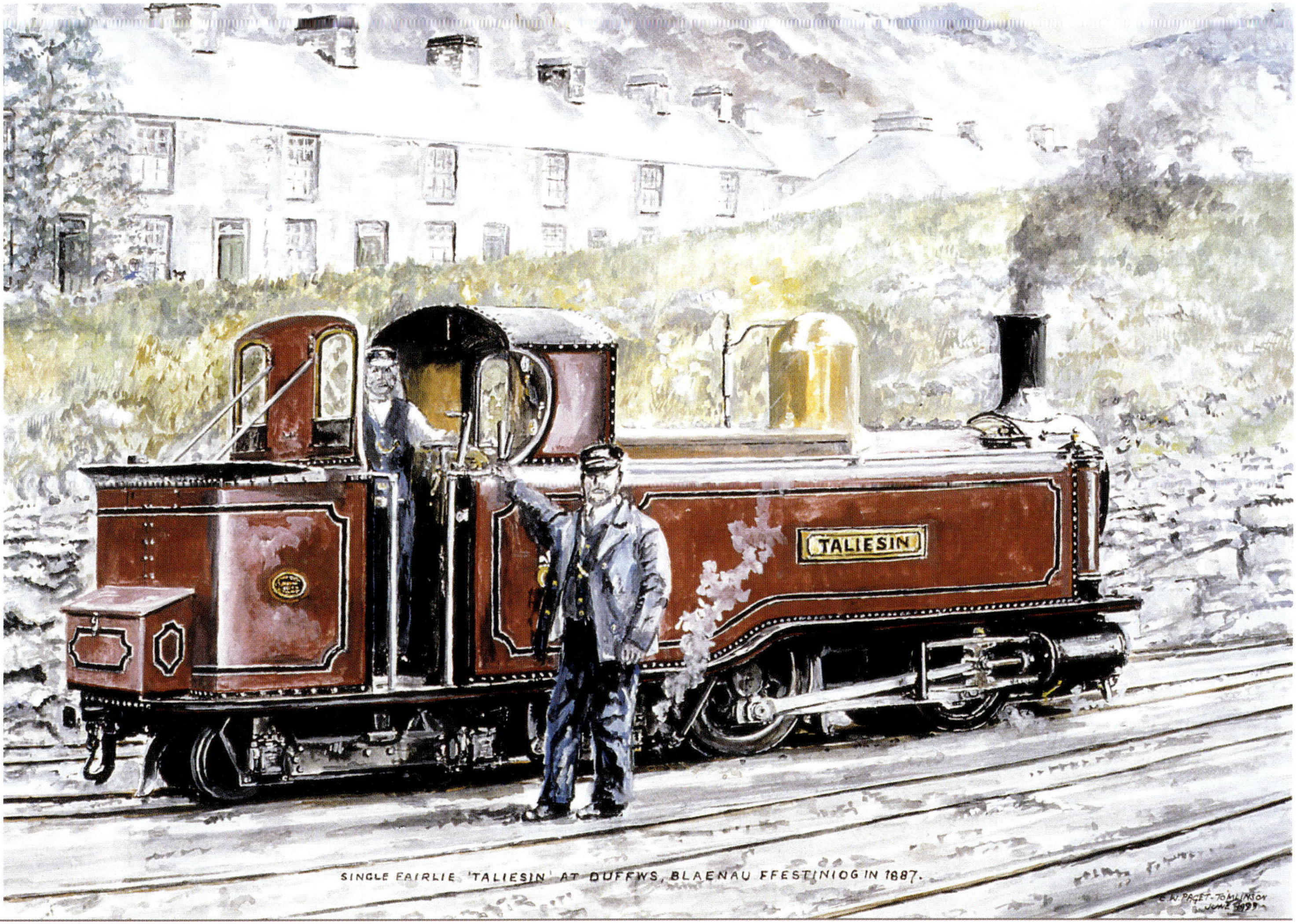
TALIESIN
SINGLE FAIRLIE 'TALIESIN' AT DUFFWS, BLAENAU FFESTINIOG IN 1887.
E.W. PAGET-TOMLINSON

Painting 15: Two Palmerstons at Minffordd Stations in 1889

Minffordd Station, two miles from Porthmadog, was an important place for the Ffestiniog Railway. Here passenger, slate and general goods traffic transferred between the narrow gauge and the coastal line of the Cambrian Railways. In earliest times the Ffestiniog had a stabling point for horses hauling empty wagons back to Blaenau and it was some years before Minffordd grew in importance.

The painting shows only a little of the complexity of the interchange arrangements. Palmerston is seen on the Ffestiniog main line, with a short rake of empty slate wagons, on Bottom Shunter duties here and at Porthmadog. The Ffestiniog's impressive stone station building is just visible to the extreme left, above the Cambrian's more modest wooden affair. Above the first carriage is the roof of the Cambrian's signal box that controlled access to the fan of standard-gauge sidings in the exchange yard, seen running into the immediate foreground. To the left and behind the artist's viewpoint was a complex network of narrow- and standard-gauge lines at different levels, including chutes and a tippler, to allow for the easy exchange of goods and minerals, designed with the usual Spooner engineering innovation. However, transfer of slate was by hand, as seen to the right of the picture.

Client's Comments

Early pictures of Minffordd Low Level in Cambrian days seem to be few and far between. The only one I can lay my hands on is the superb shot of an ancient 0-6-0 standing at the platform while shunting, in C.C. Green's Cambrian Railways Album (Ian Allan, 1977 – the pages seem to be unnumbered). Certainly I know of none showing activity on both FR and standard gauge. I have always been intrigued by the meeting of narrow and standard gauge at Minffordd, both the passenger connection down the ramp, which still fulfils its purpose, and the elaborate transhipment facilities for freight, which still existed and were in limited use when I first visited the Ffestiniog in 1957. The Ffestiniog had already been running through Minffordd without a station there for 31 years before the Cambrian Railways opened between Barmouth and Pwllheli in 1867. It took another five years before the passenger and goods facilities for interchange were opened. Eventually almost all slate traffic from Blaenau was carried to Minffordd for transhipment to the standard gauge and very little reached the harbour at Porthmadog. The last train of the old order on 1 August 1946 was of empties from Minffordd to Blaenau. So in choosing a subject for a painting I decided one showing trains on both lines at Minffordd in Cambrian days would fill a gap and provide a fascinating scene. How the idea of "two Palmerstons" originated I cannot remember, but it adds a nice touch. The FR's Palmerston, seen shunting slate wagons overhead, needs no introduction. The Cambrian's No. 54 Palmerston was one of twelve Sharp Stewart 2-4-0s which bore the brunt of passenger services for many years. It was built in 1865 and cut up in 1909. It lost its name shortly before the time of the picture. It heads a westbound train of three six-wheelers, while two Cambrian wagons are being loaded with slates from FR wagons in the yard at right.

Peter Treloar

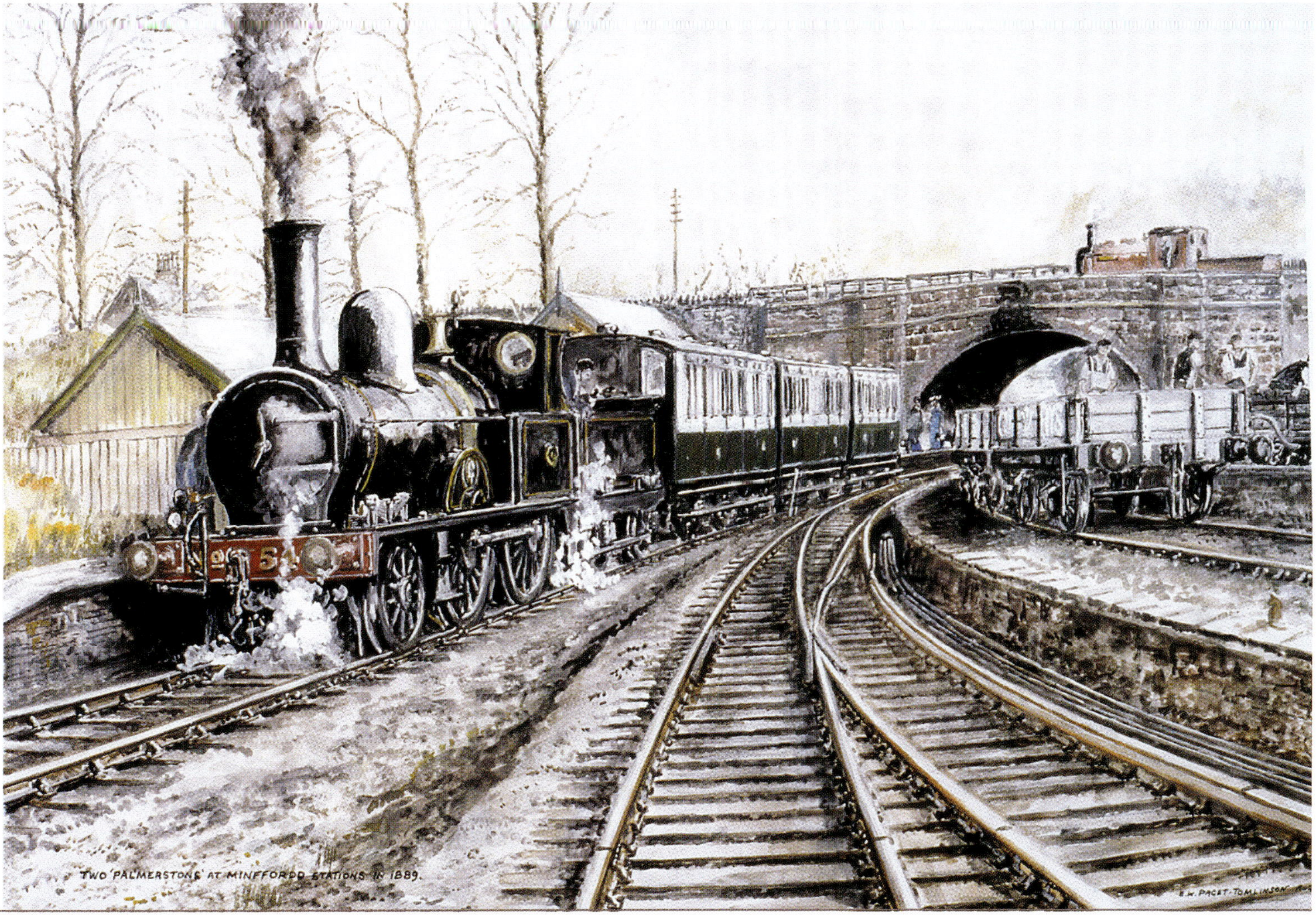
TWO 'PALMERSTONS' AT MINFFORDD STATIONS IN 1889.
E.W. PAGET-TOMLINSON

Painting 16: Up Quarrymen's Train Leaving Portmadoc Harbour Station in 1903

There are relatively few photographs of Ffestiniog Quarrymen's trains, fewer still of double-heading, and the Mondays-only 5.50am departure probably eluded the camera altogether. This train was the busiest of the week, with many quarrymen travelling back to work after a brief weekend break at home and then staying in barracks in the quarries before returning again at midday on Saturday. The Monday train was also used to position the England engine to be employed as Top Shunter at Blaenau for the week, it having come down at the end of the previous week for servicing at Boston Lodge.

The scene is of the station throat at Porthmadog Harbour Station with the train just pulling away. The two-storey station building is seen to the left above the roofs of the carriages in the siding. The masts and rigging of ships at the wharves stand in front of the dark silhouette of Moel-y-Gest rising above the town. To the right, on the line leading to Britannia Bridge and the network of lines on the wharves beyond, stands the De Winton vertical-boilered locomotive built in 1877 for the Gorseddau Junction and Portmadoc Railway, a short-lived line that served quarries in the Gorseddau and Pennant valleys. After its own line closed the locomotive was used briefly in the period from 1902 bringing granite from Moel-y-Gest Quarry to be loaded into steamers at the wharf in front of the Harbour Station. To achieve this it needed to run onto the Cob and then reverse back at about the point the artist has captured it. At this time the Ffestiniog Railway was still fully signalled and the signalman, accompanied by Paddy, in his sentry box would have had a busy time with an array of signals and points controlling complicated passenger, slate and freight train movements.

The train consists of Mk.3 Quarrymen's Carriages, which were rudimentary compared with the carriages used on the main passenger service. They were lit by oil, certainly not as brightly as Edward has shown to enhance the dramatic effect.

Client's Comments

Derek Haynes wanted a painting with plenty of action and strong dramatic effect, but he had no particular preference on location or subject. We worked though various ideas and eventually decided on a night-time scene at Porthmadog. The first draft was of a Down train arriving in the evening, but there still was not sufficient activity. We then came up with the idea of a dawn scene, with the departure of the Monday-only double-headed quarrymen's train. Later on in the process we included the ex-Gorseddau Tramway vertical-boilered locomotive for added interest. The completed painting was just what Derek Haynes wanted and is quite unlike any other in the series. Sales of copies have confirmed that the subject has great appeal.

P.J.H.

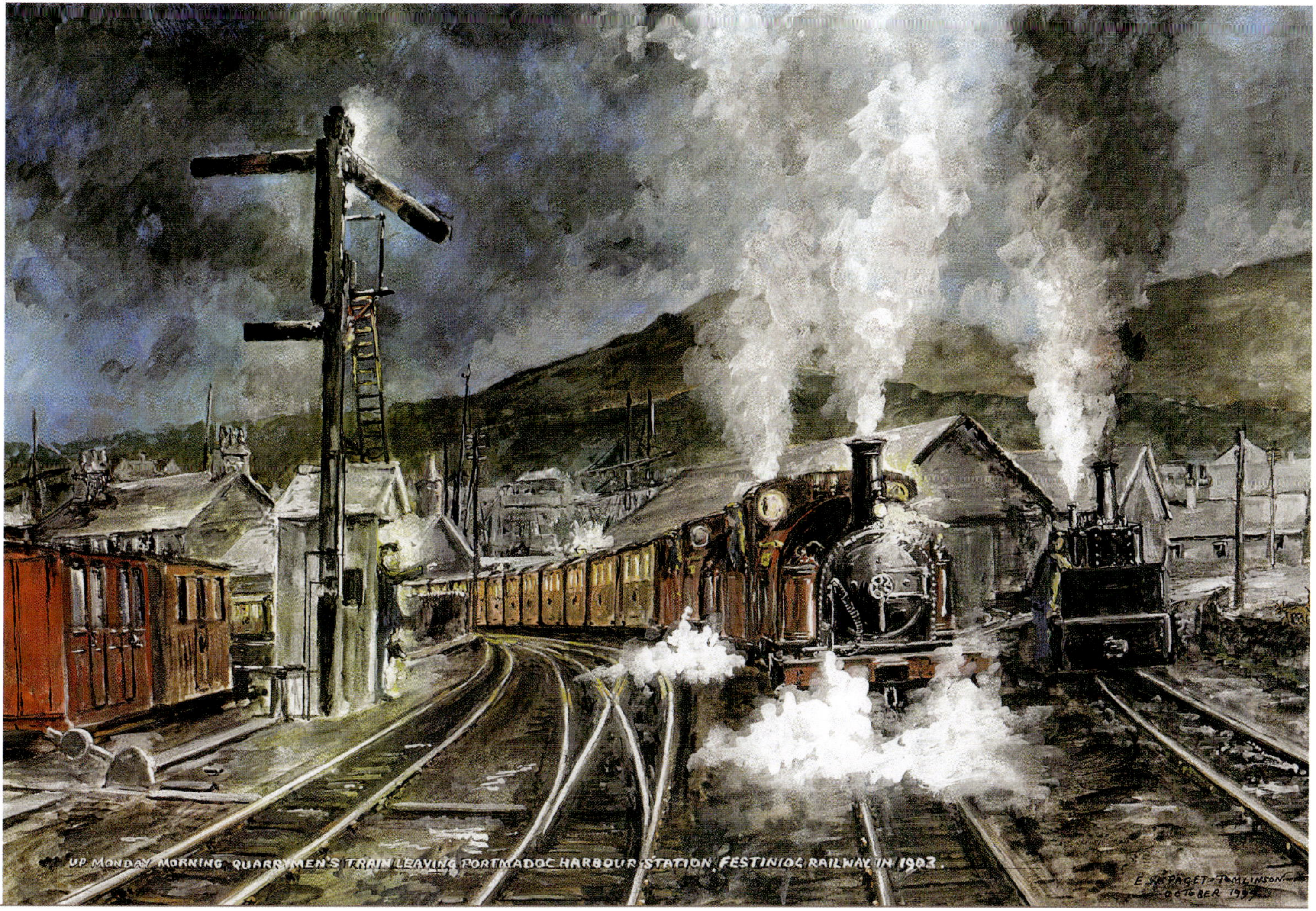
UP MONDAY MORNING QUARRYMEN'S TRAIN LEAVING PORTMADOC HARBOUR STATION, FESTINIOG RAILWAY IN 1903.
PAGET-TOMLINSON
OCTOBER

Painting 17: Kerr Stuart Diesel Locomotive No. 4415 at Boston Lodge in 1929

Kerr, Stuart & Co. of Stoke-on-Trent built a six-wheel experimental diesel locomotive in 1928, which ran trials on the Welsh Highland Railway. This was at the suggestion of Colonel Stephens, a proponent of internal combustion locomotives and railcars on the light railways in his empire. Having proved successful on the Welsh Highland, 4415 was moved to the Ffestiniog Railway in March 1929, where Colonel Stephens thought it would be well employed carrying out the duties of the Bottom Shunter. It was somewhat over the Ffestiniog's loading gauge and needed its cab reduced in height to go under Rhiw Plas Bridge above Boston Lodge. By all accounts it operated entirely satisfactorily and when Kerr Stuart decided they wanted it back in August 1929, Colonel Stephens is claimed to have remarked, "I thought they had given her to us." The locomotive was eventually exported to Mauritius, but was returned to the UK in 1999. It is now is store at Minffordd awaiting restoration to full working order by The 4415 Group.

The painting shows 4415 coming round the curve at Boston Lodge and approaching the Cob on a train of slate wagons with a brake van converted from a Quarrymen's carriage at the rear. A Double Fairlie is being steamed in the works Bottom Yard and carriages stand on the road to the Carriage Shed. The rock face at the rear of the works dates from the time when this was one of the quarries used to obtain stone for the building of the Cob in the early 1800s. Above the train can be seen the various Works buildings, built over a period of years as the railway developed. The first were Boston Lodge Cottages, the distinctive white cottages on the extreme left, in front of which were stables from the railway's horse-drawn era. The view today remains remarkably similar and one of Boston Lodge's claims to fame is that it is the oldest railway works in the world still in use for its original purpose.

Client's Comments

Apart from a few shots taken at Minffordd, there are no photographs of 4415 at work on the Ffestiniog Railway. This prompted me to commission the painting. I wanted a rear three-quarter view so as to show the unusual position of the radiator inside the cab and the distinctive shape of the engine casing. 4415 only worked between Minffordd and Porthmadog, so there weren't many possible locations. Choosing Boston Lodge curve enabled the depiction of several features, which are now history, namely the works chimney (demolished), the wall between the works and the main line (replaced by railings), the castellated pillars at the yard entrance (demolished) and the "Long Shed" behind the carriages on the right of the picture (also demolished). The lorry on the road below is also a Kerr Stuart product, using the same type of engine as the locomotive, and it was Edward's idea to include it, likewise the dog lifting its leg against the carriage. Whether the Kerr Stuart lorry ever made it to Wales is not known, but it is a nice touch.

Hugh Smith, Honorary Secretary, The 4415 Group

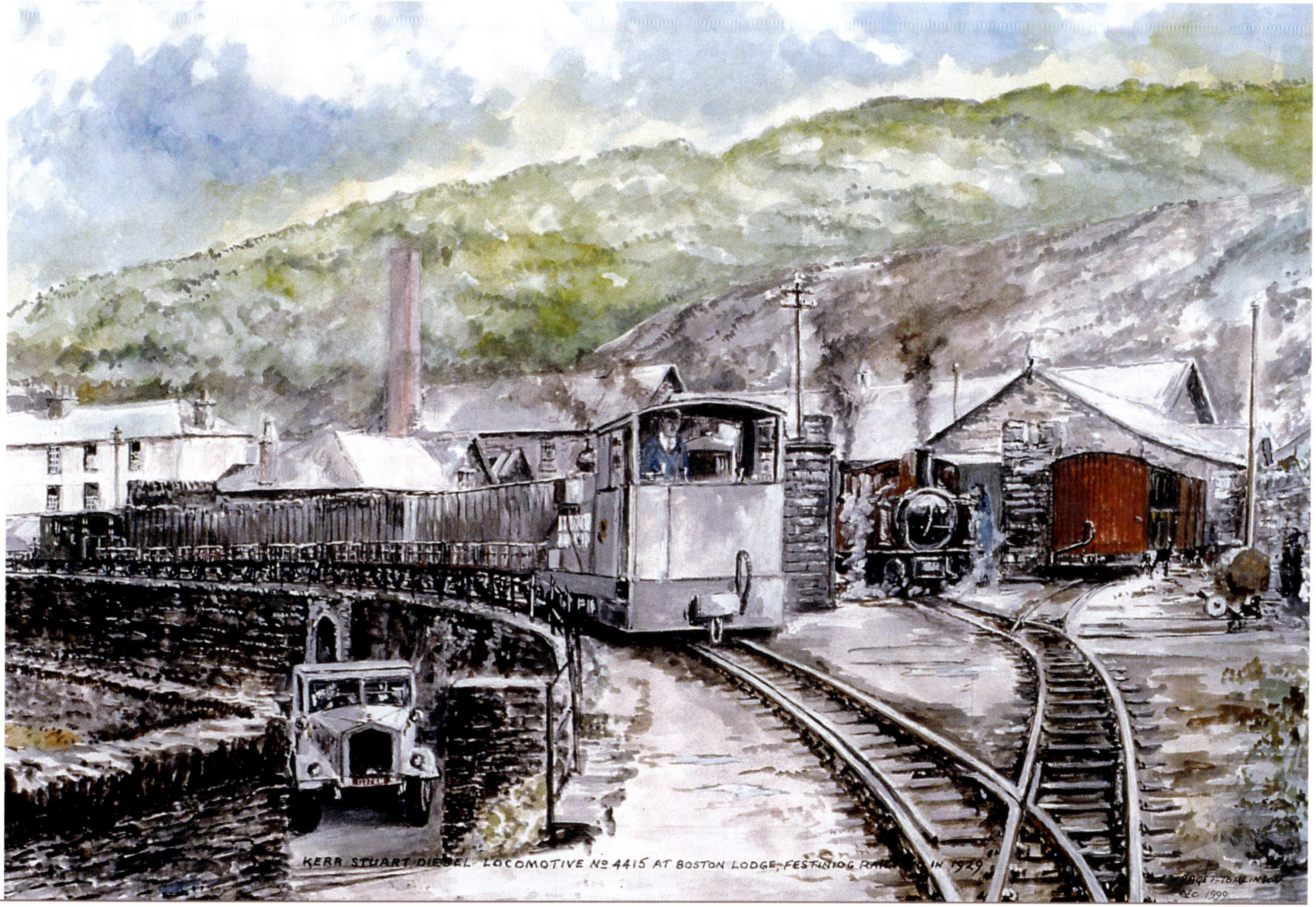
KERR STUART DIESEL LOCOMOTIVE No 4415 AT BOSTON LODGE, FESTINIOG RAI IN 1929
DEC 1999

Painting 18: Lottie's Crossing in 1963

Quarry Lane Crossing had already featured in Painting 8 when John Dobson asked if he could commission a painting of Lottie's Crossing as a memento of many happy times spent there in the early preservation days. Strictly, the request was outside the project's criteria, but as the author was also one of the young volunteers who descended on Lottie's at the end of those distant working days, he discussed the idea with Edward and it was agreed to go ahead. An aberration perhaps, but one that has brought pleasure to those who toiled away in the 50s and 60s to lay the foundation for all that has been achieved over the years.

Client's comments

In the early 1960s, the tenants of the Quarry Lane Crossing cottage were Mrs Charlotte Olive Edwards, known to everyone on the Railway as Lottie, and her husband Dai, who worked with the Ffestiniog's Permanent Way Department, having previously worked in the quarries at Blaenau Ffestiniog.

Born in Barmouth, Lottie had first got involved with railways during the Second World War, when she worked for the Great Western Railway as a ticket collector and assistant guard on the Cambrian Coast line, gaining a reputation for friendliness and helpfulness that she retained throughout her life. She left the GWR when she married Dai and they moved into the Quarry Lane Crossing house in 1956, the year that the Railway reopened to Minffordd. Dai was unfortunately killed in a road accident in Minffordd in 1963.

With her sunny, outgoing personality, Lottie soon established herself as one of the Railway's "characters". She was incorrigibly curious and knew all of the latest gossip. Volunteers who hadn't visited the line for some time could get a full update on everything that had happened on the Railway, details of any scandal in the private lives of other volunteers (and an excellent cup of tea) by paying a visit to "Lottie's" – the name that both the cottage and the crossing soon acquired. Lottie herself made firm friends with volunteers, many of whom stayed with her as B&B guests over the years. As younger volunteers finished their education and moved on to careers around the world, greetings cards would arrive at the cottage with interesting stamps and sporting some very odd addresses – "Loh Tee, Teahouse of the Wooden Spoon, Minffordd" being a representative sample . . . The local postman soon got used to these oddities.

Life on the Railway was considerably more relaxed and less rule-bound in the 1960s than it is nowadays and it wasn't unknown for train crews to play pranks on Lottie as she operated the gates. Lumps of coal would disintegrate at her feet as she waved her fist at the culprit or packages would fly through the air in her direction. She didn't mind too much as the coal helped to keep the fire in the cottage range alight and the tea kettle hot, and the packages often contained ice cream from the buffet car, or chocolate, which was even more acceptable.

The painting shows a Down train, headed by Prince and driven by Bill Hoole, negotiating the crossing in the summer of 1963. The Guard, Ross Gregory, is leaning out of Buffet Car No. 12, about to "deliver" a package to Lottie, who is clearly expecting it. Lottie is accompanied by her dog Perrot and a typical 1950s car, an Austin A90, is parked in the vestigial "lay-by" on the uphill side of the crossing. Artistic licence is evident in that No. 12 would not normally have been the first vehicle in the train at that period. It would usually have been preceded by the First Class Observation Car No. 11. We can only assume that No. 11 was temporarily out of service for some reason. **John Dobson**

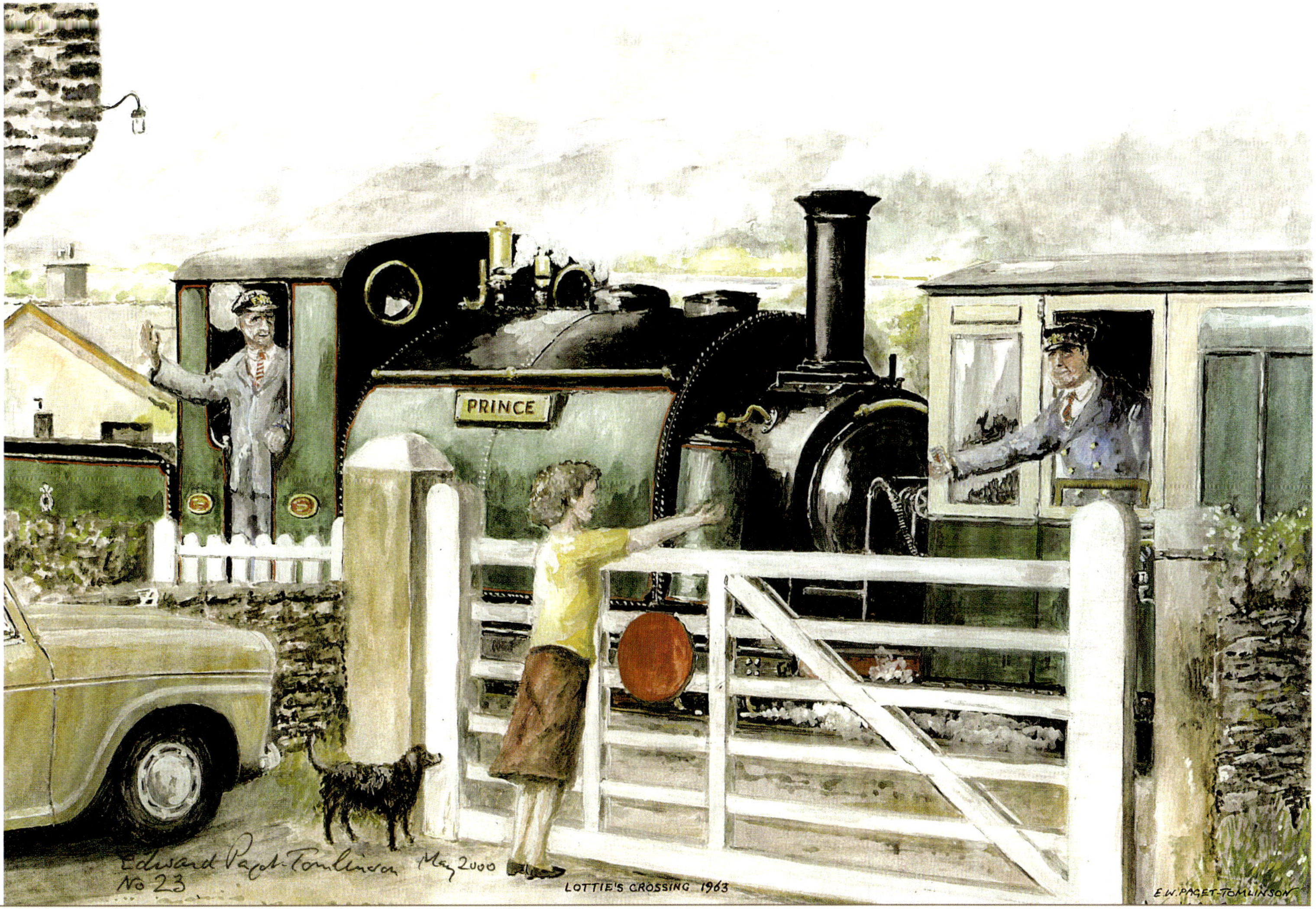
PRINCE
Edward Paget-Tomlinson May 2000
No 23
LOTTIE'S CROSSING 1963
E.W. PAGET-TOMLINSON

Painting 19: Dolgarreg Ddu Junction, Blaenau Ffestiniog in 1880

This painting depicts an area of Blaenau Ffestiniog now changed almost beyond recognition, with only the Queen's Hotel to the right and the rock outcrop Garreg Ddu to the left as reference points. Above rise the tips and levels of Maenofferen and Votty & Bowydd Quarries. The train headed by the neat little Manning Wardle Scorcher stands in the Festiniog & Blaenau Railway station, with the roof of the wooden station building just visible above the locomotive. The carriage is one of six owned by the railway, all built by Ashbury and similar to the Ffestiniog's first carriages, but slightly higher off the ground. In the centre is the coal siding, with a cart being loaded and Paddy and friends inspecting something on the ground, while in the immediate foreground is the run-round loop. Running off to the left is the connection to the Ffestiniog Railway known as Dolgarreg Ddu Junction, with the two-arm standard Ffestiniog McKenzie & Holland signal as protection. Double Fairlie James Spooner heads a Down train having just left Duffws Station and passed under the Church Street Bridge. There was no passenger interchange station here until the coming of the standard gauge.

By 1880 Blaenau Ffestiniog was a bustling town and the quarries were at the height of their activity and prosperity. In 1881 the L&NWR would open its line from Llandudno Junction. Three years later the Great Western Railway completed its line from Bala Junction and built its own station on the site of the earlier narrow-gauge one. The passing of the years has seen much further change and today the car park next to the combined Ffestiniog and Conwy Valley Line station covers this area. Nothing remains of the earlier railway arrangements and even the Church Street Bridge has been demolished.

Client's comments

The Festiniog & Blaenau Railway is one of North Wales's least-known railways, no doubt because of its short existence as a narrow-gauge line. It was built in effect as a two-foot-gauge feeder to the Ffestiniog, although quite independent. It ran the 3½ miles from Llan Ffestiniog village to a junction with the Ffestiniog at Dolgarreg Ddu, slightly to the west of the present station. It opened in 1868 and was taken over by the Great Western Railway, which converted it to standard gauge as part of its line from Bala. The F&B had two 0-4-2ST locomotives, Manning Wardle Nos. 258/9 of 1868, delightfully named Scorcher and Nipper. There seem to be very few photographs of the line and none that I know showing its proximity to the FR, so a view at Dolgarreg Ddu fills a gap.

Peter Treloar

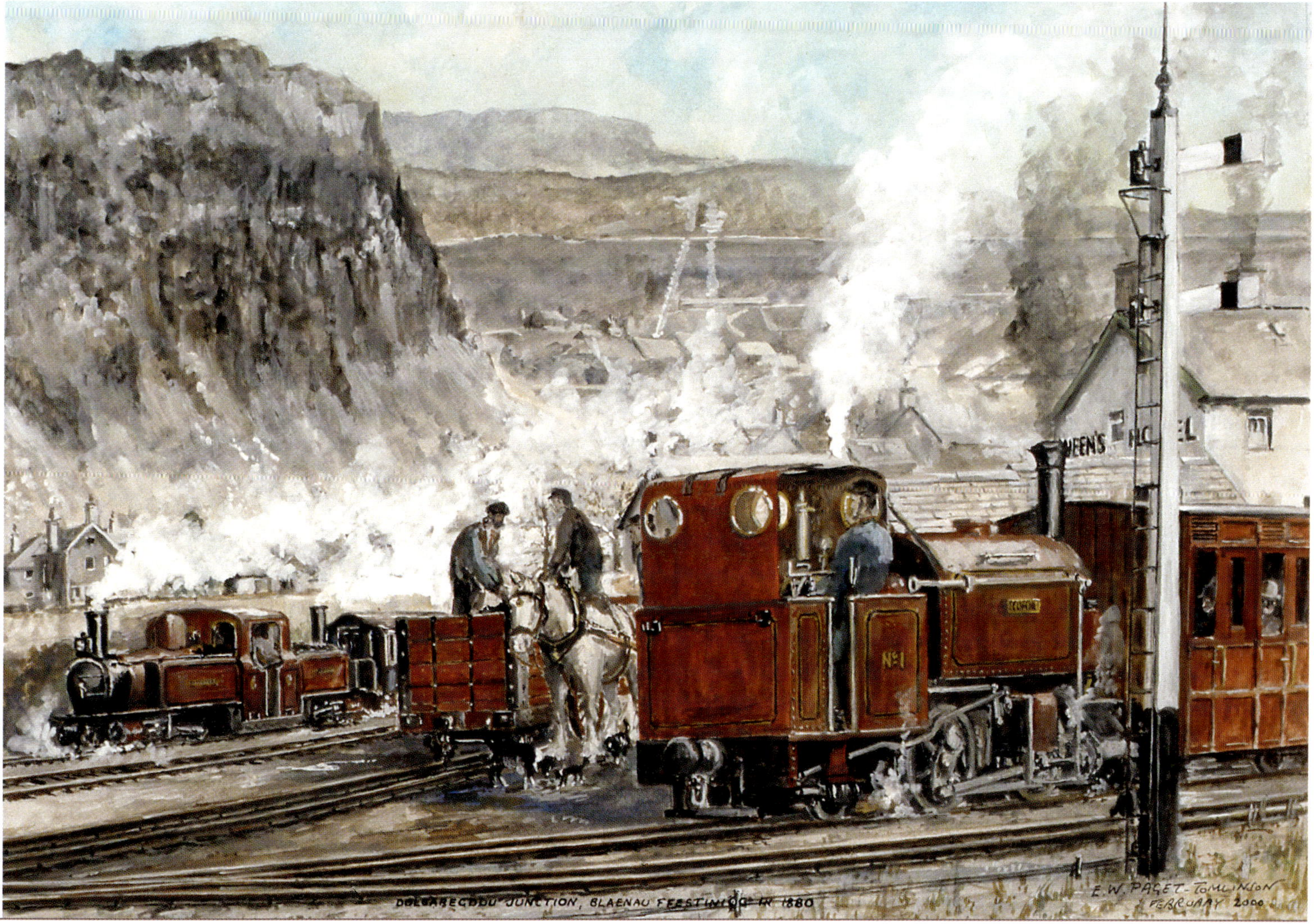
JUNCTION, BLAENAU FFESTINIOG IN 1880
E.W. PAGET-TOMLINSON
FEBRUARY 2000

Painting 20: Steam Tug Wave of Life Leaving Portmadoc Harbour in about 1890

The story of the Ffestiniog Railway and the harbour at Porthmadog, their growth and decline, are inextricably linked. As the Railway's traffic grew, so did the use of the harbour. By the 1860s shipbuilding had assumed important proportions and with increasing trade the harbour became congested for the first time in its short life. In addition the unfriendly nature of the estuary, with broad tracts of sand constantly changed by the confluence of the Glaslyn and Dwyryd, and prevailing winds unfavourable to outward-bound loaded ships, was hindering the growth of the slate trade. Samuel Holland, who was also planning the introduction of steam locomotives on the Railway, came up with the solution to all these problems by forming the Portmadoc Steam Tug Company in 1862. Thereafter the steam paddle tugs transformed the congested harbour and towed sailing vessels out to the safer waters beyond the notorious bar at the mouth of the estuary. The first four vessels owned by the Steam Tug Co. over the next fifty years were paddleboats, which were best in the tight confines of the harbour and with a shallow draught well suited to the sandy estuary.

The painting shows the Wave of Life towing the schooners the Twelve Apostles and The Oakleys out from the main harbour. To the left is Pen Cei and to the right the Britannia Foundry. Also visible to the right is the Harbour Station, with a Double Fairlie standing at the head of a train ready for departure.

Hepple in Newcastle built the Wave of Life, the second Porthmadog tug to bear this name, in 1872. At 91 feet she would have been longer than many of the ships she towed. She was sold to Joseph John King of Garston, Liverpool, in February 1914 and not long afterwards became a barge. Although the two-mast schooner Twelve Apostles was one of the better-known Porthmadog ships, she was actually built at Pwllheli. She became one of the many victims to be stranded and wrecked at Porth Neigwl (Hell's Mouth) on Pen Llyn in November 1898, although the crew escaped. The Oakleys was a three-mast schooner built by David Jones at Porthmadog. Her career was short-lived as she was stranded and became a total wreck off one of the Greek islands in December 1894.

Client's comments

Whilst my initial interest was the Railway itself, this soon grew to include the Porthmadog slate fleet and the associated industries that made the town what it is today. I became aware that in many old photographs of the harbour there were invariably paddle tugs to be seen, but without taking any particular note. Then, through the purchase of a copy of Henry Hughes's Immortal Sails, came the realisation that the paddle tugs were a crucial part of the story. The book includes a wonderfully atmospheric photograph, almost silhouette in nature, of two slate traders outward bound being towed out across the estuary by the Wave of Life. The image stuck with me, so when, chatting to Edward, it became clear that he knew all about the steam tugs, the idea of a painting depicting the Wave of Life appealed to us both. The result is full of charm and true evidence of Edward's skill as a marine artist.

P.J.H.

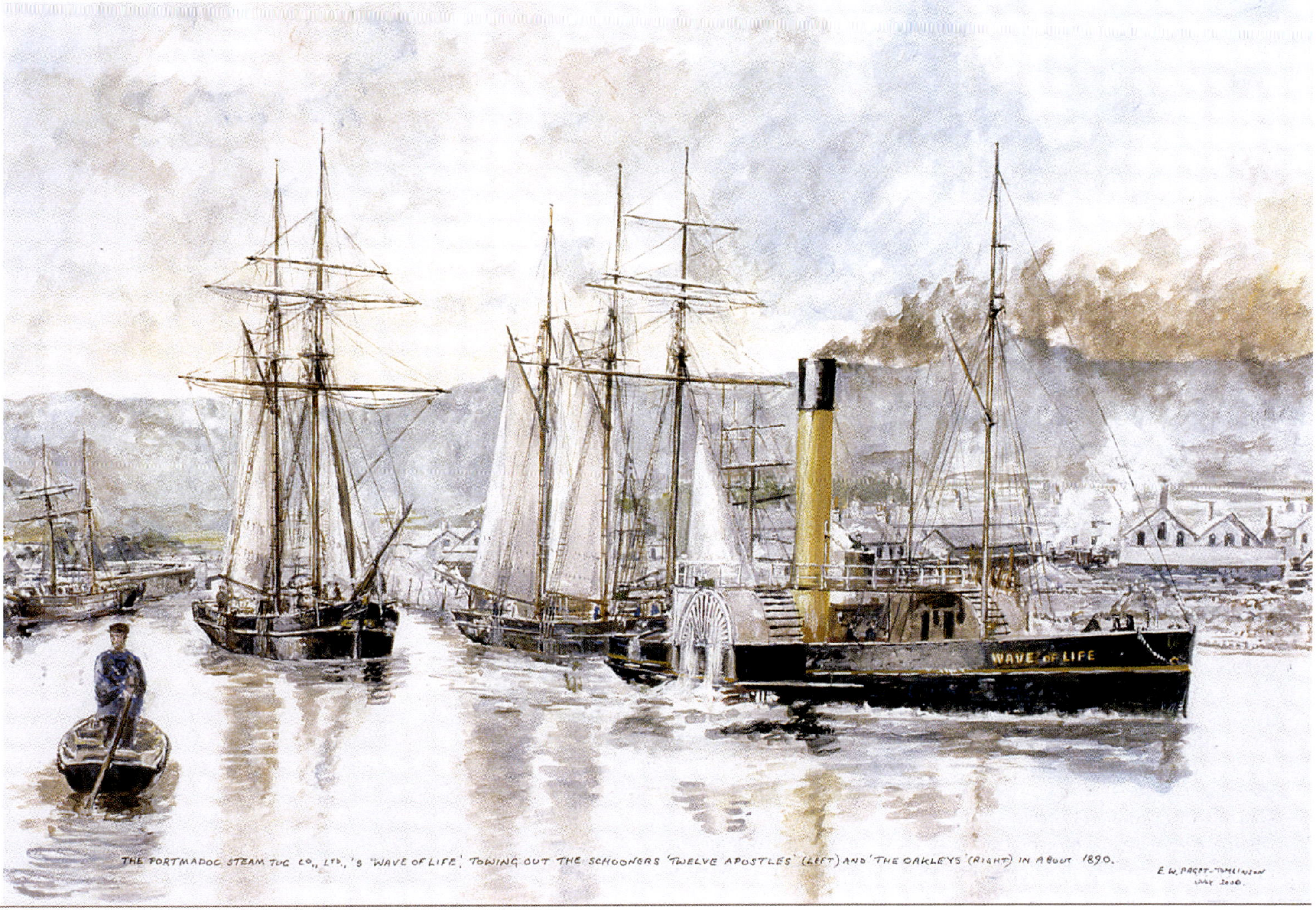
WAVE OF LIFE
THE PORTMADOC STEAM TUG CO., LTD.,'S 'WAVE OF LIFE', TOWING OUT THE SCHOONERS 'TWELVE APOSTLES' (LEFT) AND 'THE OAKLEYS' (RIGHT) IN ABOUT 1890.
E. W. PAGET-TOMLINSON

Painting 21: 590 and Palmerston at Tryfan Junction in 1923

Tryfan Junction was the first station after leaving the terminus of the North Wales Narrow Gauge Railways at Dinas Junction. Here a steeply graded branch ran to serve the quarries on the mountains beyond the terminus at Bryngwyn, while the mainline continued south to Rhyd Ddu. The branch had a passenger service until 1914 and thereafter continued to carry most of the line's slate traffic. In 1922 Tryfan Junction became part of the Welsh Highland Railway, but little change can have been noticed at this quiet spot, other than the appearance of different rolling stock.

The painting is set in 1923, the first year of through services from Porthmadog, with Ffestiniog rolling stock making regular appearances. Palmerston and a train comprising a curly roof van and two Ffestiniog bogie carriages is drawing out of the station on its way back to Porthmadog. Above the train can be seen the roof of the station building and to the right is the, by then, disused signal box. Running off to the left is the Bryngwyn Branch, with a train of loaded slate wagons hauled by the ex-War Department Baldwin No. 590, waiting by the stop sign to gain access to the main line. This locomotive had only recently been acquired and was a typical Colonel Stephens purchase. It proved to be very unpopular with footplate crews because of its rough riding and temperamental injectors, and unless required for the passenger service was most likely to be found working the Bryngwyn trains. The crossing in the foreground carried a track over the railway.

After a short and unprofitable life, the Welsh Highland Railway closed in 1937 and the track was lifted as war salvage in 1941. Thereafter Tryfan Junction lay undisturbed until 2000, when it once more saw trains running through on the revived Welsh Highland Railway. The station building remains as a roofless ruin, but there are plans to restore it. However, the station has not been reopened and it remains a tranquil spot. The Bryngwyn Branch is unlikely to be relaid, but may find a new use as a footpath.

Client's comments

Tryfan Junction must have been a dire experience for anyone stranded there on a cold, wet and windy day. The station site is situated in what was a very remote area when the Bryngwyn Branch of the NWNGR opened in 1877 and even today the locality remains thinly populated. That such a bleak spot managed to evade the visiting photographer is hardly surprising, hence pictures of the junction in use are few and far between. Palmerston is a favourite locomotive of mine, especially since its remarkable restoration and return to the Ffestiniog. I remember seeing it rusting amid the weeds in Glan-y-mor yard at Boston Lodge Works back in the early 1960s, apparently beyond all hope of repair. To see it restored and back in steam in 1993 was a wonderful moment and I have had a soft spot for it ever since. Having chosen the major player in the scene, I decided to opt for a total contrast in locomotive styles with Baldwin No. 590 bringing another run of slate down from Bryngwyn and onward to the standard-gauge sidings at Dinas. The branch revenues provided the life-blood of the NWNGR and the new WHR, although the slate traffic subsequently faded away by the early 1930s. It was Edward who had the splendid idea of including in the picture the mounted shepherd, complete with Welsh pony and sheepdog. All three look extremely wet and glum: hardly surprising given the weather conditions!

Tony Champkins

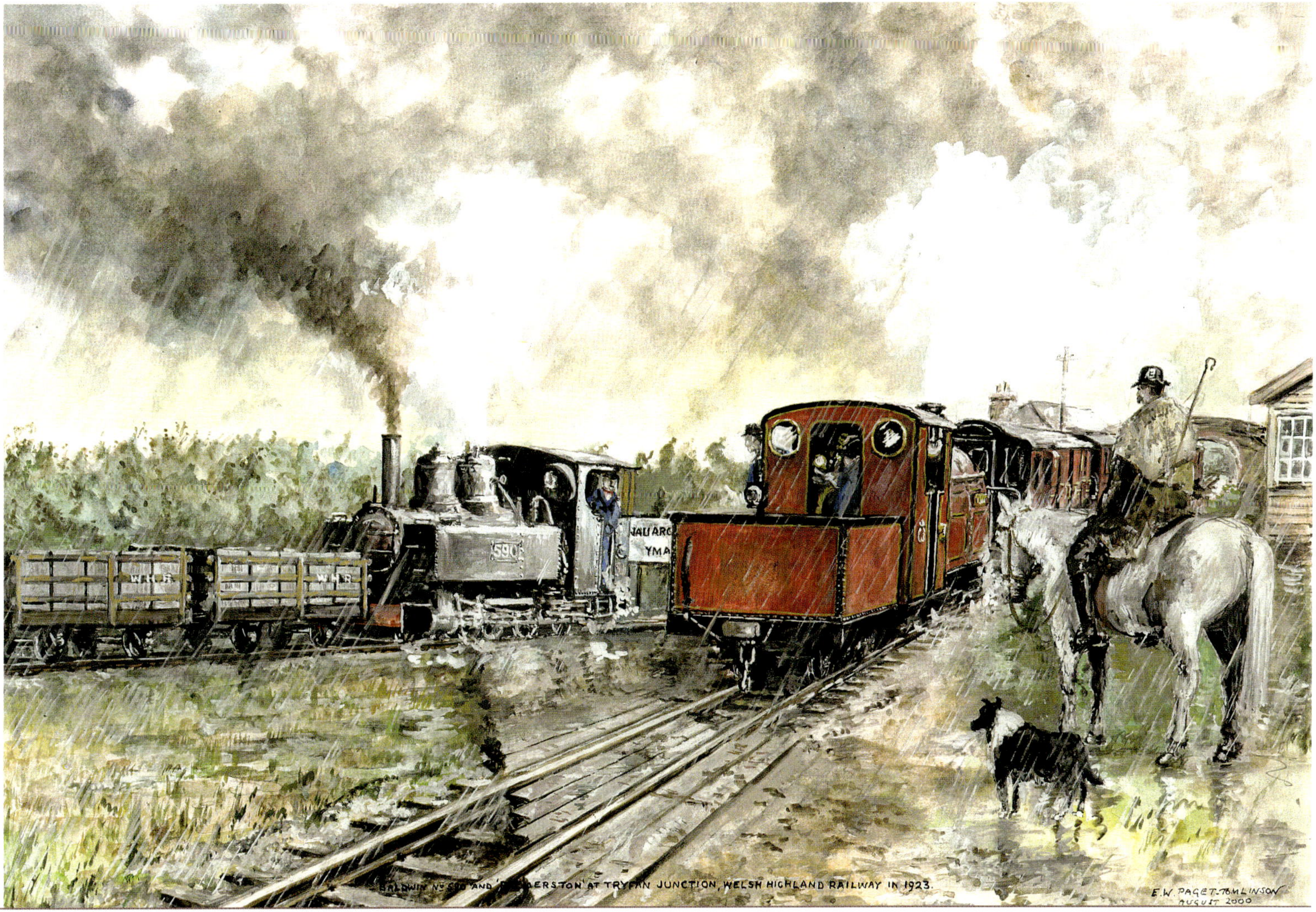
590
W.H.R.
W.H.R.
BALDWIN
AND
AT TRYFAN JUNCTION, WELSH HIGHLAND RAILWAY IN 1923.
E.W. PAGET-TOMLINSON
AUGUST 2000

Painting 22: Merddin Emrys at Tan-y-Bwlch in 1946

With the cessation of passenger services in September 1939 and the general limitations on travel and holidays during the war years, the Ffestiniog Railway entered a period when it was largely lost from sight and thus photographs of the thrice-weekly slate-only service are few. Gravity trains had ceased to run in 1940 and thereafter a locomotive brought down the loaded slate wagons from Blaenau to Minffordd. An England engine, latterly Princess, sufficed on two days, but the remaining active Double Fairlie Merddin Emrys was required on Wednesdays.

The painting depicts Merddin Emrys running through a grass-grown Tan-y-Bwlch on its final run in July 1946. There is some photographic evidence that the passing loop was not used in the final years and indeed the painting shows the train on the Up line, with the overgrown Down line to the left. Driver Tom Davies waves to Wil Jones, who lived in the station house with his more famous wife Bessie, the Welsh Station Mistress. History does not record whether indeed Wil had a Border collie which looked like Paddy, but the cart that stands to the right near the wooden station building certainly belonged to him.

A few days later driver Tom and his brother Wil Davies were putting Princess back in the engine shed at Boston Lodge when they were told that the Railway was closing the next day. Princess has not worked since and is now preserved in her final condition. Merddin Emrys has been rebuilt three times under the new order and is regarded by many as the finest Ffestiniog locomotive. Tan-y-Bwlch is now a bustling passing place, but still retains its sylvan charm.

Client's comments

I have always been intrigued by the few photographs of the Ffestiniog working in the war years, which always seem to convey how austere things were at that time and also how down at heel the railway had become. The photographs also tend to include the train crew, just quietly getting on with the job of bringing the slate down from Blaenau. I stayed with Tom and Elizabeth Davies at Bron Madoc, their home on the hill above Boston Lodge, in the early 1960s and heard first-hand about his love for the Railway and his pride in the old footplate traditions. It was easy to imagine how poignant it must have been for Tom, having struggled to keep the service going through the war, to see the Railway finally fade away, defeated by changing circumstances. I wanted the painting to convey some of those emotions.

P.J.H.

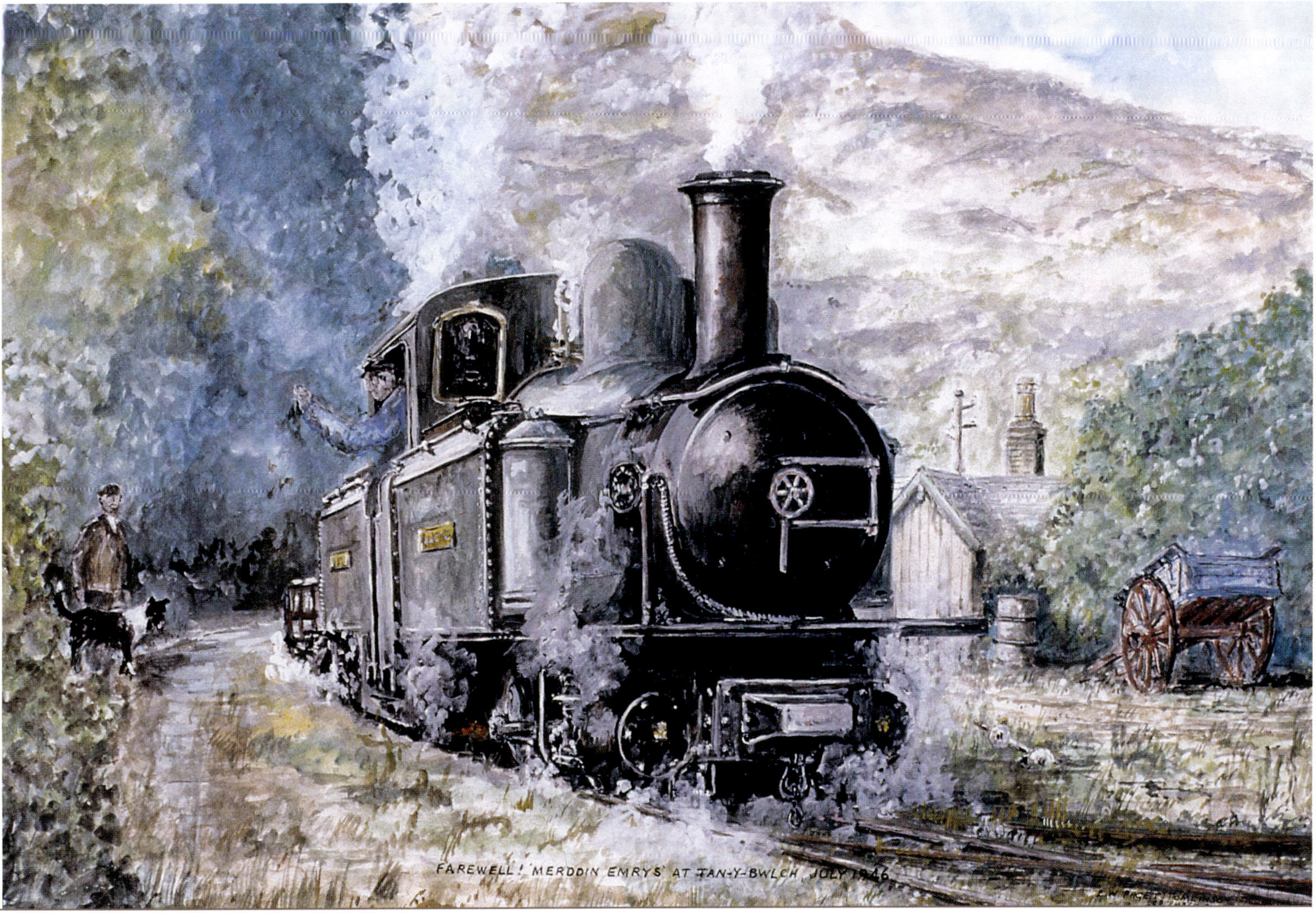
FAREWELL! 'MERDDIN EMRYS' AT TAN-Y-BWLCH, JULY 1946

Painting 23: Five Fairlies at Porthmadog

In 2001 the Ffestiniog Railway Society had a very successful appeal to raise funds to complete the rebuild of Double Fairlie Merddin Emrys, then languishing out of service with boiler problems. One of the incentives for subscribers was that they would receive a framed copy of this painting by Edward of five Fairlies, which would not otherwise be available. The original painting was later included as a prize in a raffle to raise funds for the rebuild. Merddin Emrys returned to traffic in time for the 2005 Vintage Weekend in the ornate Ffestiniog Victorian red livery, the rebuild having been funded entirely by the Society.

The painting when commissioned showed what was a highly desirable line-up of all five of the Ffestiniog's extant Fairlie locomotives, but which was unlikely ever to be achieved, since Livingston Thompson was on long-term loan to the National Railway Museum in York. The obvious location was Harbour Station with its convenient fan of adjacent lines. To the left is the newest of the Double Fairlies, David Lloyd George, built at Boston Lodge Works and completed in 1992. Next is Earl of Merioneth with its rather unconventional appearance, built at Boston Lodge and entering traffic in 1979. It replaced the former Earl of Merioneth, which regained its original name Livingston Thompson when it was eventually cosmetically restored and loaned to the National Railway Museum. In the middle is Single Fairlie Taliesin, new in 1999, but incorporating a few parts from the original locomotive scrapped in the 1930s and therefore classed as a rebuild. To the right is Merddin Emrys in the condition aimed at with the fund-raising appeal. Just visible behind is Livingston Thompson. In a rare breach of safety regulations Paddy accompanies his master, the hammer-carrying Permanent Way Ganger. Overseeing it all is the Duty Controller leaning out of the Control Office's dormer window.

At the time it was painted such a scene in real life was an improbability, yet in October 2005 during the Vintage Weekend, the five Fairlies did indeed pose for a line-up at Harbour Station, with Livingston Thompson briefly released from York as part of the celebrations to mark fifty years of Ffestiniog preservation.

This painting is one of only two in the Heritage Paintings Project depicting scenes in the preservation era, but the cause of restoring Merddin Emrys greatly attracted Edward and he saw it as his way of assisting the appeal.

Client's comments

When the Ffestiniog Railway Society was first asked to raise the funds to restore Merddin Emrys to service, I was the Society Director responsible for fund-raising.

We were not sure that simply appealing for funds to restore the superstructure would attract donations. Instead, as there was a partly-constructed Fairlie power bogie in existence, I came up with the idea that completing this and building a ninth bogie would really give members a dream to aspire to, as it would potentially allow five Fairlies, four Double and one Single, to be arranged at Porthmadog, something the "old company" could never do. The financial and practical benefits were that the FR Company could take a much more structured approach to maintenance and rebuilds.

To help achieve this, the Society commissioned Edward Paget-Tomlinson to paint what we thought would be an impossible scene, Five Fairlies at Porthmadog – impossible because there was considerable resistance to the idea of taking Livingston Thompson out of the National Railway Museum at York.

Needless to say, when the scene in the painting was finally realised in 2005, it created an historic moment full of emotion and quite beyond words.
Dave Charlton

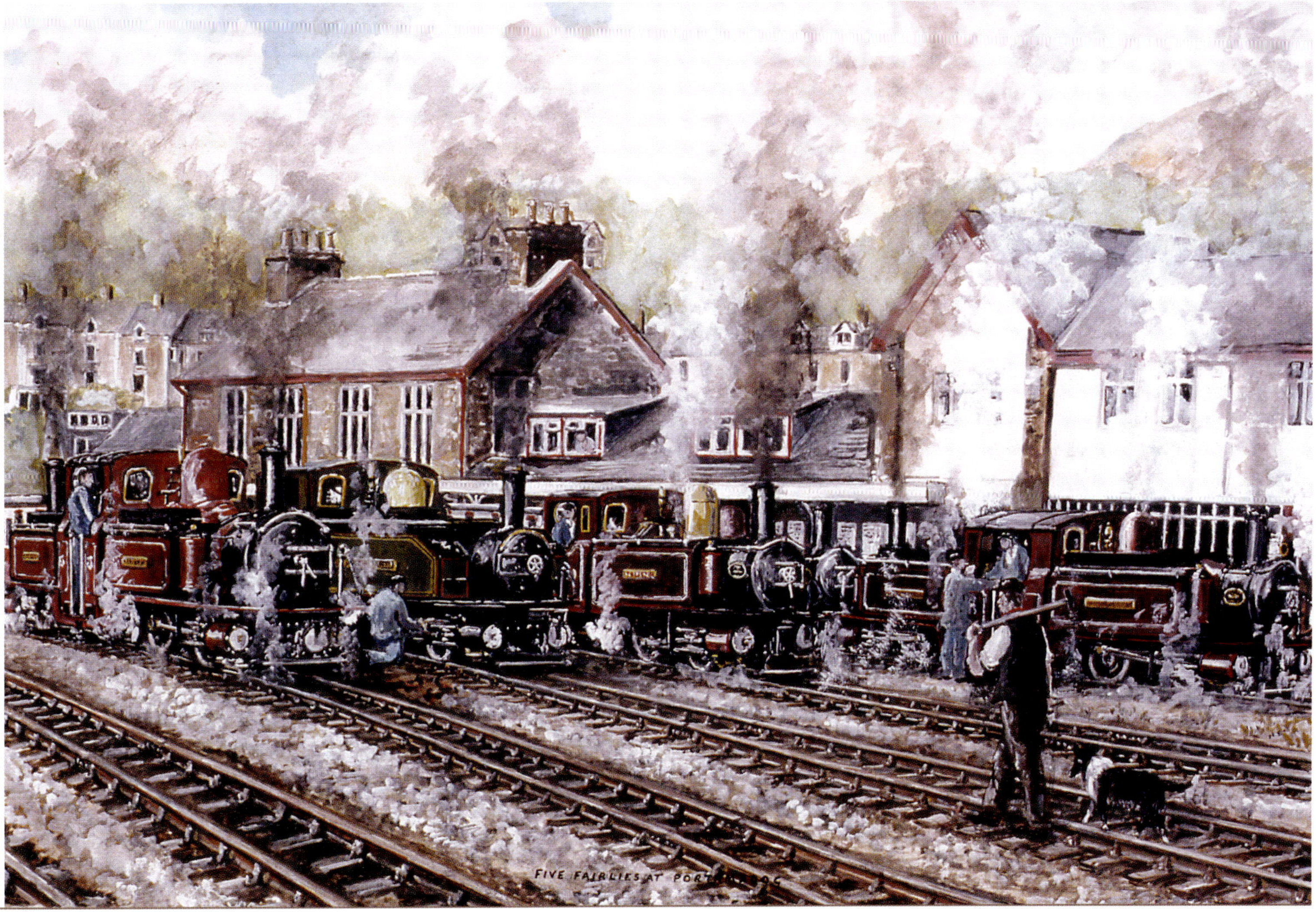
FIVE FAIRLIES AT PORT

Painting 24: Mountaineer Approaching Three Gates Crossing in 1875

The Heritage Group again wanted a painting for their 2001 Christmas card and another slightly romanticised scene was devised. The location is Three Gates Crossing, where one of the Oakeley Estate's tracks crossed the Railway on the hillside above Tan-y-Bwlch. Here the Railway hugs the hillside, following the contours though a series of cuttings and along drystone embankments. As it approaches Three Gates, the line is indeed as sharply curved as the painting shows. Mountaineer is as built by George England in 1863. It is remarkable that engines specially designed for a railway with a notoriously wet upper terminus took so little account of the footplate crew's comfort. The driver, in the then traditional light-coloured jacket, stands exposed to the elements and the fireman too can be glimpsed. Mountaineer never received the fully enclosed cab fitted to all the other England engines when they were rebuilt, being withdrawn in original condition as worn out in 1879 and used as a source of spare parts. By 1879 the Railway had three Double Fairlies and Single Fairlie Taliesin available for traffic and the need for the smaller engines was reduced. At the rear of the short passenger train is the usual long rake of empty slate wagons being retuned to Blaenau Ffestiniog.

A surprising amount of traffic is held up by the train. As was his wont, Edward used this painting to include a number of real animals as models. Nearest the camera, Astrakhan, a Dales Pony, hauls a loaded Oakeley Estate cart, accompanied by both Paddy and Meg. On the far side, the Hon. Mary Oakeley rides side saddle on an Anglo-Arab, modelled on Print, who belonged to Sue Davis, the author's partner. Edward with his usual sense of humour, upon hearing that Print was frightened of donkeys, decided to include one with a pair of pannier baskets. To complete the scene Sparkle, Sue's springer spaniel, peers through the far gate.

The crossing at Three Gates remains today, but is now two gates with stiles, and a partly blocked opening where a third gate to the right once led to a further track beside the line.

Client's comments

Three Gates is a favourite spot on our walks along the network of paths in the woods around Tan-y-Bwlch. The scene is now transformed, and not for the better, by conifers planted on the hillside above the line in the 1960s. Even the native mountain oaks and other broadleaf trees below the line are now far more mature, with the woodlands being far less managed than in the great days of the Oakeley Estate. Oakeley Estate oaks provided much of the timber for the Porthmadog shipbuilding industry. Given a fairly free hand, the scene evolved and Edward took his usual pleasure in including our animals and his own dogs.

Sue Davis & P.J.H.

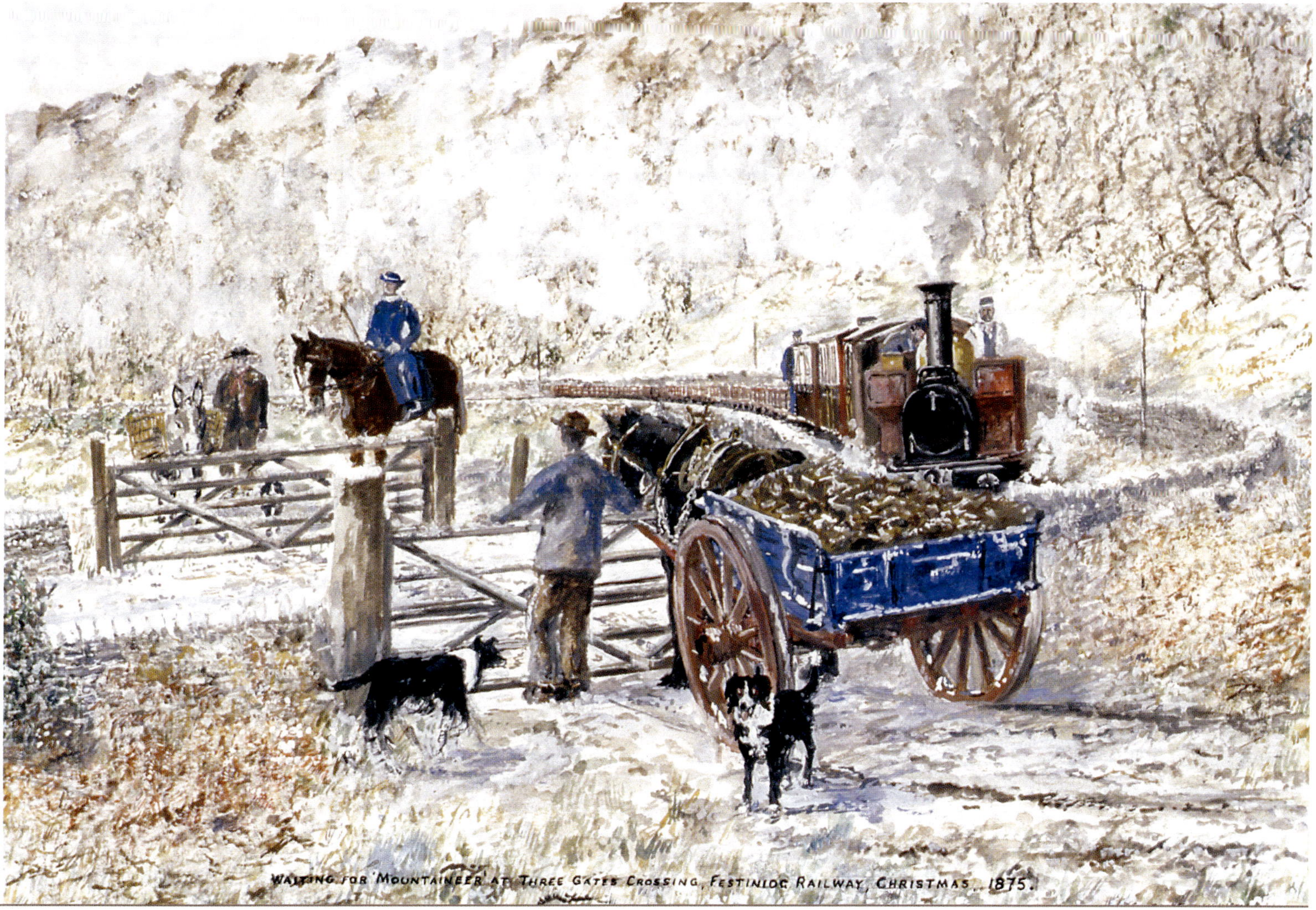
WAITING FOR 'MOUNTAINEER' AT THREE GATES CROSSING, FESTINIOG RAILWAY, CHRISTMAS, 1875.

Painting 25: Welsh Pony and K3 MG at Penrhyn in 1934

At the top end of Penrhyn Station is Fron Goch foot crossing, leading to a house of the same name, which is now the home of the author of this book. When Roger and Linda Butler, friends of Edward, wanted a painting with road transport and railway interest, the main road at Penrhyn, where it runs alongside the railway, seemed a good choice, with the chance to include Fron Goch too tempting to resist. The house is on the right of the painting with its two distinctive full-height white bay windows grafted on to a much older cottage that existed before the railway was built in 1832. There is a degree of artistic licence, since the bays were not in fact added until 1946, but they give the house some of its character. In pre-war days Fron Goch was one of the village bakeries and the baker can be seen outside the house. In the middle of the painting is the station building and to the left, the houses of the village on the hillside below.

The choice of MG was left to the author and he has always thought the K3 MG to be the quintessential pre-war sports car. At the time he had just sold his own MGA to someone who also owns a K3. The other vehicle also has a story. Ffestiniog supporters Judy and Ron Walker are in the process of restoring this 1934 Austin 7 van that once belonged to William Williams of Bangor. Paddy takes his usual interest in its rear wheel. The other dog, a springer spaniel, belonged to Sue, the author's partner, who is included too in period costume.

The train is a rare view of a freight working, since wagons were usually attached to the rear of passenger trains and therefore special workings were seldom caught on camera. Added interest is that the first wagon is the unique Cleminson six-wheel wagon, which was at this time used to transport flour to local bakeries. Welsh Pony is also of interest, since it is in the light blue livery, weathered to rather a pea green, which it alone sported in the 1930s. Further artistic licence has the train and car racing each other to the level crossing a couple of hundred yards further up the line.

Client's comments

Linda and I first became acquainted with Edward when seeking factual verification of detail in respect of Inland Waterways related material. As so many before, we found Edward to be most generous in sharing his encyclopaedic knowledge and living as we did in Somerset, he and Pam kindly invited us to their home near Wells. We immensely enjoyed visiting his garden "studio" and witnessed work in progress for another book. On a reciprocal visit they listened with great interest as Linda's mother, Mrs Ivy Broomfield, related memories of her childhood in Tardebigge next to the Worcester–Birmingham Canal and we sensed that Edward really valued such first-hand recollections.

Linda's brother, Roger Broomfield, has been a keen supporter of the Ffestiniog Railway since his youth when he first visited with his father, Mr William Broomfield. He has been a Society member for over fifty years now and, being the one-time owner of an MGB GT V8, is also a former member of the MG Owners' Club.

With his retirement approaching we pondered over a suitable gift to mark the occasion and decided to approach Edward with a view to commissioning a painting that might encapsulate the two key elements – the railway, of course, and an MG of the period. The result was as you see: a painting which more than realised our expectations, delighted Roger and now hangs in his home, a happy reminder, whenever we visit, of a talented and kindly man, whom it was a pleasure to know. **Dr Roger Butler**

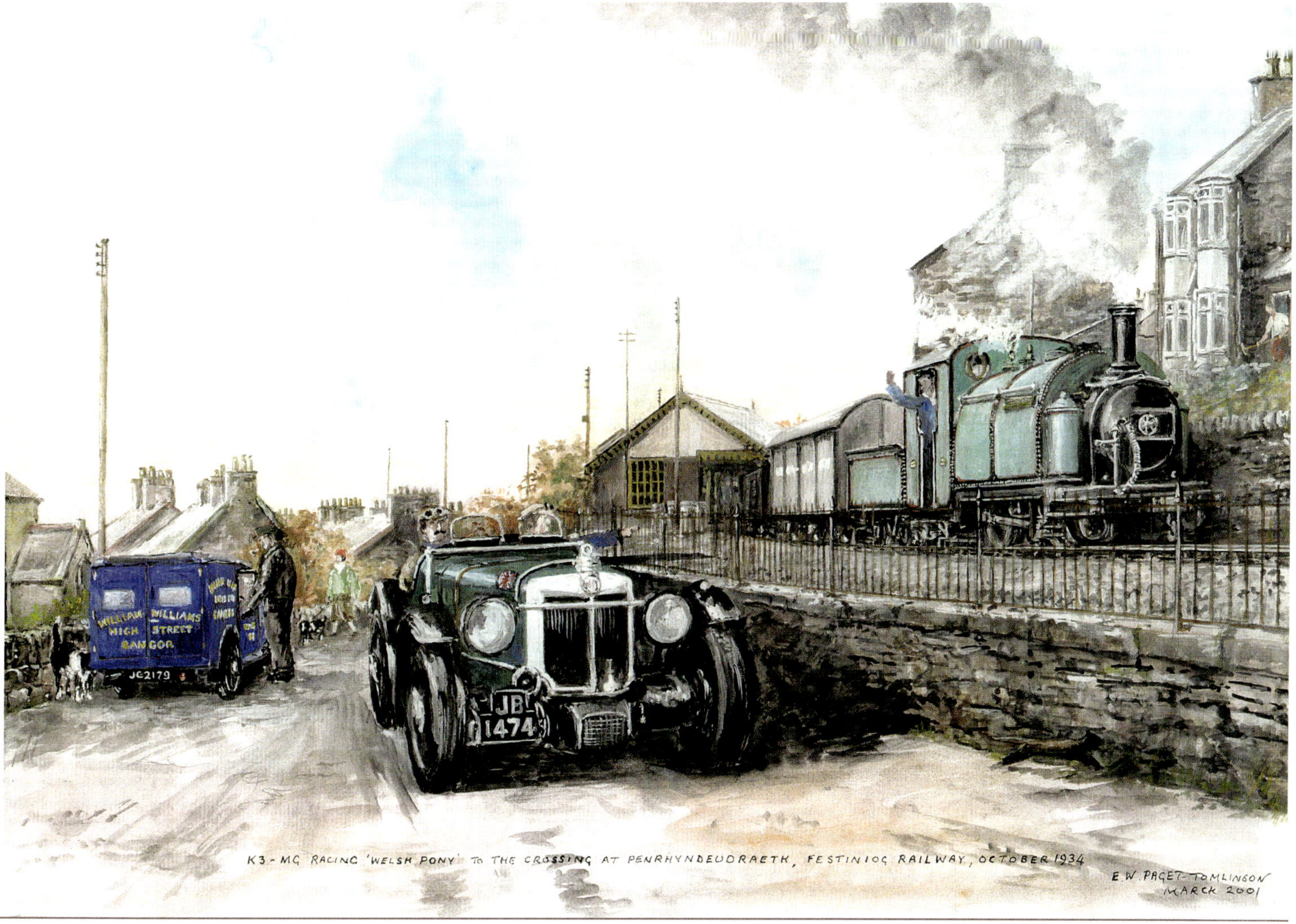
WILLIAM WILLIAMS
HIGH STREET
BANGOR
JC2179
JB
1474
K3-MG RACING 'WELSH PONY' TO THE CROSSING AT PENRHYNDEUDRAETH, FESTINIOG RAILWAY, OCTOBER 1934
E.W. PAGET-TOMLINSON
MARCH 2001

Painting 26: Prince on a P.W. Train at Minffordd in 1892

Because of its importance to the overall Ffestiniog Railway operation, Minffordd Station is well represented in the photographic archive. Thus many of the features included in the painting are well recorded, but the train is of a type seldom, if ever, caught on camera. The Permanent Way train stands on the Up line, perhaps waiting for a Down train, Minffordd being a regular passing place. It is hauled by Prince, just out-shopped from Boston Lodge after the fitting of a new boiler and a complete rebuild. Behind it is one of the Railway's two bogie coal and ballast wagons, which remained in service until the early 1900s. Next is a bolster set loaded with rails. One of these timber-framed sets survived into the preservation era and has been rebuilt with longer frames and remains available for service.

To the left is the small wooden station building that sufficed from 1872, when Minffordd opened, and to the right is the impressive stone station building and stationmaster's house built in 1887. The wooden shelter was beyond saving by the 1950s and has now been replaced with a superb replica. The now lost double-arm signal may also one day be replaced. The variety of luggage and parcels on the platform gives some idea of the traffic that passed through the station, with much interchange between the Ffestiniog and Cambrian stations keeping the porters fully employed. The Stationmaster in frock coat is in conversation with a passenger, but it is not recorded who is responsible for Paddy.

Some of the paintings contain details that cause debate. As the researcher, the author is prepared to concede that it is unlikely that the top of Prince's tank would have been painted black at this period and, as an experienced P.W. volunteer himself, he should have spotted that Ffestiniog double head and bull head rails are normally loaded on their sides on bolster wagons, not standing up.

Client's comments

The subject of "our" painting is very personal to our family, as it brings back many happy memories of holidays in the 1980s and 90s. With a little artistic licence it includes the smallholding of Bron Turnor in the background. The annexe at Bron Turnor was used by some of the Ffestiniog Railway directors in the 1960s as a base and was recommended to us by Les Smith who, as well as being one of the founders of the modern railway, was also my wife's godfather. My wife's family spent wonderful holidays with the Smiths in the 1950s and she recalls a gravity train ride back to Minffordd Station in the dark. After the arrival of our sons, we returned to the area spending many school holidays and weekends at Bron Turnor. Minffordd Station was and is special to our family.

Prince was chosen as it was the motive power for the charter train to celebrate our Silver Wedding anniversary with family and friends. We were advised that it had been rebuilt in 1892, hence the dating of the painting. As a track volunteer and as there had not been a previous painting featuring the subject, it was an obvious choice for us to include a P.W. train. Finally the replica Down platform shelter was just being completed by the Heritage Group at the time of the commission and we felt it important to project its image to the outside world as another reconnection to the Railway's history.

Mike & Diana Colville

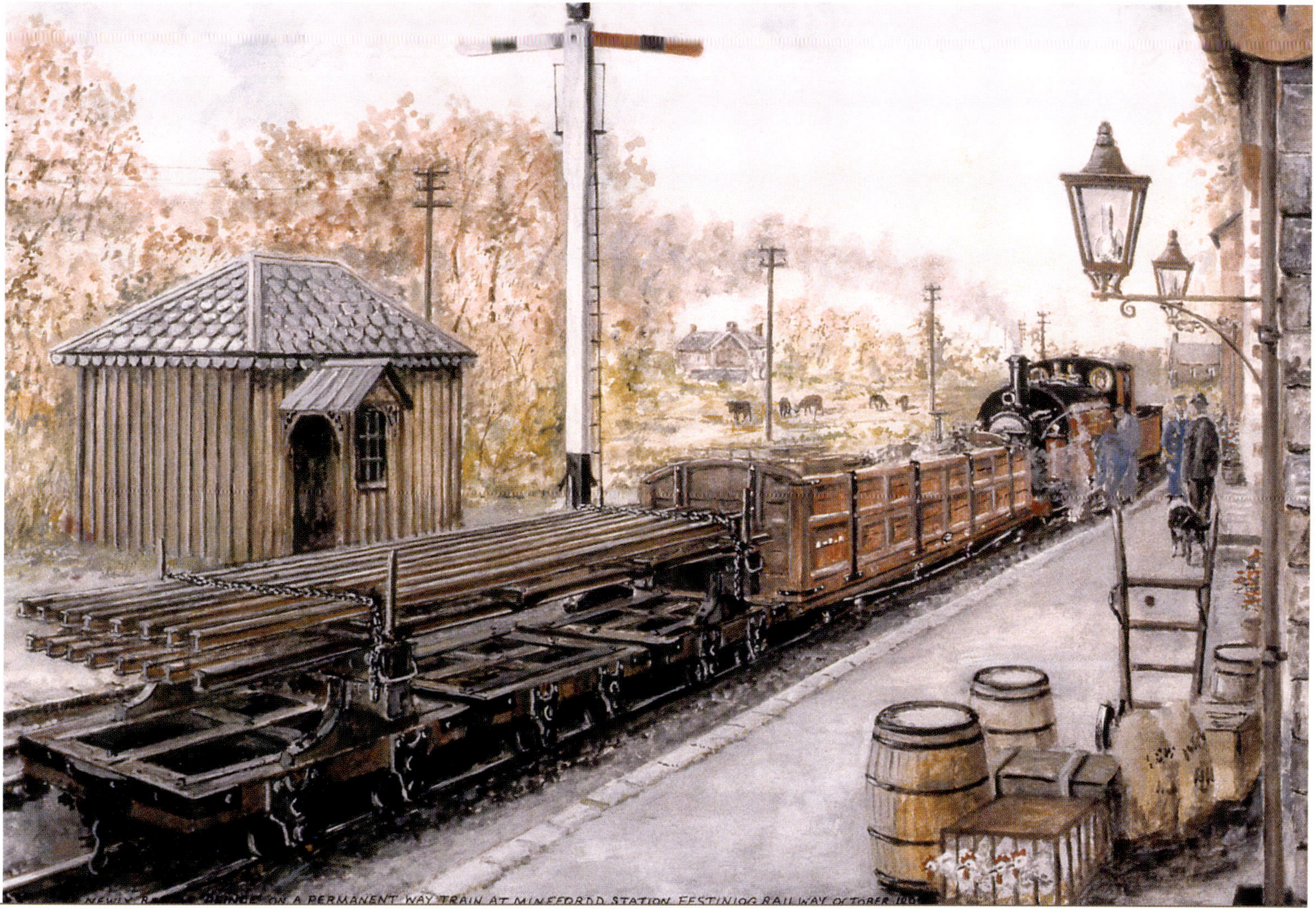
ON A PERMANENT WAY TRAIN AT MINFFORDD STATION FESTINIOG RAILWAY OCTOBER

Painting 27: Up Quarrymen's Train near Tanygrisiau in 1891

Just below Tanygrisiau Station the Railway's original 1832 route was altered in 1852 to ease a particularly sharp curve. In the painting, looking down the valley, the old route is in the foreground and is being used by a photographer as a vantage point. The train is on the new route with its easier curve on a high drystone embankment, deviating from the old line roughly where the building stands near the rear of the train. The waterwheel and leat, prominent features in the early years, powered the Tanygrisiau Foundry. All trace of the railway on this alignment was obliterated by the power station in the 1960s and the approach road now runs roughly along the 1852 route, but the foundry manager's house survives. The present line climbs well to the right to gain height around the lake, which now fills the valley and covers the old route.

The train is the Monday morning Up Quarrymen's, already seen in Painting 16 a few years later, and once more it is double-headed. Leading is The Prince, which has the distinctive open back cab carried only from 1890 and 1891, prior to a major rebuild to what would become the standard outline for these locomotives. Behind is Double Fairlie Livingston Thompson as built only five years earlier. The train comprises over 20 Mk.3 Quarrymen's carriages, which would be packed, for the slate industry was still not far from the height of its prosperity in the mid-1880s. Some quarrymen will alight at Tanygrisiau and climb to the quarries in Cwmorthin and on the slopes of Moelwyn, while the rest will carry on to the three stations in Blaenau. The scene is in summer, since it can be no later than 6.45am, but already the sun is up and casting long shadows. Edward's own explanation of the two dogs is that both should be with the shepherd in the right foreground, but that Meg in some agile way has climbed the embankment and is in danger of barking at the shrouded photographer. Paddy, however, remains with his master.

Client's Comments

This is a photographer's picture, showing probably the only scheduled double-headed train operated by the pre-restoration Ffestiniog Railway; the Monday morning quarrymen's train often had the week's top shunting loco coupled to the front. The picture is based on a poor photograph taken by a local resident in the 1950s, recording landscape features that would be lost, including two alignments of the FR, by the construction of the Tanygrisiau pumped-storage power station. As a photographer it appealed to me for a location, showing features no longer in existence, a typical target for a photographer who calculated that the light would be best for photographing it from this vantage point in the summer, although it would have been a brave man who'd try to stop a moving train with the slow emulsions available in 1891.
Peter Johnson

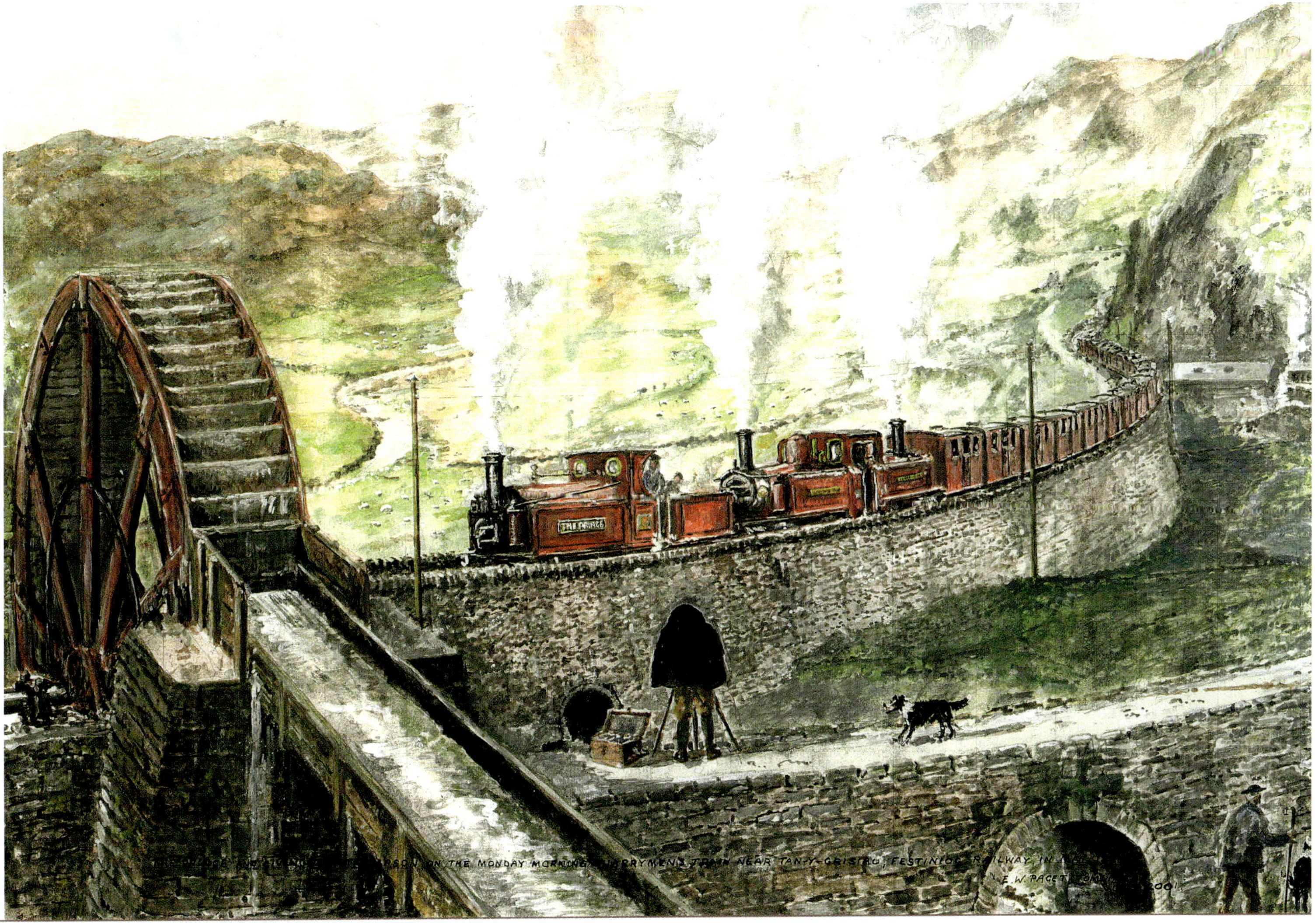
ON THE MONDAY MORNING
TRAIN NEAR TAN-Y-GRISIAU, FESTINIOG
E.W. PAGET

Painting 28: Merddin Emrys at Dduallt in 1895

Dduallt Station, midway between Tan-y-Bwlch and Blaenau Ffestiniog, is the most isolated and, therefore, probably the least recorded of locations on the Railway. Few photographs exist and all confirm that even in the Railway's heyday it was a lonely spot, which is hardly surprising since it has no road access and is hidden away in the midst of the mountains. Its one time stationmaster, poet Gwilym Deudraeth, expressed the boredom of his job – "The poet's spirits start to fall, waiting for a train to call." The station served a few isolated farms and houses, one of which, Rhoslyn, is shown in the painting standing right beside the lake of the same name. The station building was a particularly charming wooden structure that sadly failed to survive into the preservation era. Thus a painting of the station was always one intended as part of the project, so when David Bussey wanted a view of Merddin Emrys in original condition, but without a specific location, Dduallt was an obvious choice.

The painting shows Merddin Emrys on an Up train passing though the station, with the stop signal at clear, meaning that no passengers were waiting. The engine is in almost original condition as built in 1879, prior to being taken into Boston Lodge in 1896, the year after the painting, for a complete refit and new boiler.

The station remains a quiet spot even in the preservation era. After a brief period as the temporary upper terminus from 1968 to 1978, tranquillity returned to Dduallt. Its surroundings are, however, much changed, with the new line to Blaenau Ffestiniog commencing just behind the artist's viewpoint and climbing in a spiral around the station and crossing the line where the footbridge can be seen above the back of the train in the painting and then running above the lake to the right. The station building has been replaced with a stone structure better suited to the elements, but Rhoslyn house remains, albeit in a sad state of repair at the time of writing.

Client's comments

This picture was a 60th birthday present from my wife Julie. Like many other people Merddin Emrys is my favourite Ffestiniog steam engine, so the choice of subject was not difficult. When our children were young one of our favourite trips was to take the train from Porthmadog to Dduallt, walk down to Tan-y-Bwlch and then catch the train back. I particularly remember when trains passed at Dduallt, which was idyllic with the Down side of the loop wandering in a very picturesque setting behind a few trees at the valley side of the station. The cat in the right foreground of the picture is mine, also called Merddin Emrys, but just Merddin most of the time, and we all now live in Penrhyndeudraeth, about one hundred feet from the railway. So I can see all the trains go past! I count myself as being very lucky.

David Bussey

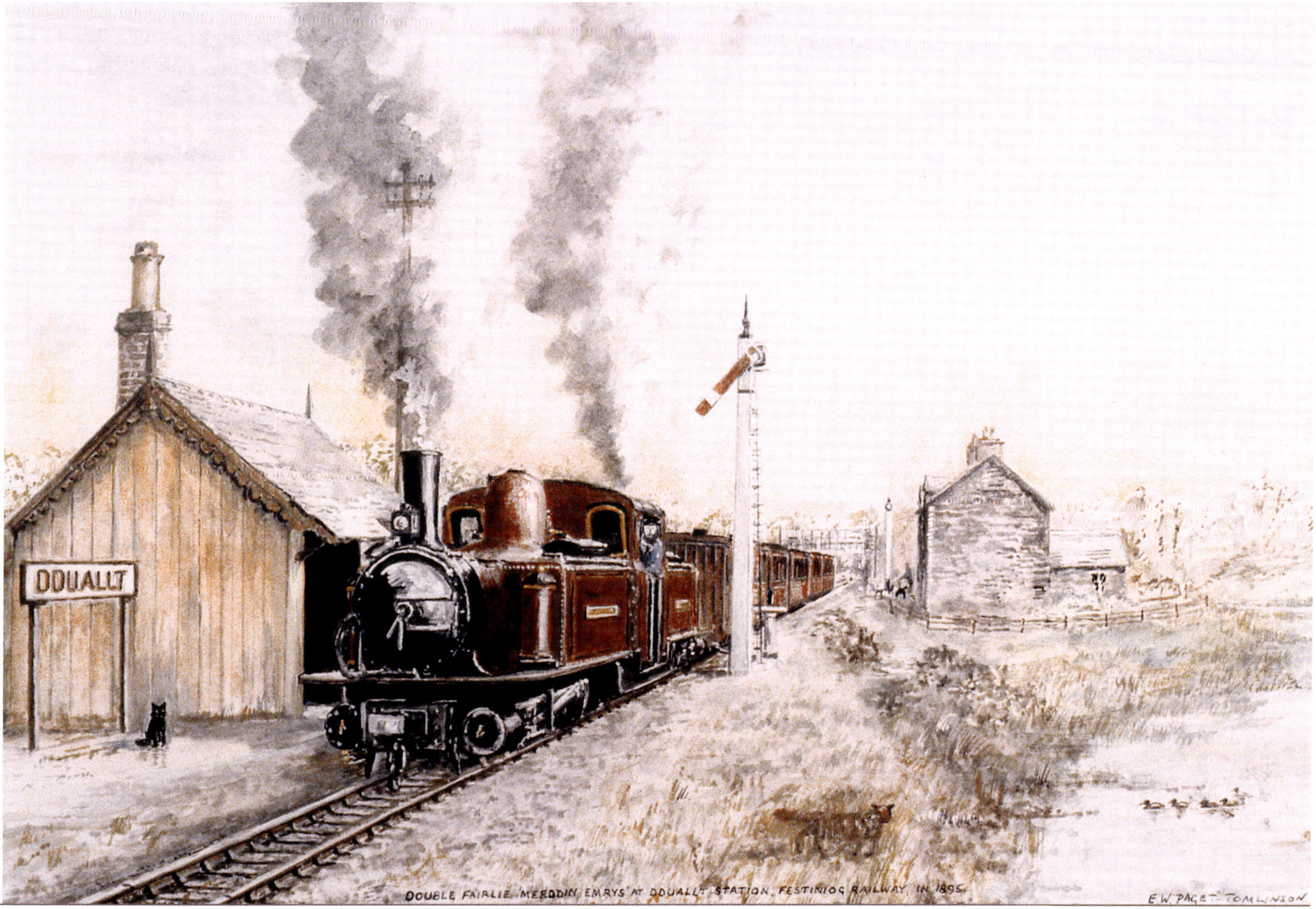
DDUALLT
DOUBLE FAIRLIE 'MERDDIN EMRYS' AT DDUALLT STATION, FESTINIOG RAILWAY, IN 1895.
E.W. PAGET-TOMLINSON

Painting 29: Portmadoc, Beddgelert and South Snowdon Railway in 1910

The view in this painting was indeed "beyond the reach of the camera", since the railway depicted was never completed. The Portmadoc, Beddgelert and South Snowdon Railway was an intriguing part of the complex history of 2ft-gauge railways in Caernarfonshire which culminated in the completion of the Welsh Highland Railway in 1923. The line was planned by the North Wales Power & Traction Co., starting in 1900 and petering out in 1909. It was to use three-phase electricity generated at the company's hydroelectric power station at Cwm Dyli in Nant Gwynant and would have linked the North Wales Narrow Gauge Railway at Rhyd Ddu with Porthmadog. Not inconsiderable work was done around Beddgelert before funds ran out. Some sections, most notably the tunnels in the Aberglaslyn Pass, were later used by the WHR, but others were unsuitable, since the gradients planned for the PB&SSR's electric locomotives were far too steep for the WHR's steam locomotives. These unused sections remain as fascinating and mute reminders of the abortive scheme. The most impressive is the bridge over the road near the Royal Goat Hotel and this was chosen for the painting, which along with the two walls of an unfinished accommodation bridge standing in isolation in the nearby field are the most obvious remains.

Edward was particularly interested in this commission and did careful research to get the detail of the locomotive and its overhead current collection arrangements correct. The overhead collection arrangements are to some extent conjecture, but are generally reckoned to be likely. The design of the locomotive is based on a photograph and drawings of the one loco actually known to have been completed by Bruce Peebles & Co. before the project folded. The carriages are based on the NWNGR's Ashbury "Corridor Coaches" of 1893. It is assumed that the PB&SSR would have used the stock it inherited from the NWNGR, although the specification for the line included ten trailers of unknown design.

The scene below the bridge, with roadworks in progress watched by Paddy and Meg, adds interest. It is worth noting that this painting has the distinction of being the most popular of all those in the project in terms of selling out quickest, no doubt because of its combination of charm and whimsy. A final note for students of historical accuracy is that Caernarfonshire did not actually require road locomotives to be registered until 1921, which is a minor irritant to the author as researcher and in no way the fault of the artist.

Client's comments

The never-used railway formations around Beddgelert have always fascinated me ever since first coming across them on a family holiday in 1969. At that time not knowing the history of the failed Portmadoc, Beddgelert and South Snowdon Railway I was unable to understand why there were bits of railway formation going nowhere. Since then, having read the history of the PB&SSR and being employed in the railway electricity industry, my interest has grown in "what never was". If the scheme had been completed it would have been unique in Britain, with three-phase electrics requiring two overhead conductors and the third conductor through an earthed running rail. I know of only one other similar proposal in Britain. This was for the Metropolitan Railway, but it did not come to fruition due to the need for the electrification to be the same as the District Railway's. We do know that one of the PB&SSR's electric locos was completed at the factory of Bruce Peebles in Edinburgh, but it was scrapped during the First World War. **Rodney Thorp**

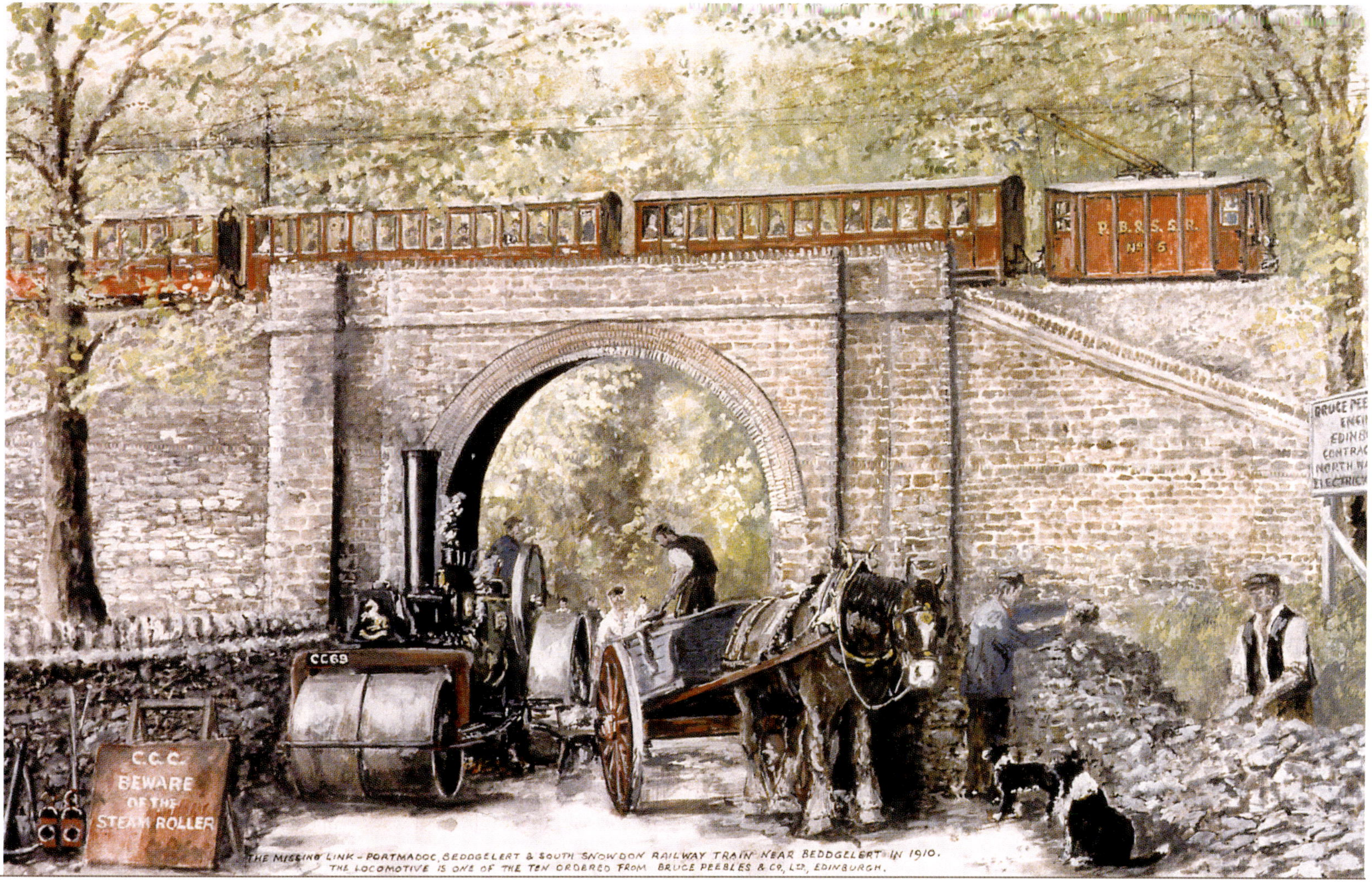
P.B.&S.E.R.
No 6
CC69
C.C.C.
BEWARE
OF THE
STEAM ROLLER
THE MISSING LINK – PORTMADOC, BEDDGELERT & SOUTH SNOWDON RAILWAY TRAIN NEAR BEDDGELERT IN 1910.
THE LOCOMOTIVE IS ONE OF THE TEN ORDERED FROM BRUCE PEEBLES & CO., LTD., EDINBURGH.

Painting 30: The Topsail Schooner C.E. Spooner off Harlech

During the project, potential commissioners sometimes suggested topics that were really outside the guidelines, but a couple of these were allowed to slip through because they particularly appealed to Edward. This was certainly the case when Julie Bussey asked about a painting of a Portmadoc ship. The subject is in fact not divorced from the Ffestiniog Railway, since most of the ships sailing from Portmadoc were carrying slate brought down from the Blaenau quarries by gravity.

The ship is the C.E. Spooner, built at Cei Newydd, Portmadoc, in 1878 by David Jones, 103.2ft long and with a registered tonnage of 171.77 tons. She was a typical product of the various yards at Portmadoc and Borth-y-Gest, which from 1824 until 1913 produced over 260 vessels. Of these some forty were three-masted topsail schooners like C.E. Spooner, described by Basil Greenhill, Director of the National Maritime Museum at Greenwich, as "the ultimate development of the small wooden sailing ship in Britain" by the end of the nineteenth century. The C.E. Spooner was one of five Portmadoc ships built between 1873 and 1878 known as "Jack Barquentines", halfway between the regular barquentine and the three-masted schooners that followed in later years. She was regarded as one of Portmadoc's finest ships, once crossing the Atlantic in thirteen days. Typically the Portmadoc ships, with a crew of only five or six, would carry slate outward bound and then a variety of cargoes between European, Baltic and North Atlantic ports on voyages lasting many months, eventually returning to Portmadoc either in ballast or with a cargo. Her Portmadoc career lasted 34 years, before she was sold to the Portuguese in 1912, not long before the already much reduced ship-borne slate trade was finally curtailed by the First World War. She eventually sank at the end of April 1919.

The C.E. Spooner was named after the railway's engineer, who, it is said, appreciated the compliment and rarely missed the opportunity of coming into his garden overlooking the Glaslyn estuary to admire her and wave his greeting as she sailed by the rocky headland of Bron-y-Garth on an outward voyage.

The location of the painting has a degree of artistic licence, since the shore at Harlech is really further from the castle and there is a dangerous shoal south of the Porthmadog bar, but Edward wanted a local landmark to give the painting more relevance to the project. It was a commission which gave him particular pleasure and one where rivet counters study it at their peril!

Client's comments

I was very sad when I heard Edward had died. He was a lovely man, and had an enviable talent. I loved all of his paintings, and we have many of his prints. His particular use of light very much reminded me of my favourite painter of all time, J.M.W. Turner, whose watercolour of Caernarfon Castle is reminiscent of Edward's interpretation of Harlech Castle! I asked for a painting of a ship for my 50th birthday because I am fascinated by all things nautical, and knew anything Edward did would be superb. I was not disappointed, and my painting of the schooner C.E. Spooner takes up prime position along with the other two originals we own. I wrote to Edward thanking him for my painting and he was very pleased that I compared him with Turner, as he was also a fan! I miss seeing Edward at the Ffestiniog Railway events, but even more I regret that there will be no more paintings from a fantastically talented man.

Julie Bussey

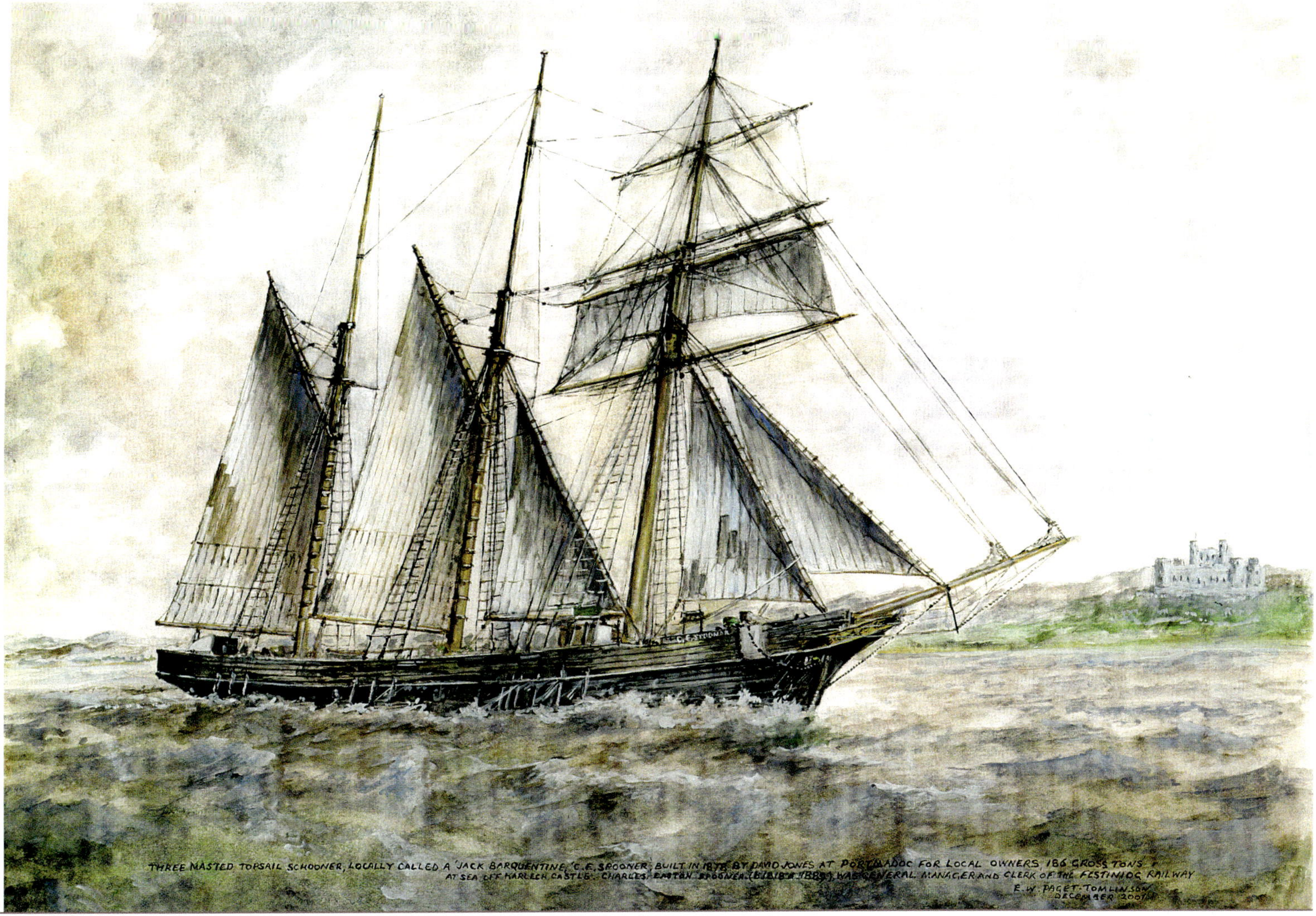
THREE MASTED TOPSAIL SCHOONER, LOCALLY CALLED A 'JACK BARQUENTINE,' C.E. SPOONER BUILT IN
BY DAVID JONES AT
FOR LOCAL OWNERS, 186 GROSS TONS
AT SEA OFF HARLECH CASTLE. CHARLES EASTON SPOONER
WAS GENERAL MANAGER AND CLERK OF THE FESTINIOG RAILWAY
E.W. PAGET-TOMLINSON
DECEMBER

Painting 31: Taliesin and Gravity Train at Minffordd in 1902

This painting of Minffordd Station was commissioned by the FR Heritage Group in 2002, for that year's Christmas card. It shows an Up passenger train, waiting on the Main line while a Down gravity slate train runs onto the Mineral line. The subjects were requested to reflect a wealth of heritage projects then underway on the railway, together with one important aspiration.

The Heritage Group's own project was the replica of the Down shelter, seen on the left of the picture. This wooden structure, the original Minffordd station office of 1867, had survived until 1956, when it was deemed to be both beyond repair and too close to the former Mineral line that would shortly be opened for passenger trains.

Slate wagons and gravity trains were highly topical. With support from the Heritage Lottery Fund some fifty wagons (the FR had a stock over one thousand before the Second World War) had just been restored to a state fit for use on the main line and several demonstration gravity trains had been run. This re-creation of sights and sounds that had been lost for nearly half a century had given those Group members lucky enough to work as brakesmen an extraordinary insight into an essential part of the nineteenth- and early-twentieth-century Railway.

The Heritage Lottery Fund had also supported the thorough restoration of carriages Nos. 15 and 16. With this pair of iron-framed bogie carriages built in 1872, the FR pioneered the use of bogie carriages in the UK and gained much publicity in the contemporary technical press. It was a minor detail, but neither carriage was restored in the single-colour livery shown in the painting.

At the rear of the train is one of the distinctive curly roof bogie brake vans, delivered in 1873, just after the two carriages. When the painting was commissioned re-creation of one of these vans was still an aspiration, for which the Group had a modest fund. Within a year or two a private sponsor had come forward and the aspiration was soon realised.

Client's comments

The locomotive at the head of the passenger train is Taliesin, the FR's Single Fairlie. Re-creation of this locomotive, the original having been dismantled in 1932, had recently been completed. This fulfilled the dreams of many with an interest in the history of the Railway as the original had been the subject of many admiring stories told by enginemen of the old Company. The money to build the replica was raised by taking modest quarterly subscriptions from about 200 people for a period of ten years and the work was done by a combination of paid staff and volunteers in the Railway's workshops at Boston Lodge.

Adrian Gray – Hon. Secretary, FR Heritage Group

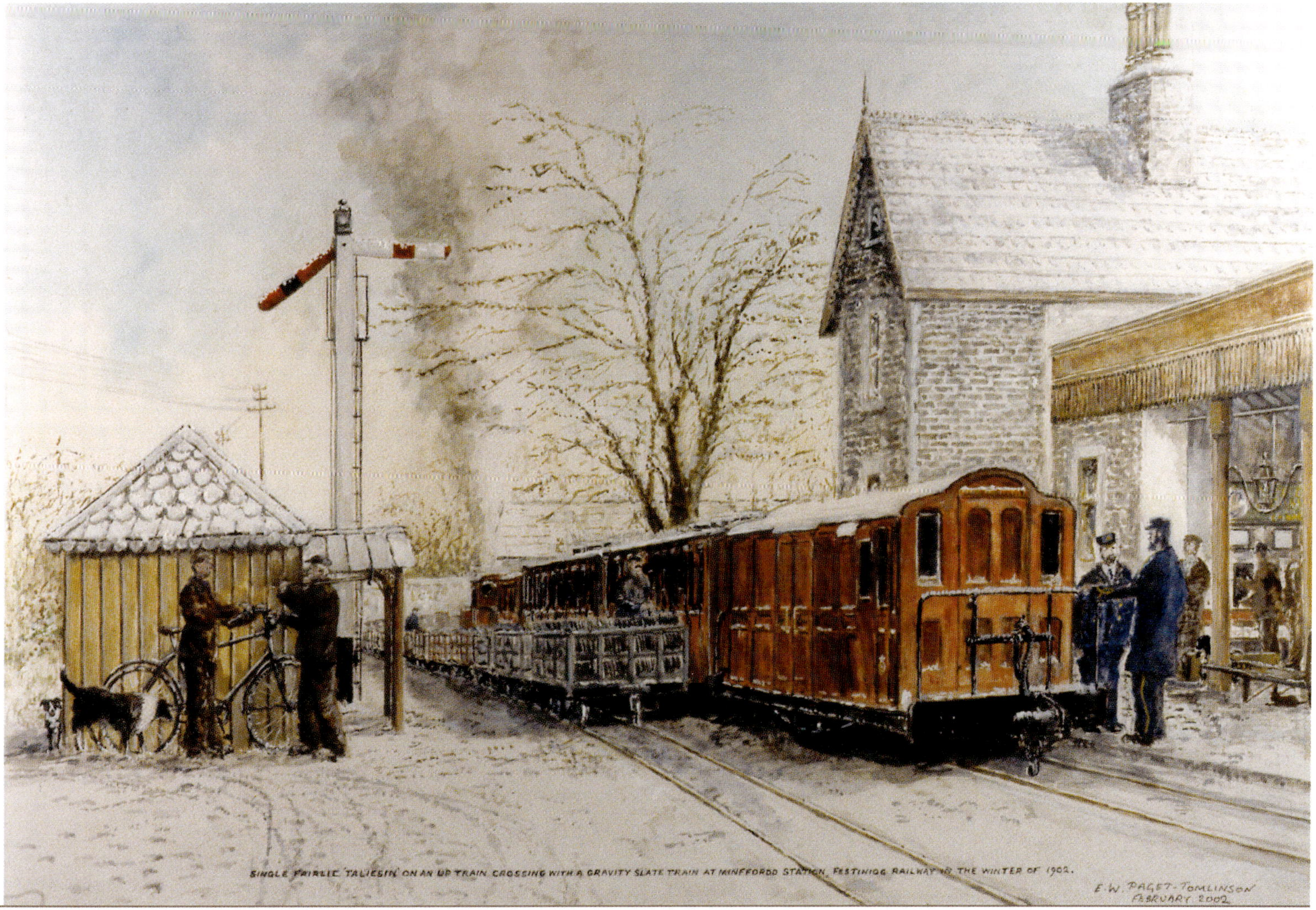
SINGLE FAIRLIE 'TALIESIN' ON AN UP TRAIN CROSSING WITH A GRAVITY SLATE TRAIN AT MINFFORDD STATION, FESTINIOG RAILWAY IN THE WINTER OF 1902.
E.W. PAGET-TOMLINSON
FEBRUARY 2002

Painting 32: Little Wonder passing Boston Lodge Works in 1881

Boston Lodge Works stands at the opposite end of the Cob to Porthmadog, built in a former quarry used as source of rock for Madocks's great embankment. The works started as a smithy and workshops for the Cob Tramway, and then as one of the stables in the Railway's horse-drawn days, and developed progressively over the years until in its heyday it was capable of erecting the two final Double Fairlies. It now has a great claim to fame as the world's oldest surviving railway workshops still in use for their original purpose. Only a small portion of the works appears in this painting, but it is a part that was seldom photographed, since the main Top Yard and erecting shop always had more activity and interest. In the immediate foreground is the scrap siding containing several of the early wooden slate wagons, then the road to the carriage shed with recently built Bowsider bogie carriage, together with both Spooner's Boat and the Oakeley private coach. Little Wonder is just approaching the gates to the Top Yard, with its distinctive corrugated-iron fence and the Paint Shop or "long shed", used in the early preservation days as the loco running shed, but now sadly demolished. To the extreme left of the painting is Pen Cob signal box, the last vestiges of which were not demolished until 2005.

Photographs of Little Wonder are few, particularly in its latter years, and those of it working trains still fewer. It is seen working a train of the period, comprising three Birmingham four-wheelers, unusually only a single bogie carriage and a Curly Roof Van, all in the ornate deep purple and ivory livery. At the end of the train would almost certainly have been a long line of empty slate wagons. Little Wonder is only a year from final withdrawal, having been put back into service after an initial period of withdrawal in 1879.

In the foreground is the beach, which has only grassed over in quite recent times. A rowing boat is being hauled out of the water, watched by Paddy and his mistress. In the middle distance cattle graze on the salt marshes of Traeth Mawr and above them rise the Mynydd Gorllwyn and Moel-ddu range.

Client's comments

I was prompted to choose this setting as I am a volunteer at Boston Lodge. I try to work one day a week but I achieve less than this in practice. For me, one of the most enjoyable moments is to sit in the yard at lunchtime with my sandwiches and a cup of tea and enjoy what I believe is one of the best views anywhere. Hence the painting. I asked for the mountains and scenery to be prominent with the railway elements in the foreground. With the benefit of hindsight I think a little less emphasis on the mountains and scenery would have resulted in a better picture. However, I got what I asked for; the fault was mine, not Edward's.

David Bussey

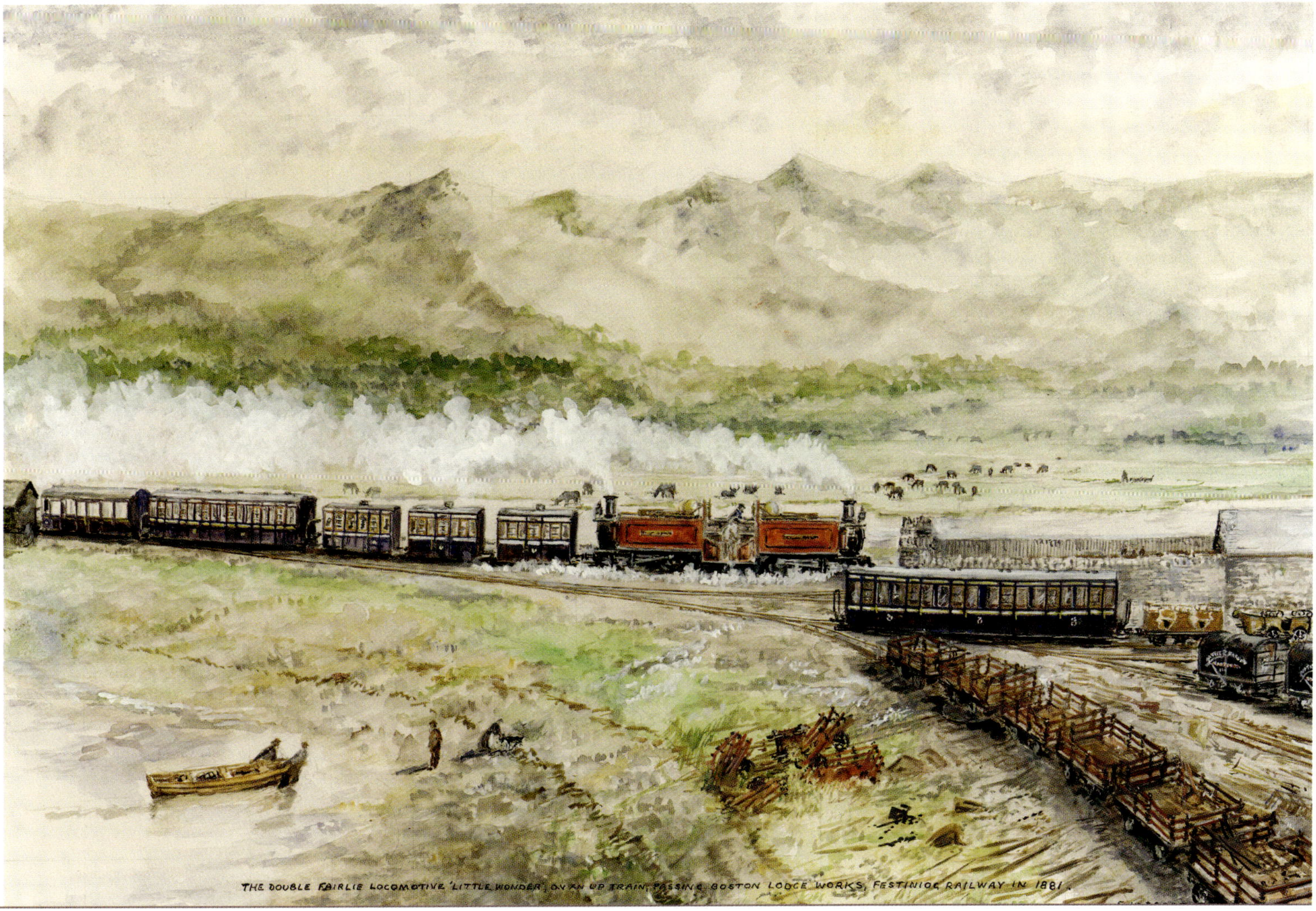
THE DOUBLE FAIRLIE LOCOMOTIVE 'LITTLE WONDER', ON AN UP TRAIN, PASSING BOSTON LODGE WORKS, FESTINIOG RAILWAY IN 1881.

Painting 33: Crossing the High Street, Portmadoc, April 1923

The south end of Porthmadog High Street was from the earliest days a scene of railway activity. The Ffestiniog lines from the Cob to the slate wharves are seen to the left with a couple of bolster wagons and a Double Fairlie standing beside the woodyard. Crossing the street is a horse-drawn train on the Croesor Tramway. This direct Croesor route to the wharves is in the process of being replaced by "The Junction Railway", the short length of line built to link the Welsh Highland Railway, which used the Croesor Tramway route to gain access to Porthmadog, to the Ffestiniog Railway at Britannia Bridge, behind the artist's viewpoint. The line of workmen is lifting a rail in to form the curve. Paddy and his mistress inspect what is going on.

In the distance can be seen the impressive tower of the Market Hall and Council Offices, now sadly replaced with Woolworth's. The building to the right is No. 1 High Street, then slate quarry offices but now a gift shop.

The date is April 1923, when work to build the new Welsh Highland line from Rhyd Ddu to Croesor Junction and upgrade the Croesor Tramway was nearing completion. The Welsh Highland opened throughout on 1 June 1923 and various photographs over the next decade or so show the unusual scene of trains and road traffic mingling on the High Street. The Welsh Highland Railway never prospered and closed to passenger traffic in 1936 and completely the year after. It was dismantled in 1941 to produce war salvage, but the Junction Railway section survived, being Ffestiniog property, and was not finally lifted until 1958. In the early preservation days it was used to take the Simplex petrol tractor to get petrol from the garage that had by then been built on the woodyard site.

Now a new link between the Ffestiniog and Welsh Highland Railways is due to open in 2009, but taking a less congested route beside Llyn Bach and deviating from the Junction Railway immediately after Britannia Bridge. Thus nothing remains of all the railway activity in this busy scene.

Client's Comments

Given the increased availability and popularity of photographic equipment in the 1920s it is quite remarkable that no photographs exist of the construction works that went into completing the Welsh Highland Railway in 1922/3. Similarly, there are no photographs of the Croesor Tramway trains crossing Portmadoc's High Street. On the other hand, a photograph does exist that shows a Double Fairlie in the siding on the left although it must have been a rare event; they were banned from crossing the original bridge. The inspiration for the painting came whilst I was completing my book, An Illustrated History of the Welsh Highland Railway.

Peter Johnson

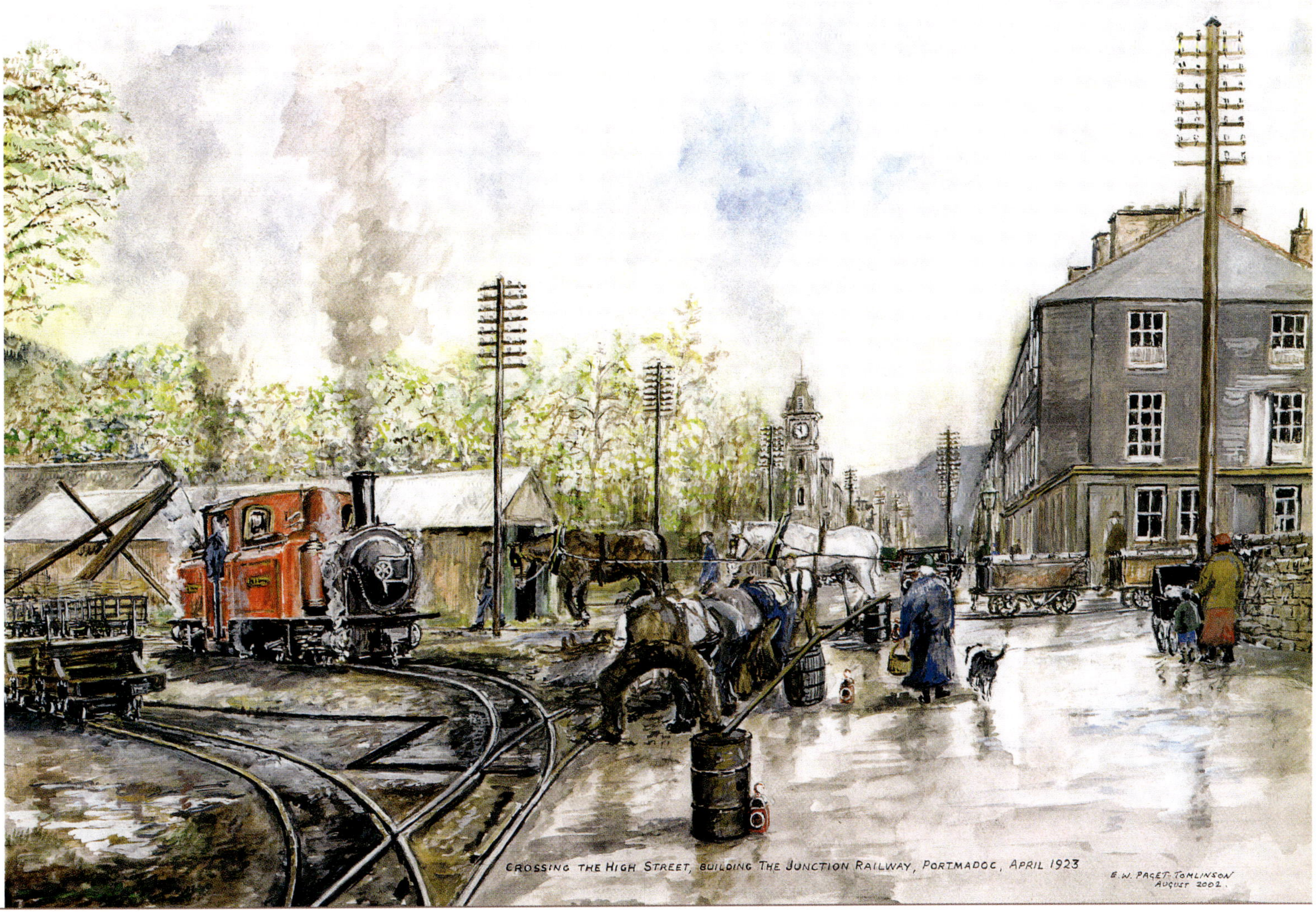
CROSSING THE HIGH STREET, BUILDING THE JUNCTION RAILWAY, PORTMADOC, APRIL 1923
E.W. PAGET-TOMLINSON
AUGUST 2002.

Painting 34: The Welsh Slate Company's Viaduct at Rhiwbryfdir in 1887

Beyond the original upper passenger terminus at Dinas, the Ffestiniog Railway ran for another few hundred yards to the bottom of inclines serving the Oakeley, Welsh Slate Co. and Llechwedd quarries, source of much of the Railway's slate traffic. This area is Rhiwbryfdir, named after the farmhouse and hamlet that once stood here.

The painting shows The Princess propelling empty slate wagons towards one of the inclines, while to the left a couple of wagons are already being hauled up. Below is the farmhouse and smithy, with a horse being shod and slate wagons awaiting repair. In 1879 the LNWR branch line from Llandudno Junction was also squeezed into this tight valley, with a complex series of bridges to take it over narrow-gauge lines and the river. A train of LNWR six-wheeled carriages hauled by a Webb Coal Tank has just left the two-mile long tunnel from the Lledr valley and heads for the terminus at the Exchange Station, where passengers could transfer to the Ffestiniog Railway. Dominating the scene is the horse-drawn train on the remarkable viaduct belonging to the Welsh Slate Company, which linked the quarry to the left to the Glan-y-Don slate mill to the right. Originally carried on three timber piers, the right-hand two were rebuilt with masonry at the LNWR's expense for safety reasons. Above the viaduct can be glimpsed Plas Weunydd, originally the house of J.W. Greaves, owner of Llechwedd Quarry, and now its offices.

One of the problems facing the quarries in this narrow valley was space to tip slate waste and a visitor today will see that it was achieved in part by tipping over most of the left-hand part of the scene as far as the Ffestiniog boundary. Thus the whole of Rhiwbryfdir, including the incline, is buried under tips. The Ffestiniog line has long been lifted, but the track bed remains and there have been embryo plans to reinstate it as a link to the tourist attraction in the Llechwedd Slate Caverns. The viaduct has been demolished except for the stub of the wooden pier and the tip to the right was removed during landscaping work in the 1970s. The standard-gauge Conwy Valley line is the only surviving feature still in use today in this bleak industrial landscape.

Client's Comments

I often comment that for every one ton of finished slate comes ten tons of waste, which has to go somewhere, and almost this whole scene is now buried under waste rock. The great waste tips that dominate the entire landscape around Blaenau Ffestiniog are mute testament to man's ravaging of the mountains around the town. It was the northern end of the valley where the Ffestiniog Railway terminated originally that I asked Edward to capture for me. In the draft the LNWR Coal Tank was in the foreground, with the narrow gauge below and behind, but Edward realised the value of the farmhouse and smithy and how right he was. He has created a domestic and pastoral scene amid the industrial setting so well captured you can easily imagine the crash of slate waste above the sound of the farm and the trains. Again Edward has captured a piece of history. I know that he "lived" each of his paintings, and perhaps that is why, in a rare forgetful moment, when Edward signed it upon completion, he dated it November 1887 and not November 2000!

Richard Pyatt

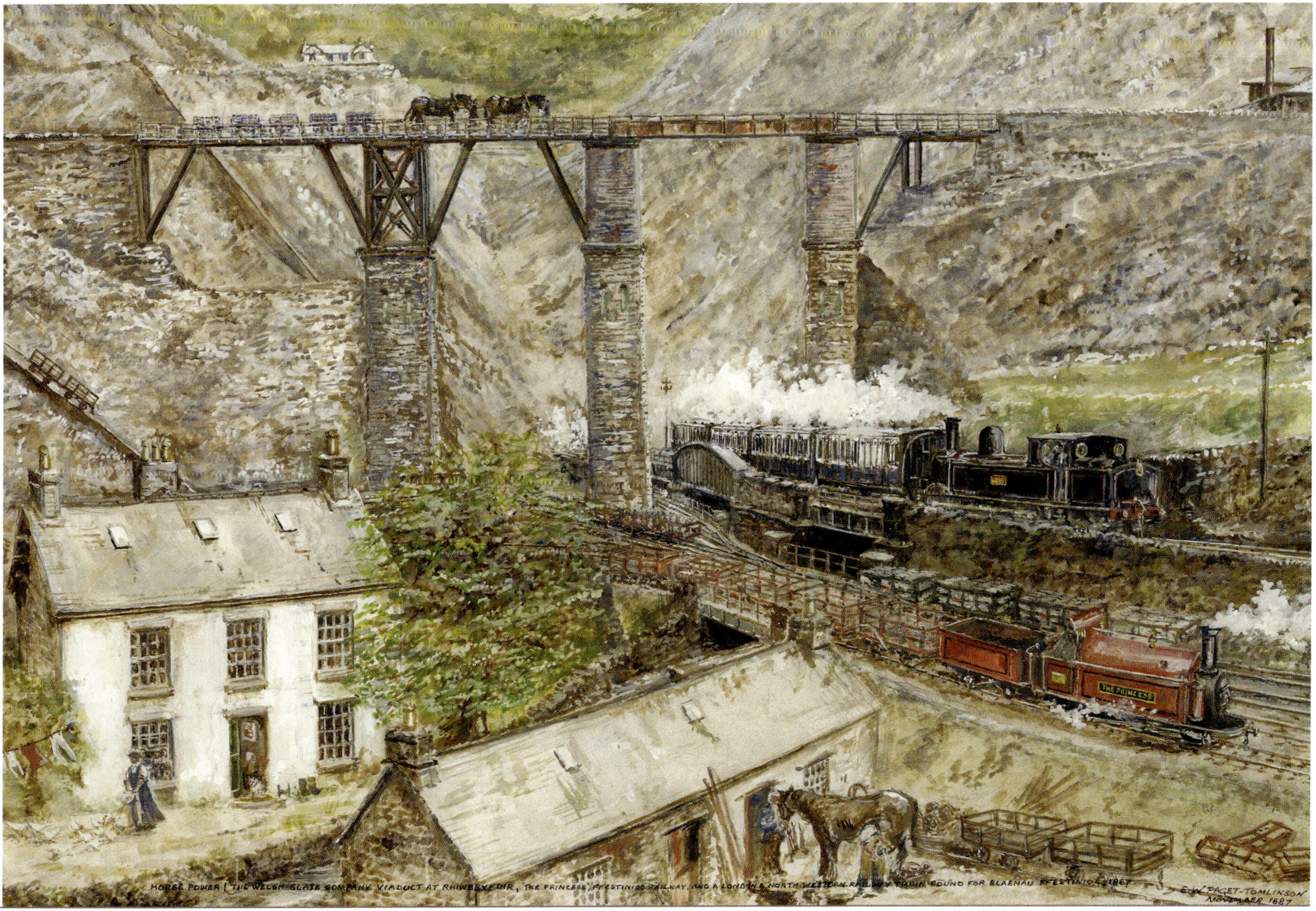
HORSE POWER! THE WELSH SLATE COMPANY VIADUCT AT RHIWBRYFDIR, THE PRINCESS, FFESTINIOG RAILWAY, AND A LONDON & NORTH WESTERN RAILWAY TRAIN BOUND FOR BLAENAU FFESTINIOG, 1887.
THE PRINCESS
E.W. PAGET-TOMLINSON
NOVEMBER 1887

Painting 35: Beddgelert at Bryngwyn in 1892

Bryngwyn, the southern terminus of the original main line of the North Wales Narrow Gauge Railway, when opened in 1877 aspired to be the justification for the railway's existence, being at the foot of the incline from the slate quarries on the slopes of Moel Tryfan. It was only after the opening that the line to Rhyd Ddu became the main line and the line to Bryngwyn the branch. The branch ran for almost 2½ miles from Tryfan Junction through open country before entering Bryngwyn Station. There was no village and the casual visitor would have alighted from the train and briefly pondered at the purpose of the journey until observing the incline rising 245ft from the end of the station to Drumhead half a mile in the distance. However, this didn't deter a nineteenth-century guide book from recommending the branch for its "scenic attractions" and "the commanding views across Caernarfon and Anglesey". Down this incline, with the silhouettes of the slate tips beyond, descended the finished products from the quarries of the Moel Tryfan area ready for Beddgelert to haul to Dinas and transfer to the LNWR for onward shipment.

The painting depicts Beddgelert and an "Ashbury" guard's composite coach (No. 1 or 2) waiting to depart for Dinas having brought a mixed train which included the empty slate wagons waiting to ascend the incline. Perhaps the crew will wait for a full load to descend before leaving. The year is 1892 and the engine has recently been turned to run bunker-first up to Bryngwyn, to improve adhesion on the steeply-graded branch. Despite the provision of Westinghouse brakes in 1892, the practice, at this time, was to marshal the full slate wagons between the engine and the coach.

Client's comments

Bryngwyn was an isolated location and, despite the enthusiasm of the guidebooks, failed to attract the attention of the tourist and much less the cameras of nineteenth-century photographers. Beddgelert (built by Hunslet in 1878) was also something of an enigma, avoiding the lens that seemed to favour its slightly more photogenic contemporaries Snowdon Ranger and Moel Tryfan, both 0-6-4T Fairlies of 1877. This trio of locos provided the motive power for the NWNGR for almost thirty years until Beddgelert was scrapped, reputed to be worn out, in 1906. It was the lack of photographs and information and the air of obscurity that originally attracted me to Beddgelert many years ago, the only loco of its class. For a narrow-gauge engine in North Wales it was probably, also, one of the largest running on two-foot gauge. Beddgelert, it is said, was built to work the traffic on the Bryngwyn branch so, in discussion with the artist, it seemed fitting to place the engine at this location considering that no known pictorial evidence exists to confirm this report.

Karl Westlake

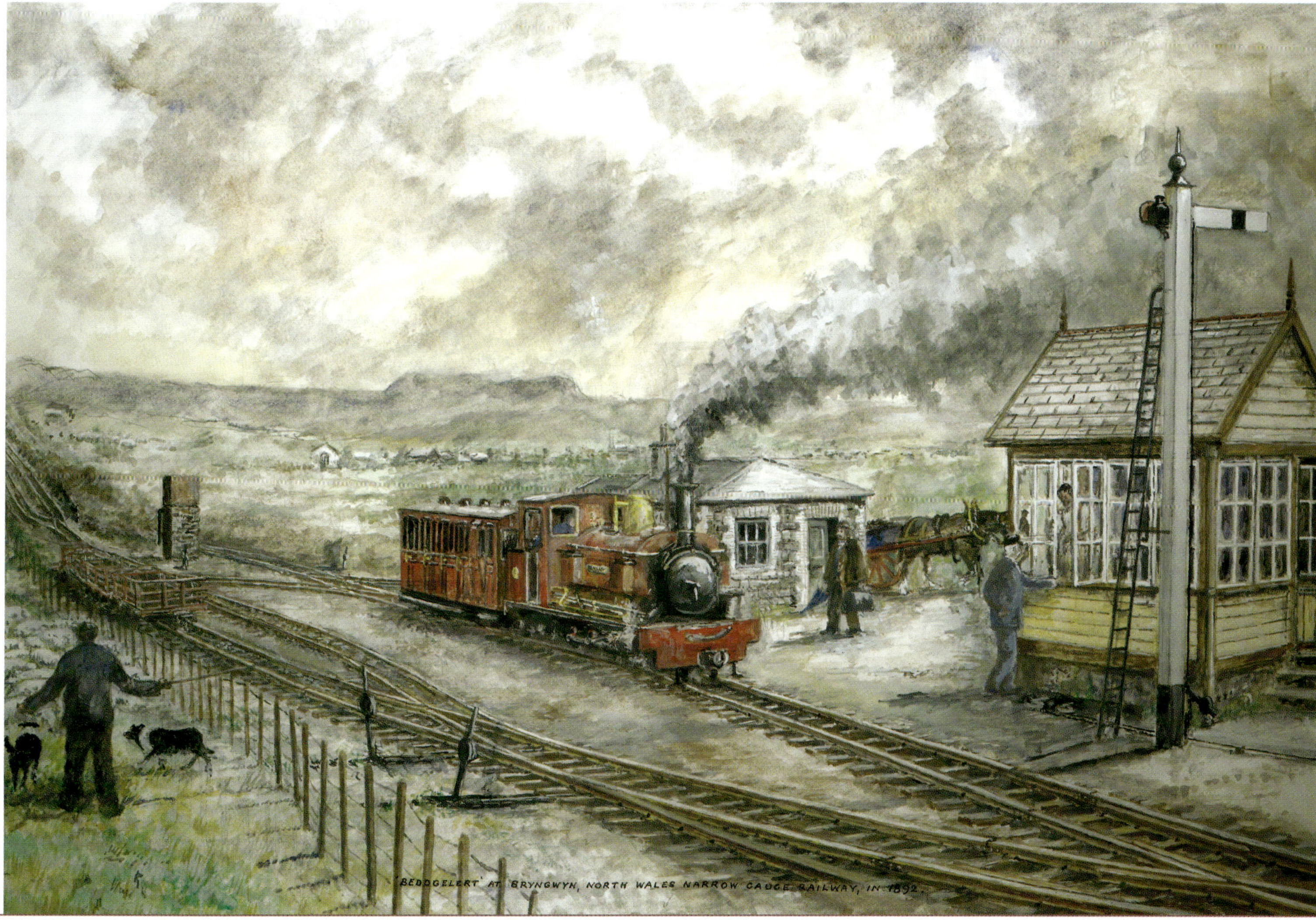
'BEDDGELERT' AT BRYNGWYN, NORTH WALES NARROW GAUGE RAILWAY, IN 1892.

Painting 36: Spooner's Boat at Portmadoc Harbour Station in 1871

In pre-locomotive days the Chief Engineer of the Ffestiniog Railway, Mr Charles Easton Spooner, had a gravity-powered inspection vehicle constructed to allow him to travel along the line at the back of a horse-drawn train of empty slate wagons, and then drift back down to Portmadoc under the power of gravity. The boat-shaped prow reputedly allowed the vehicle to push open the light field-boundary gates across the line as the carriage perambulated down. In addition a sail was provided in order to traverse the Cob, the only horizontal stretch of line. Due to its strange design, being part boat and part railway vehicle, it was christened Ni L'un Ni L'autre, this name supposedly being painted on the prow, though in common parlance it was known as "Spooner's Boat".

The painting is of the original Harbour Station before the present stone buildings were erected. The wooden station building was roughly where the later Goods Shed, now Spooner's Bar, is located. Mountaineer, representing the England engines in original condition, stands at the head of a train of early four-wheeled carriages, including one of the open type with leather aprons and canvas roof to provide passengers with some protection from the weather. To the right there is another carriage standing on the line to Britannia Bridge and the slate wharves, and a corner of the original water tank is just visible, with its brick base, unusual in an area with so much natural rock. Above rise the masts and rigging of topsail schooners standing at Holland's Wharf.

On the nearer line stands Spooner's Boat, which C.E. Spooner himself is readying for a wind-powered trip across to Boston Lodge. His faithful hound is being lifted into the dog box at the rear of the Boat by the driver, while Paddy, accompanied by Meg, watches with interest from beside the water tank.

Client's Comments

There are only two known engravings that show Spooner's Boat, with one appearing to be derived from the other, and no known photographs, the vehicle being destroyed in an accident on the railway in 1886. From this engraving, and research into similar road vehicles of the period, I formulated a set of drawings in order that the Festiniog Railway Heritage Group could construct a full-size replica of The Boat for use during special occasions on the railway. This reconstruction was completed in 2005. With my interest in the early years of the Ffestiniog Railway and my research on Spooner's Boat, when the opportunity arose for a commission with Edward, this inspection carriage had to form a central feature.

Stuart Baker

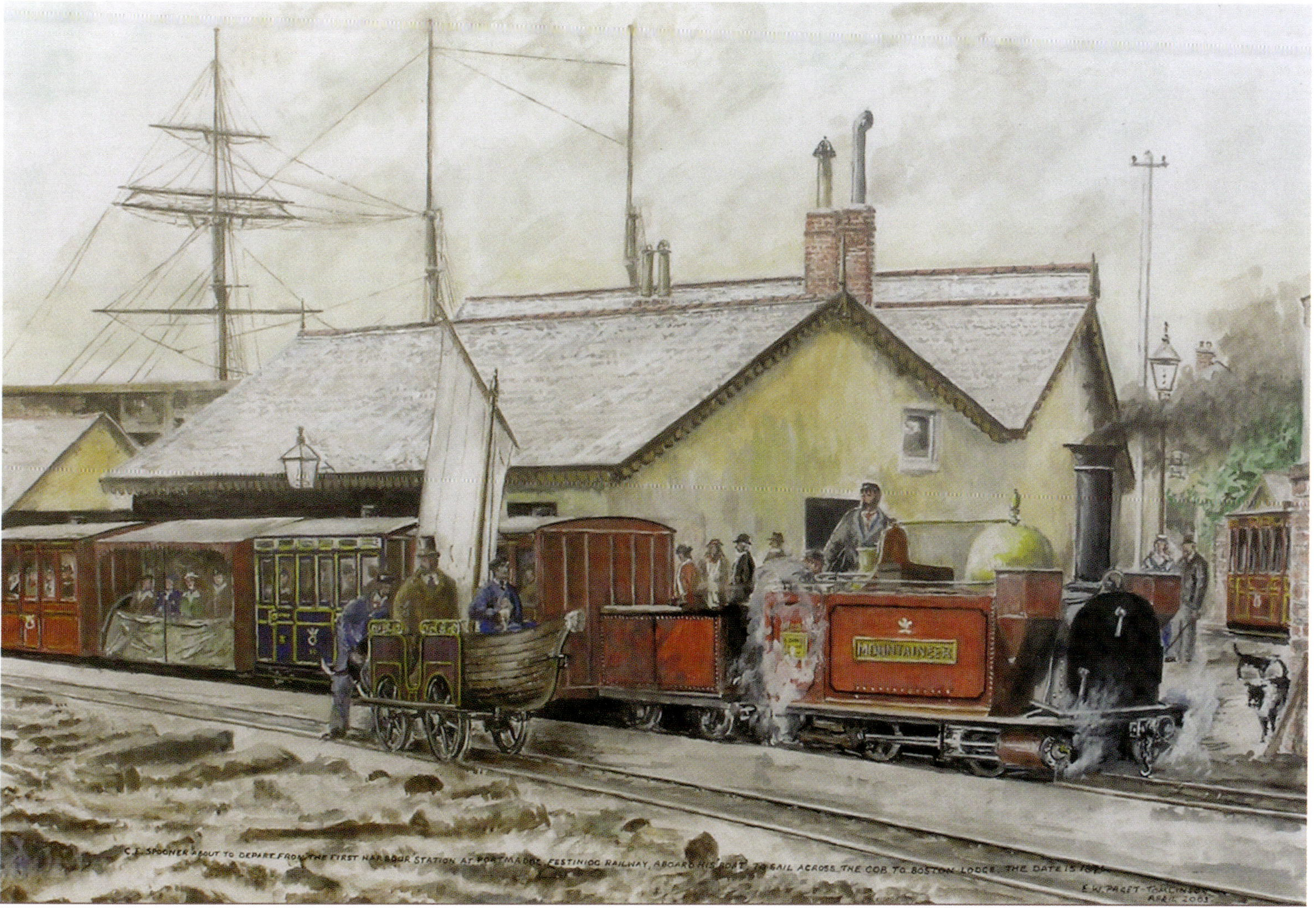
MOUNTAINEER
C.E. SPOONER ABOUT TO DEPART FROM THE FIRST HARBOUR STATION AT PORTMADOC, FESTINIOG RAILWAY, ABOARD HIS BOAT, TO SAIL ACROSS THE COB TO BOSTON LODGE. THE DATE IS
APRIL 2003

Painting 37: The New Arrivals at Boston Lodge in 1923

The year 1923 was one of great change for the Ffestiniog Railway, with the opening of the Welsh Highland Railway through to Portmadoc, the adoption of Light Railway powers, the start of Colonel Stephens' influence, and the appearance of "foreign" rolling stock for the first time. The painting shows Boston Lodge locomotive shed with, in the middle, new arrivals Russell from the Welsh Highland and the ex-War Department Simplex petrol tractor, a typical Colonel Stephens purchase for use as Bottom Shunter between Minffordd and Portmadoc. Paddy watches his master carrying out adjustments on this strange machine. An England engine stands on the left being cleaned and another passes on the right with loaded slate wagons being worked from Minffordd down to Portmadoc. A Double Fairlie is having its smoke box cleaned outside the shed.

The locomotive shed, the main running shed for the Railway, is located beside the main line just above Boston Lodge Works. The stone shed to the right dates from the 1880s and the corrugated iron extension to the left was erected soon after to cope with the increased locomotive fleet. In the background can be seen the Minffordd granite quarry, still in operation today, but with its skyline now much reduced in height.

Russell was cut down in height soon after in the unsuccessful attempt to get it to fit the Ffestiniog loading gauge, but after a varied career can be seen on the Welsh Highland Railway, Porthmadog, now restored to its original outline. The Simplex tractor has also survived and has recently been restored to original condition, apart from the cab roof. The locomotive shed is now used as carriage shed, shorn of its fine vents and roof lights, but plans are being drawn up to restore this most historic of buildings to original condition. A first step in the right direction has been the re-erection of the disc signal seen just to the right of the Double Fairlie.

Client's Comments

As a teenager in the late 1960s I was a volunteer every year on the FR with Brambleton Model Railway Club, the "Brambles", from Harpenden in Hertfordshire. We used to camp at Boston Lodge, just above the line. In the evening after a hard day at work we walked down the line to use the facilities in Boston Lodge Works. The old loco sheds on the valley of the railway always fascinated me, especially when the doors were open! Thus the location for my painting was chosen.

I wanted Russell to be in the painting as it is one of my favourite narrow-gauge engines. I first saw Russell when I was about 10 years old, looking very sad and neglected in cut-down form outside the Narrow Gauge Railway Museum at Tywyn on the Talyllyn Railway. So the choice of locomotive was easy, but it had to be in original condition. I did not want the painting showing it in its later butchered form as I first saw it. That gave the date as 1923, when coincidently the ex-WD Motor Rail Simplex petrol loco arrived on the line. It was suggested that this should be included in the painting. The first sketch showed the Simplex on the Down train, but after some discussion the Simplex was moved onto a siding and an England engine took over the Down train. The final result looks better, I think, and the original painting gives me much pleasure. **Dan Keen**

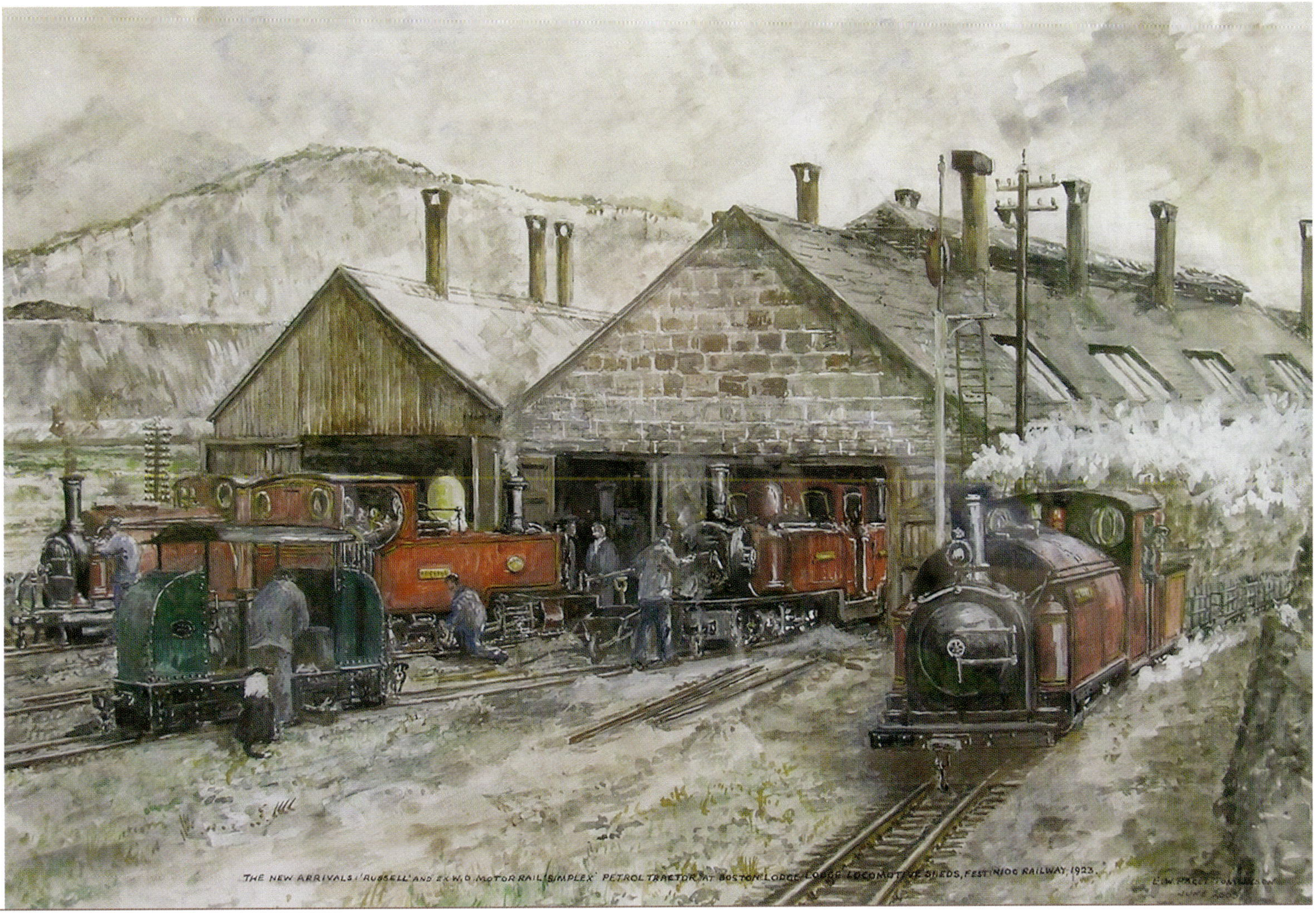
THE NEW ARRIVALS: 'RUSSELL' AND EX W.D. MOTOR RAIL 'SIMPLEX' PETROL TRACTOR AT BOSTON LODGE LODGE LOCOMOTIVE SHEDS, FESTINIOG RAILWAY, 1923.

Pen and Ink Drawings

At his own suggestion, Edward produced a series of pen and ink drawings that have been used as the cover illustrations on the quarterly newsletter of the London Area Group of the Ffestiniog Railway Society. They have a special charm, since they were produced very much for internal enjoyment, and whilst historic accuracy was still a factor, humour and artistic licence were allowed a greater place.

The first eight drawings were all of the same location, a typical Ffestiniog drystone embankment, and show the evolution of the railway and its motive power. Thus they range from horse-drawn days through to the classic outline Double Fairlie, finishing with Taliesin Single Fairlie and Spooner's Boat. Edward could not resist adding humorous touches, in one having a carriage full of shepherds and their Border collies and with The Boat pursued by C.E. Spooner's own dog.

There then followed a series of three drawings depicting a variety of trains and horse-drawn road transport at Penrhyndeudraeth, with the author's own house prominent on the right in each case. This series would have continued, but Edward tactfully explained that he was getting rather bored with drawing the railings that are a distinctive feature of this section of line. There followed a rather charming view of an England engine shunting at the Welsh Highland Railway's Bryngwyn branch terminus, but London Area Group folk soon made it clear that they prefer to have Ffestiniog scenes on their newsletter cover.

For the next few drawings in the series Edward decided to produce pen and ink versions of the latest paintings, but in each case with some subtle variations. One variation which will not be missed by experts on Ffestiniog locomotives, and not just rivet counters, is that in the drawing of the New Arrivals at Boston Lodge, Edward, with a rare lapse of concentration, has shown how a Double Fairlie would appear with a buffer beam!

The final pen and ink drawing was Edward's own idea, showing a gravity slate train in full cry, but with a couple of dogs playing a prominent role. It is apt that Edward's usual humour is there, for this was his last piece of work for the Ffestiniog, being received at the end of October 2003, just prior to his admission to hospital.

1. Horse drawn slate train

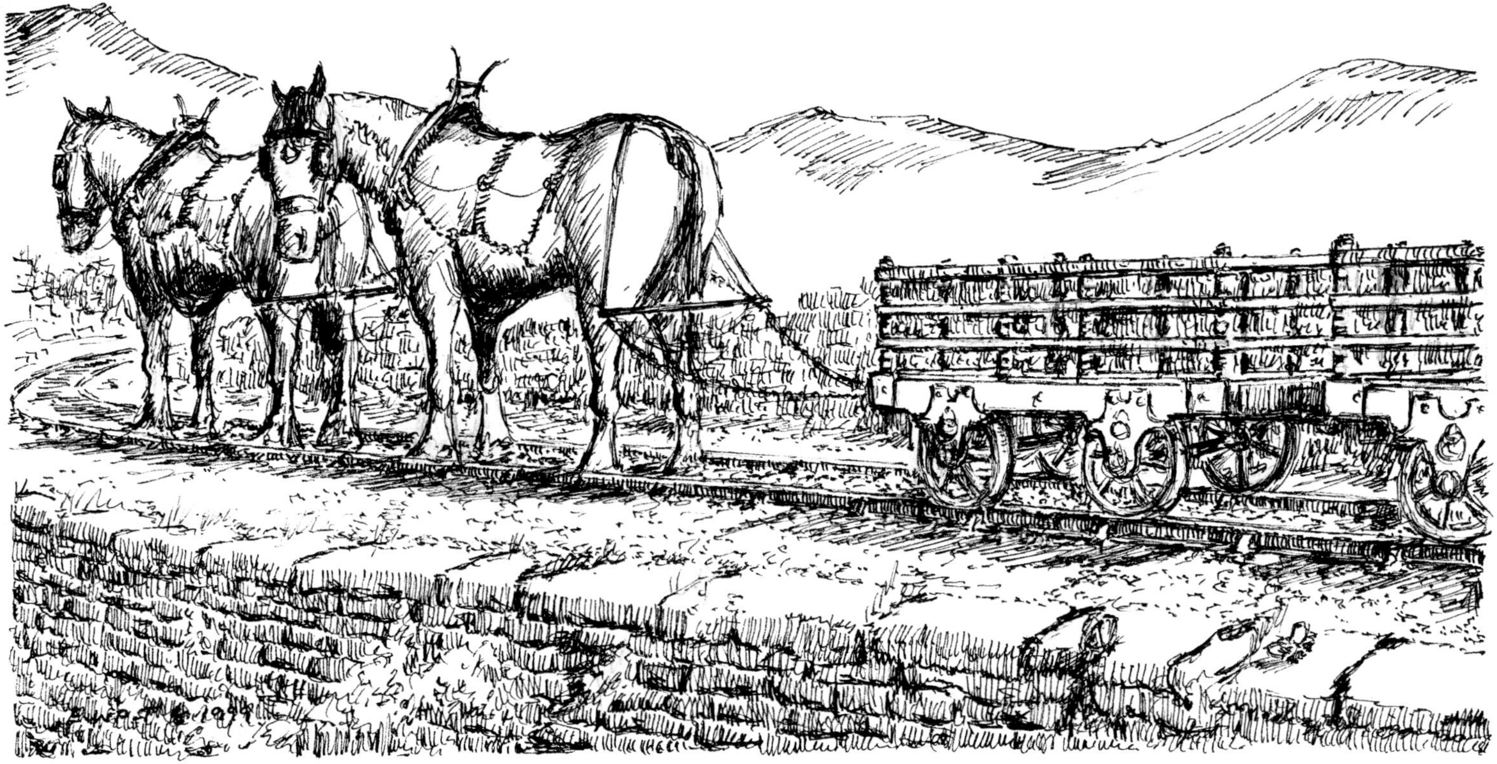

2. Gravity train with horse dandy wagon

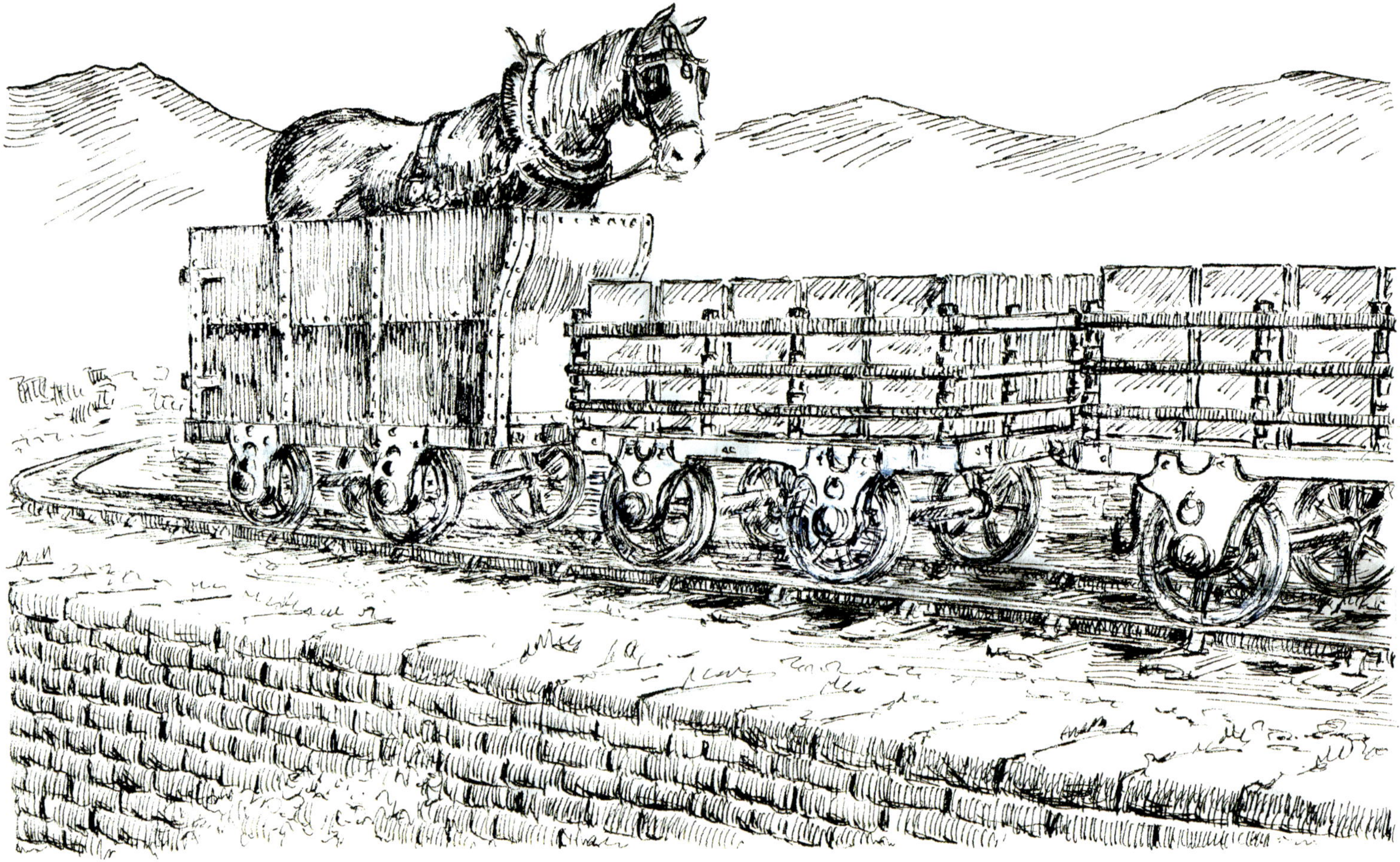

3. The Princess hauling slate empties

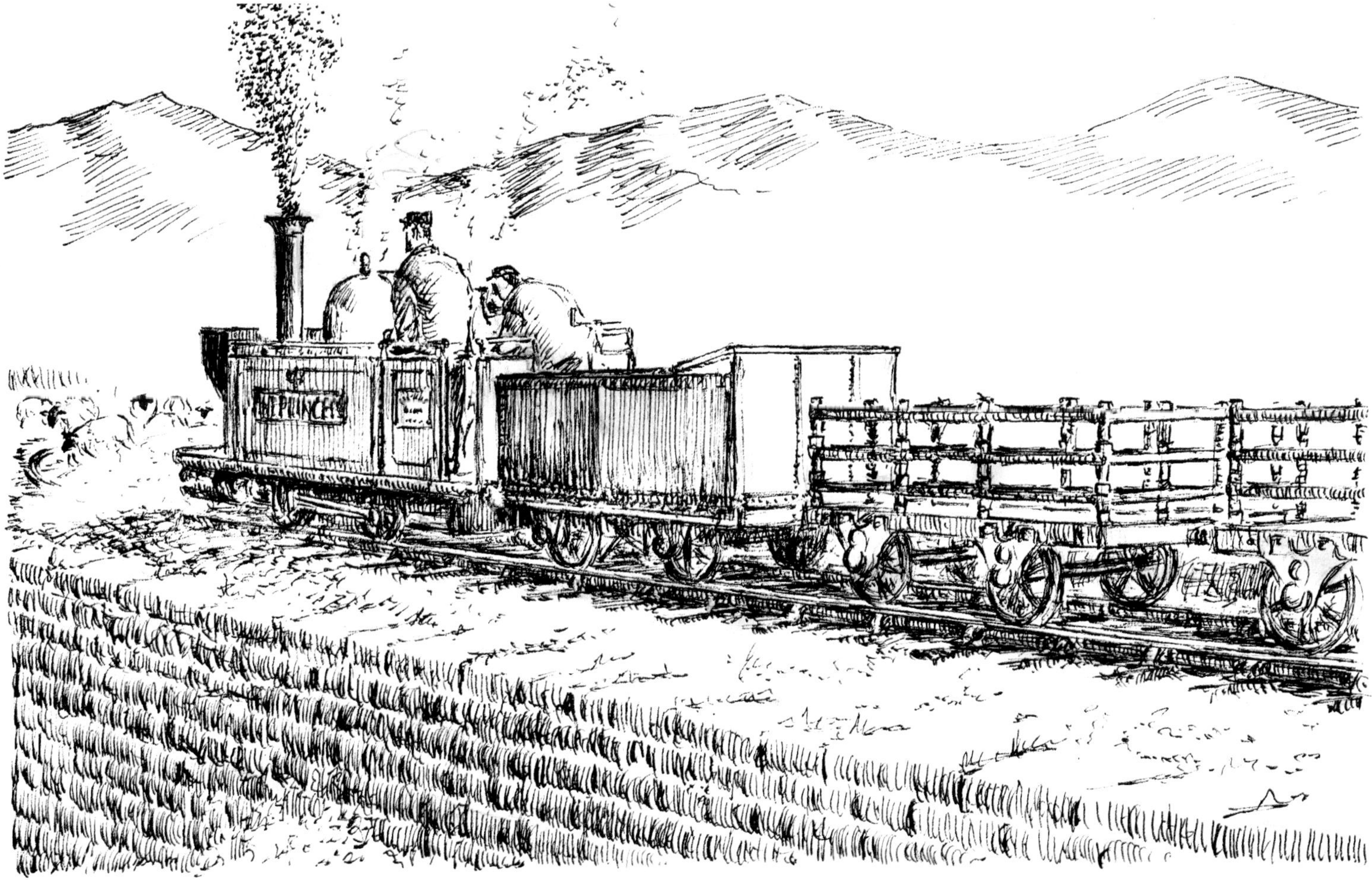

4. Welsh Pony and shepherds in open Birmingham coach

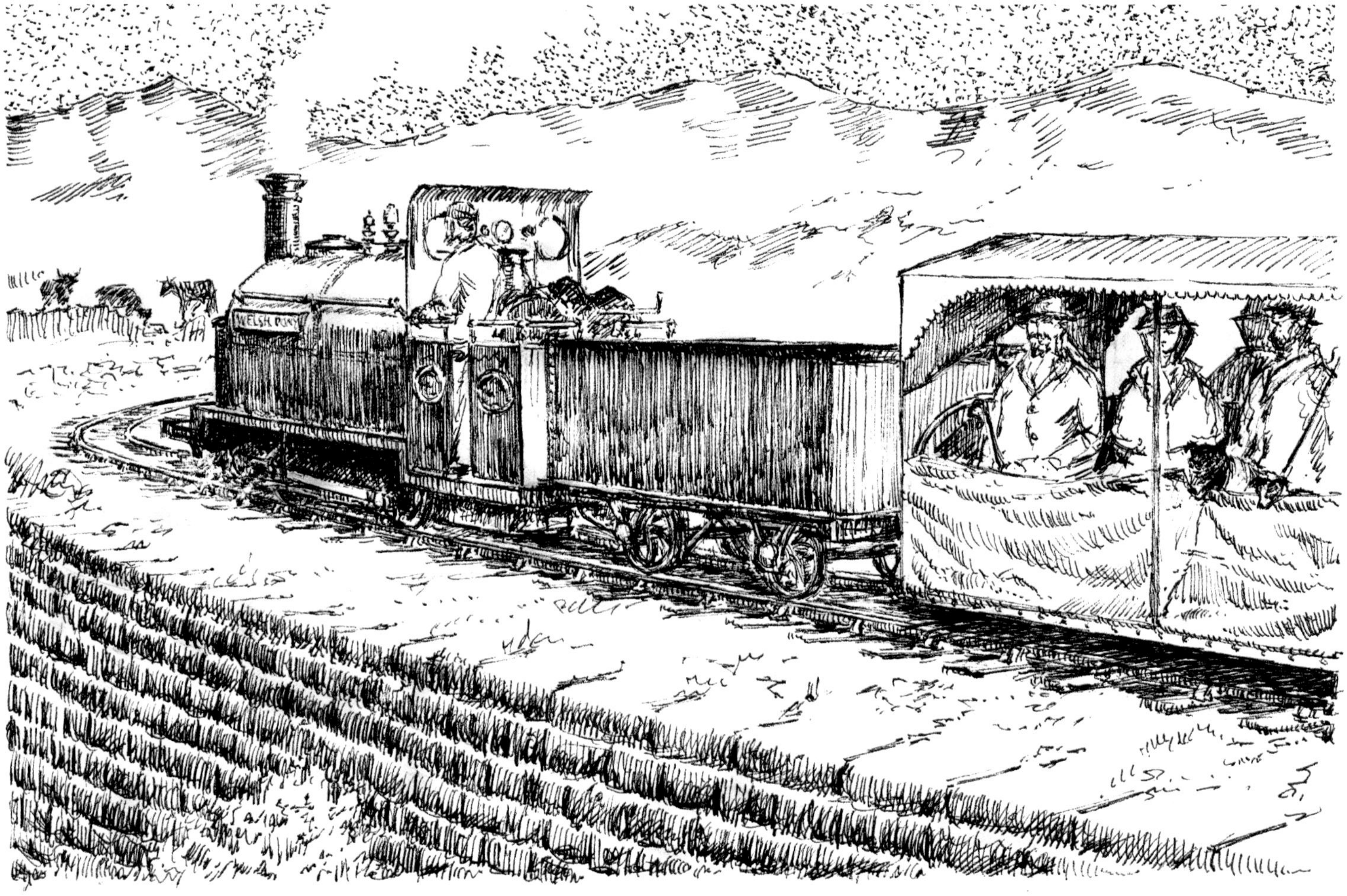

5. Little Wonder and bogie ballast wagon

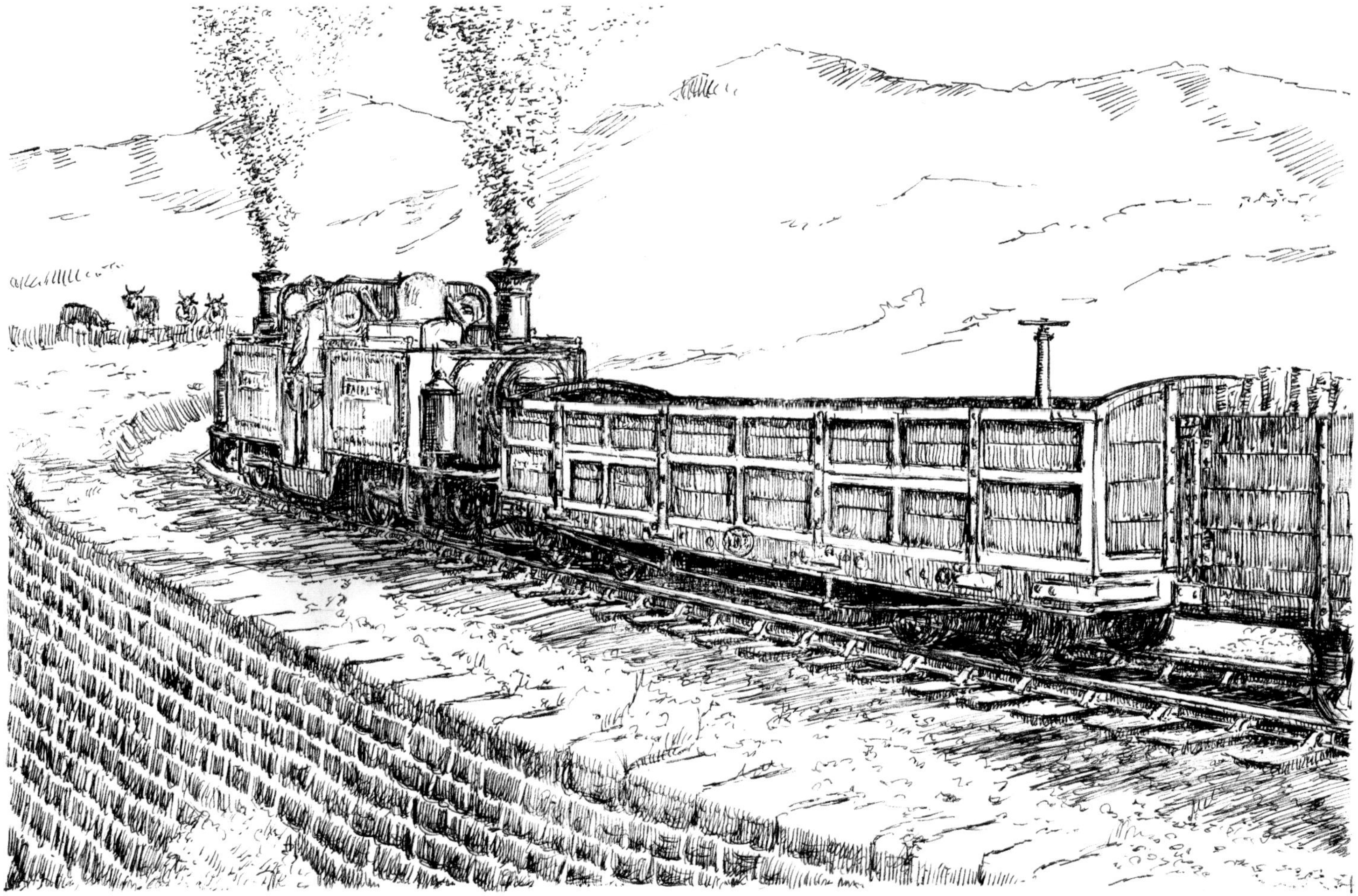

6. James Spooner and Birmingham coach

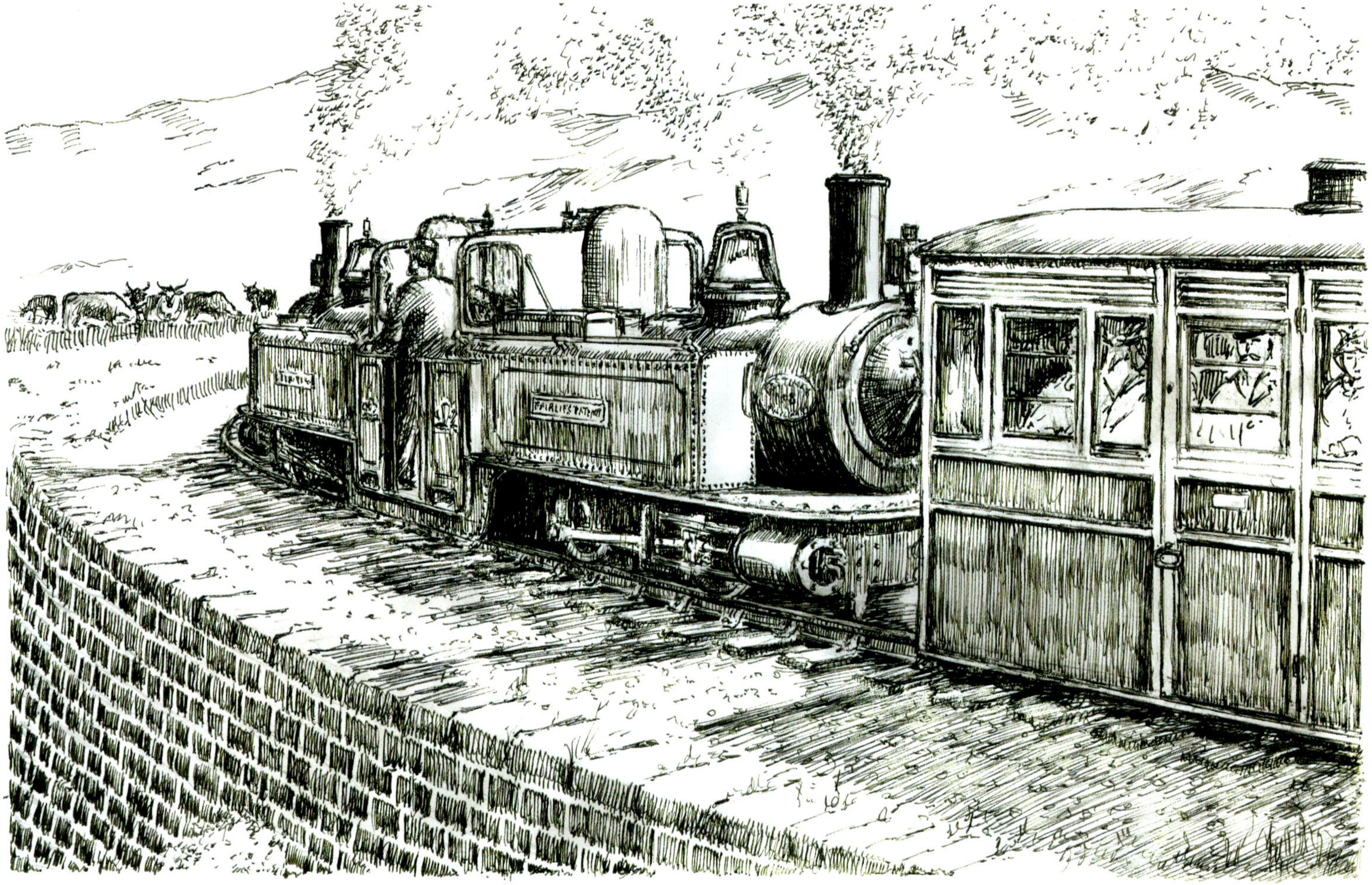

7. Taliesin and the Oakeley family carriage

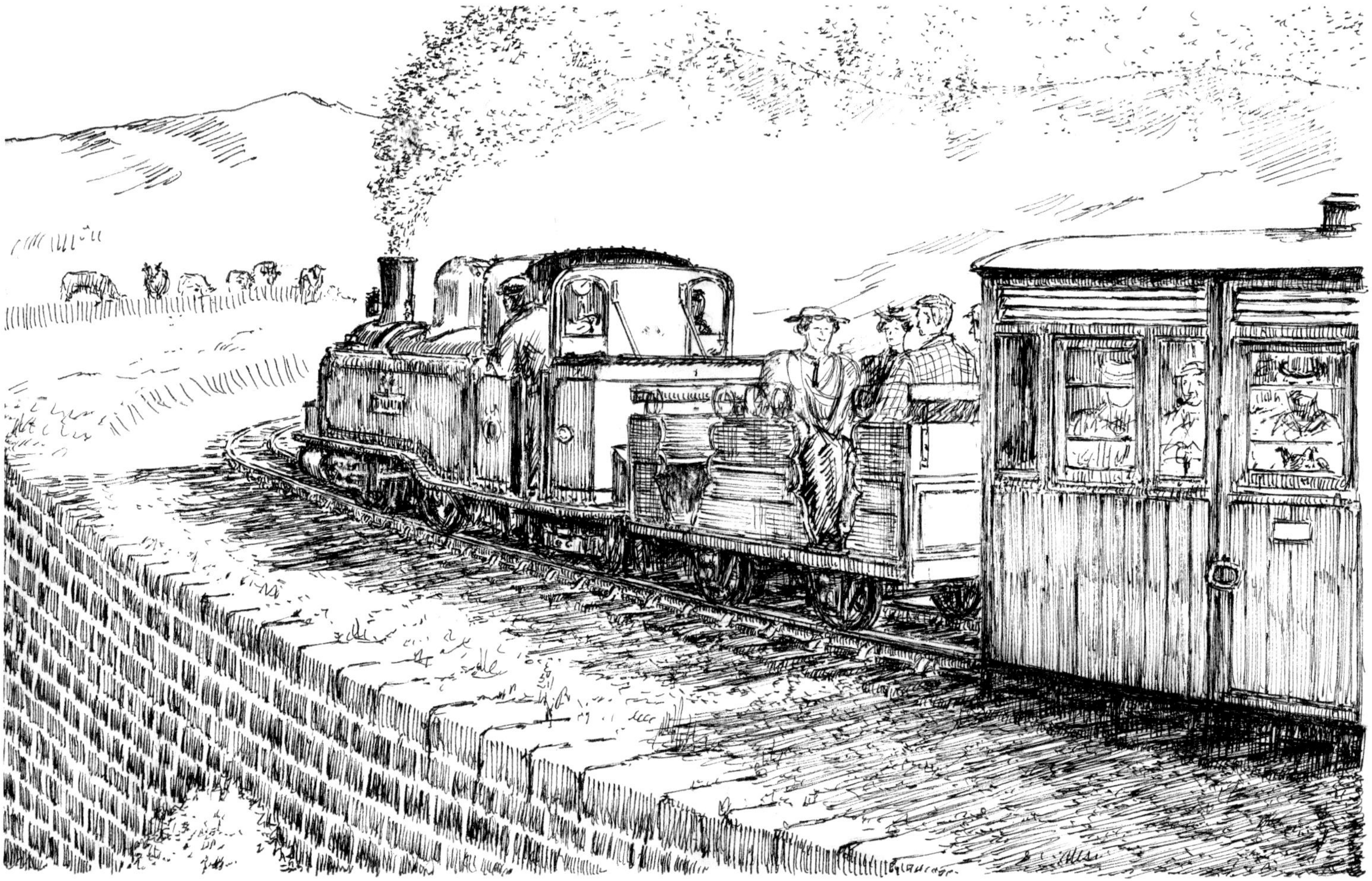

8. Spooner's Boat

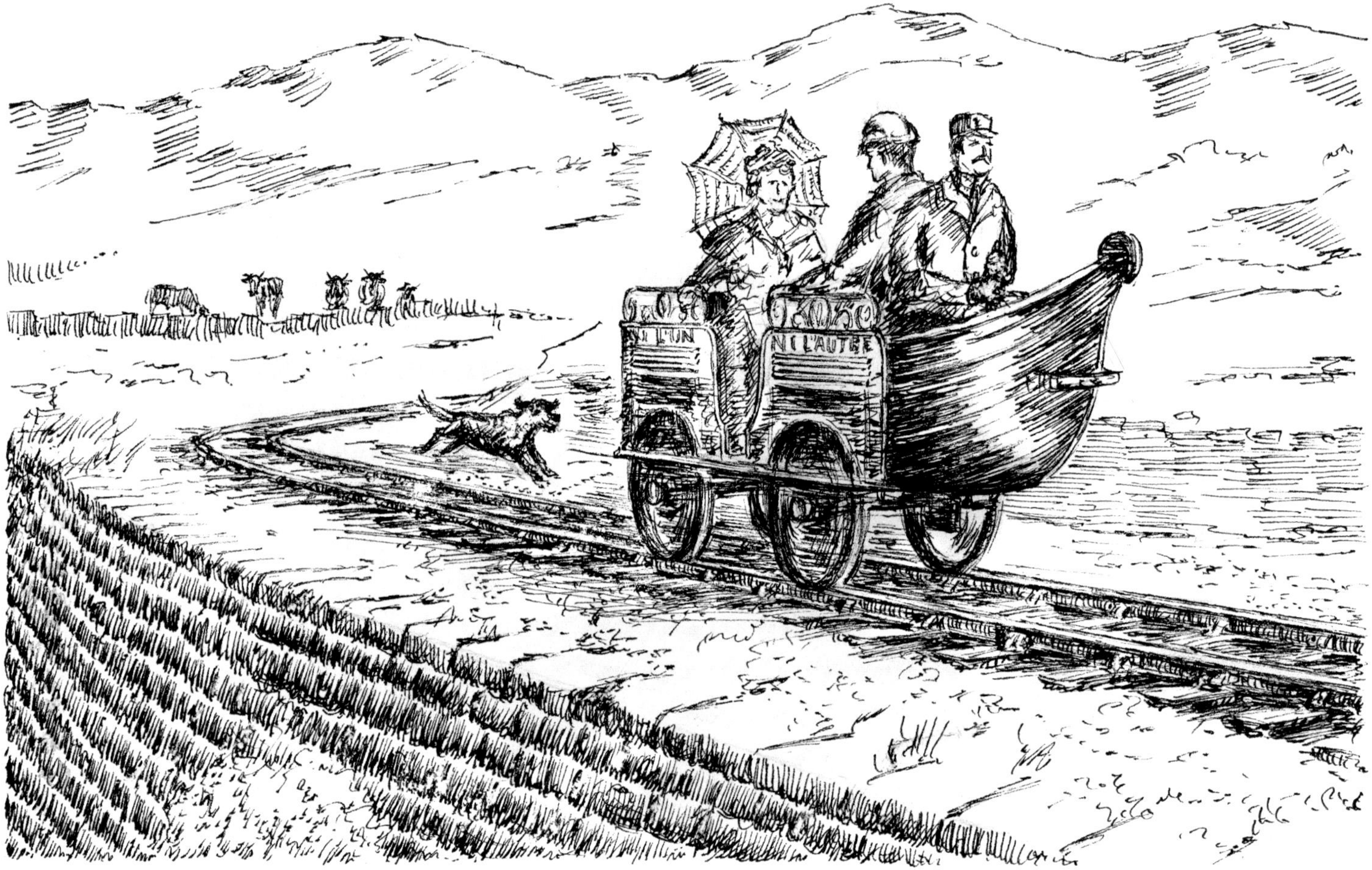

9. Welsh Pony at Penrhyndeudraeth

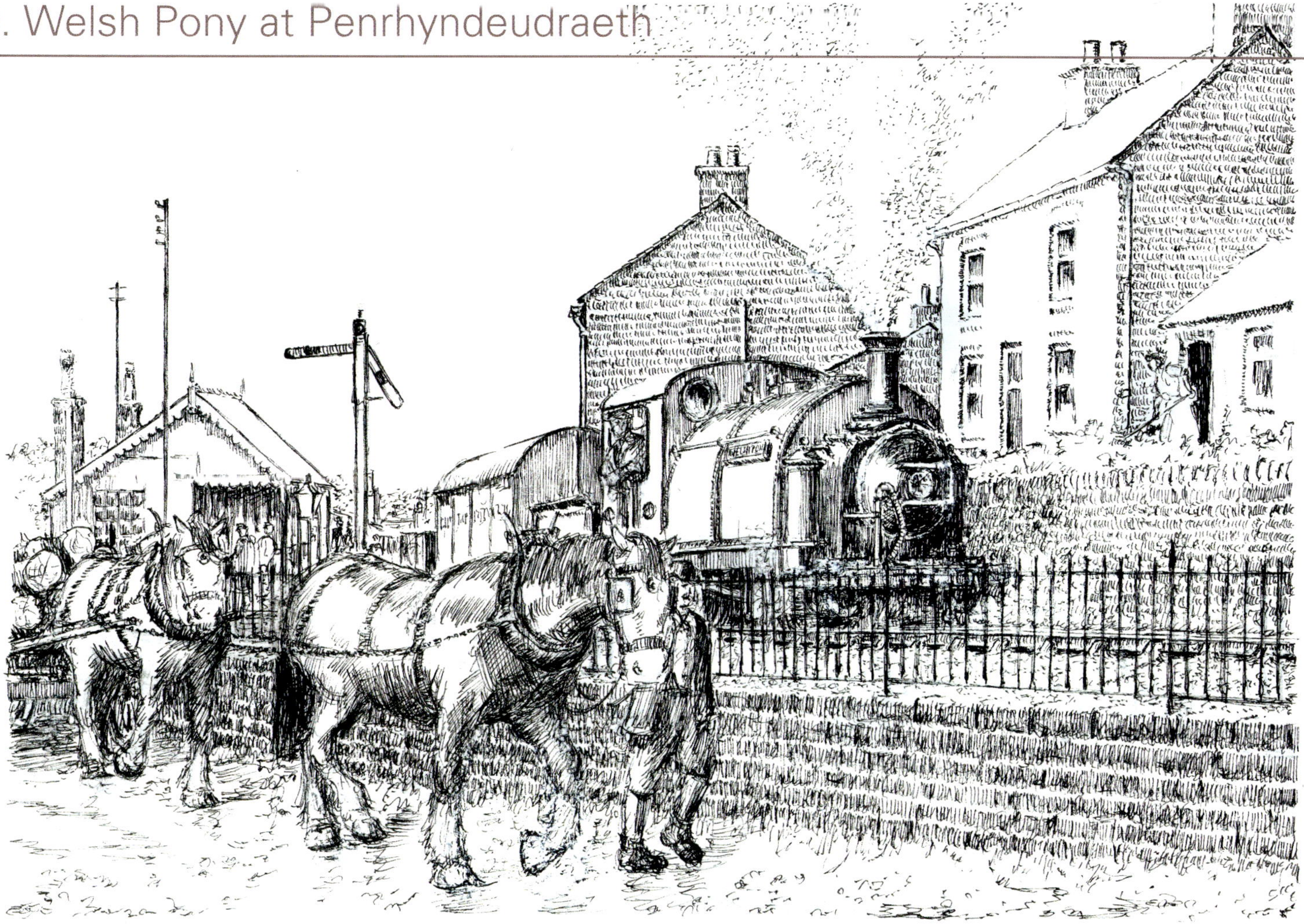

10. Merddin Emrys at Penrhyndeudraeth

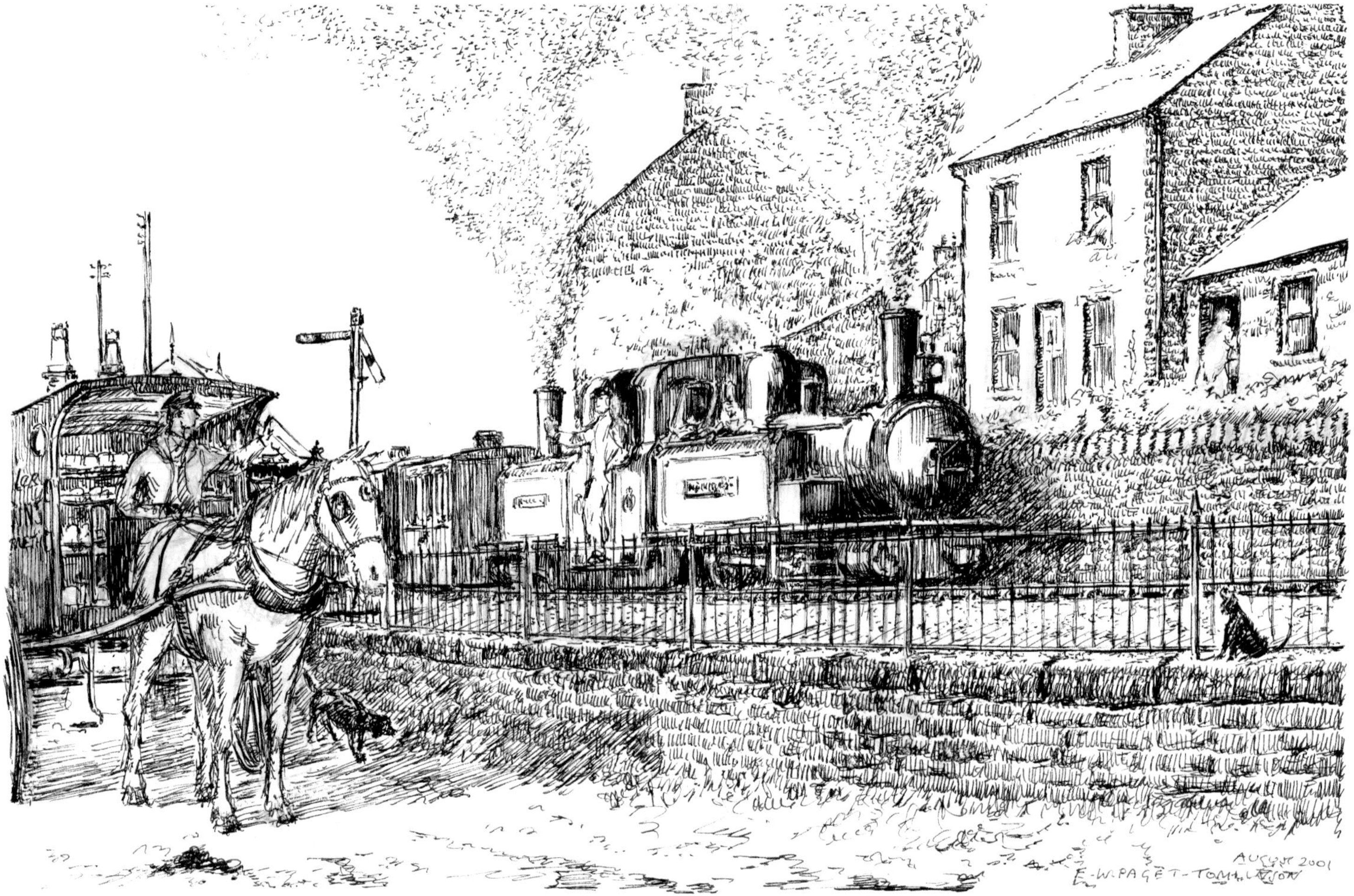

11. Gravity train approaching Penrhyndeudraeth

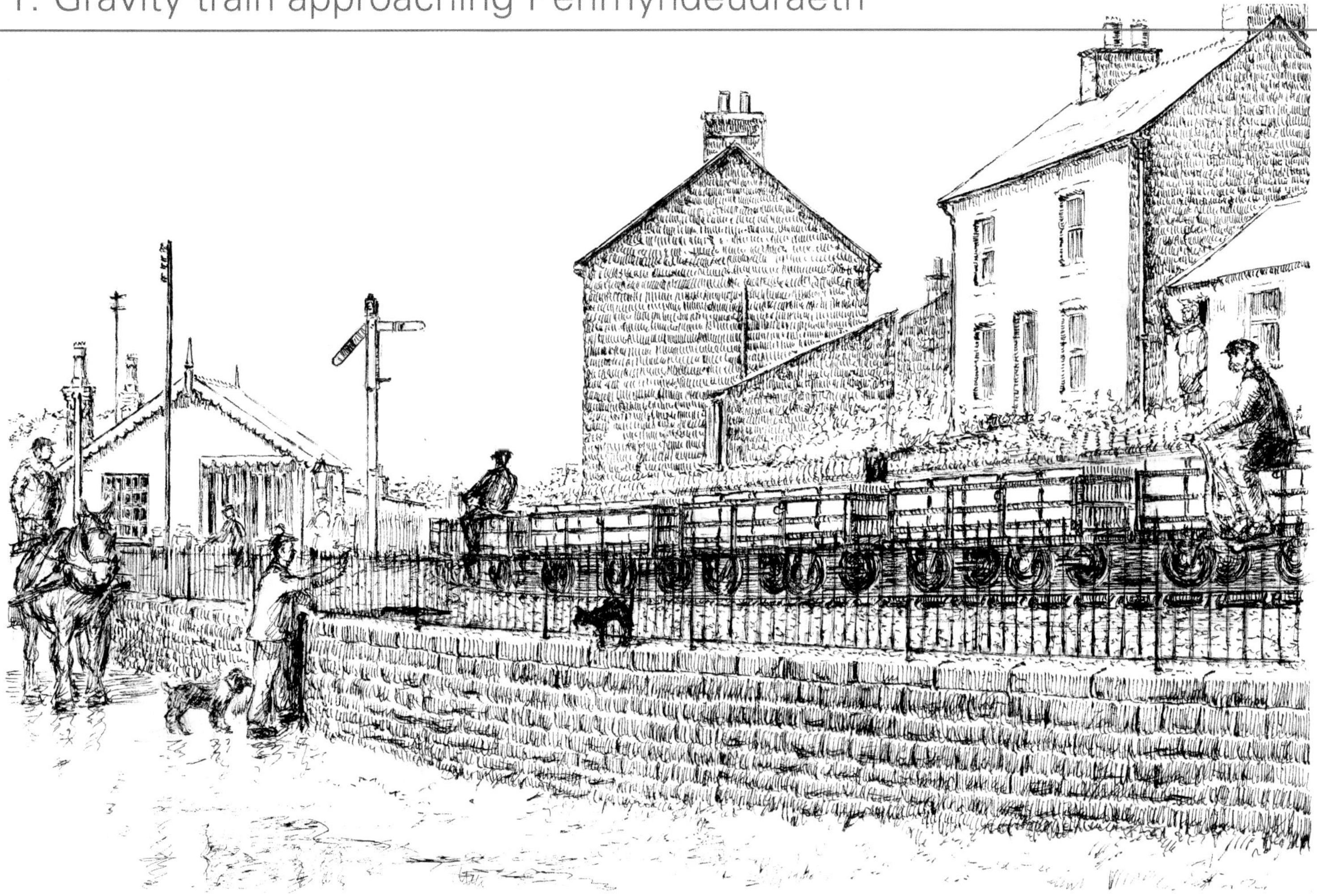

12. Prince shunting at Bryngwyn, Welsh Highland Railway

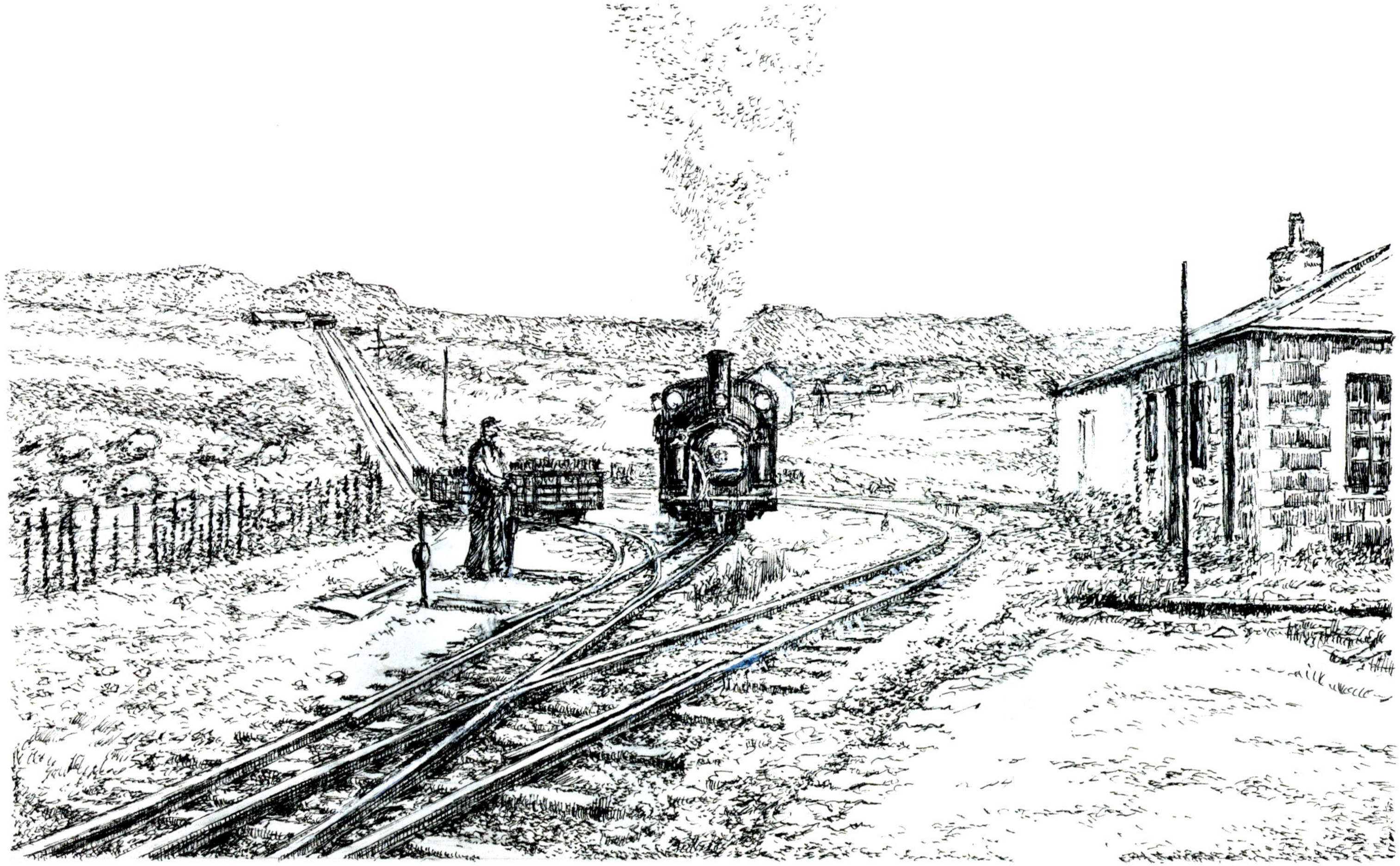

13. Little Wonder passing Boston Lodge Works

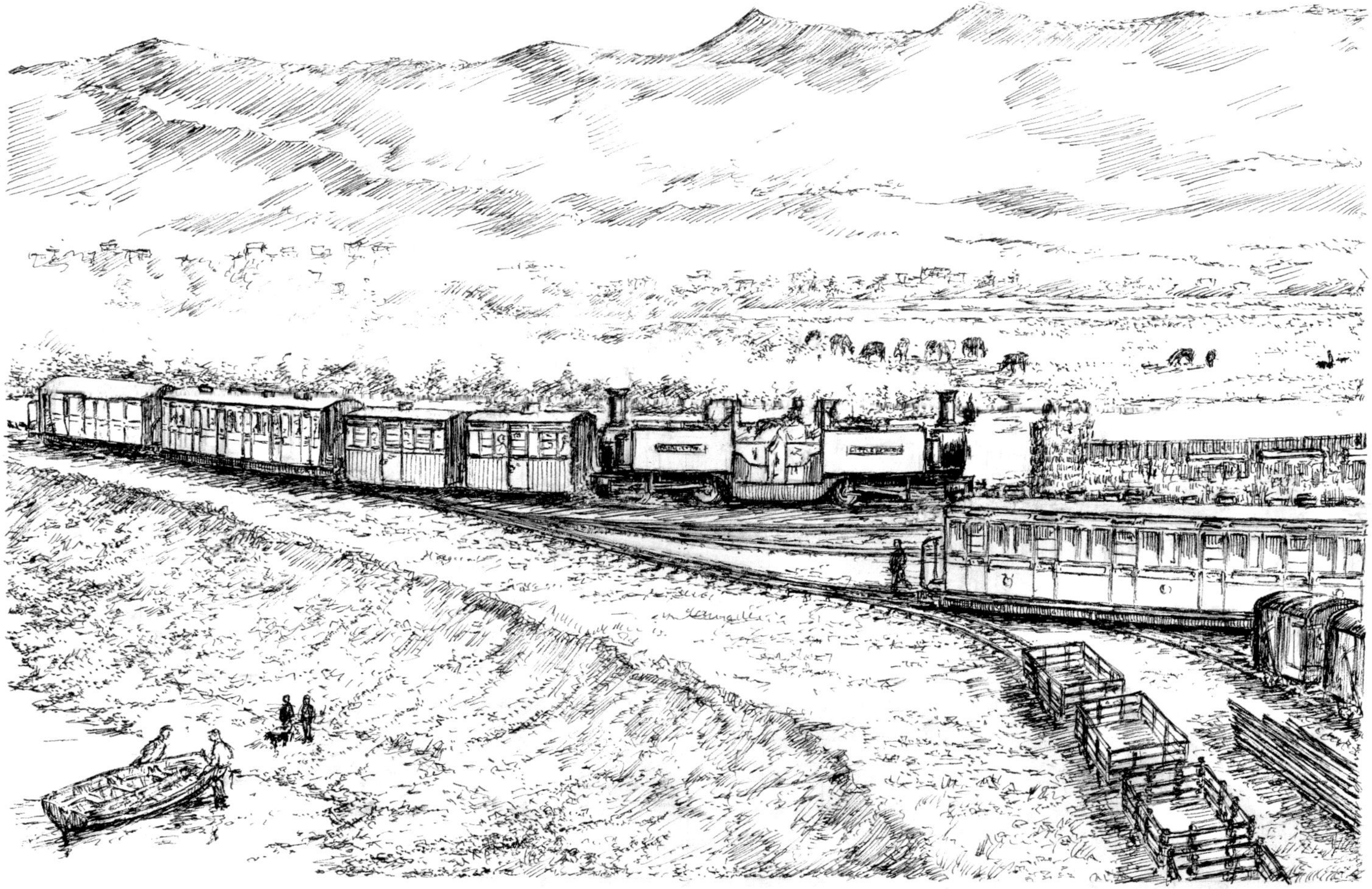

14. Building the Junction Railway at Portmadoc

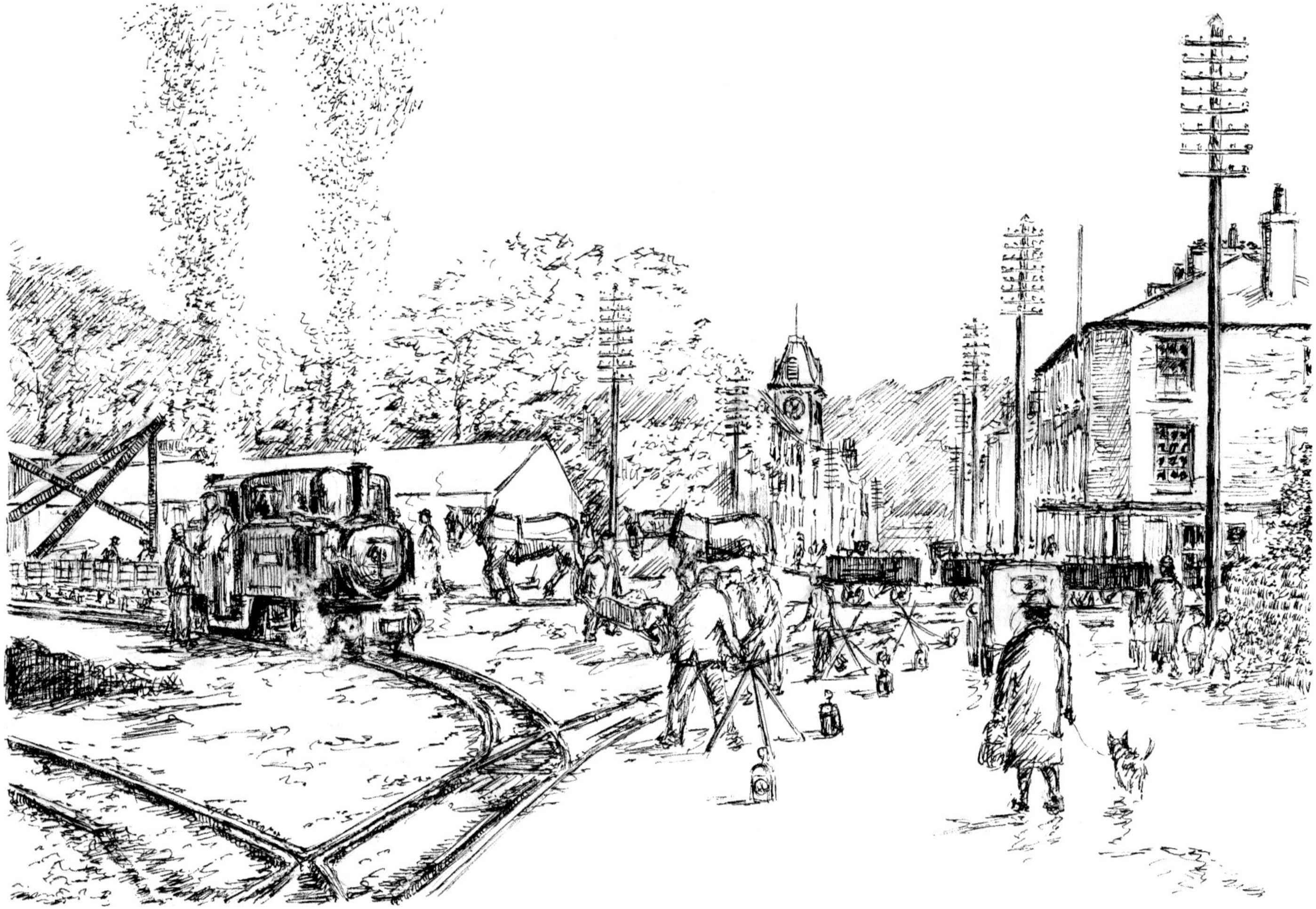

15. The Welsh Slate Company viaduct at Rhiwbryfdir

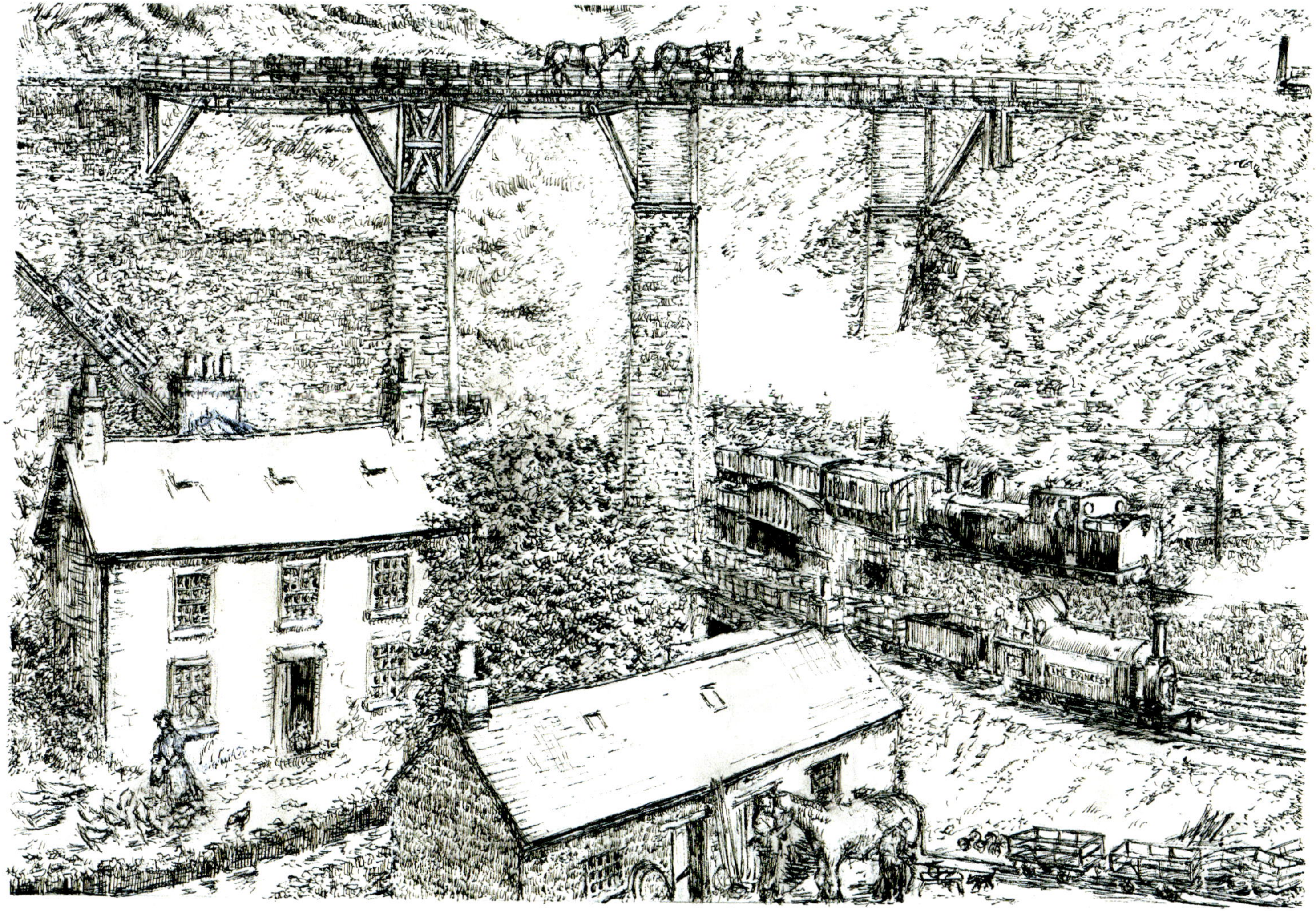

16. Spooner's Boat and Mountaineer at Portmadoc

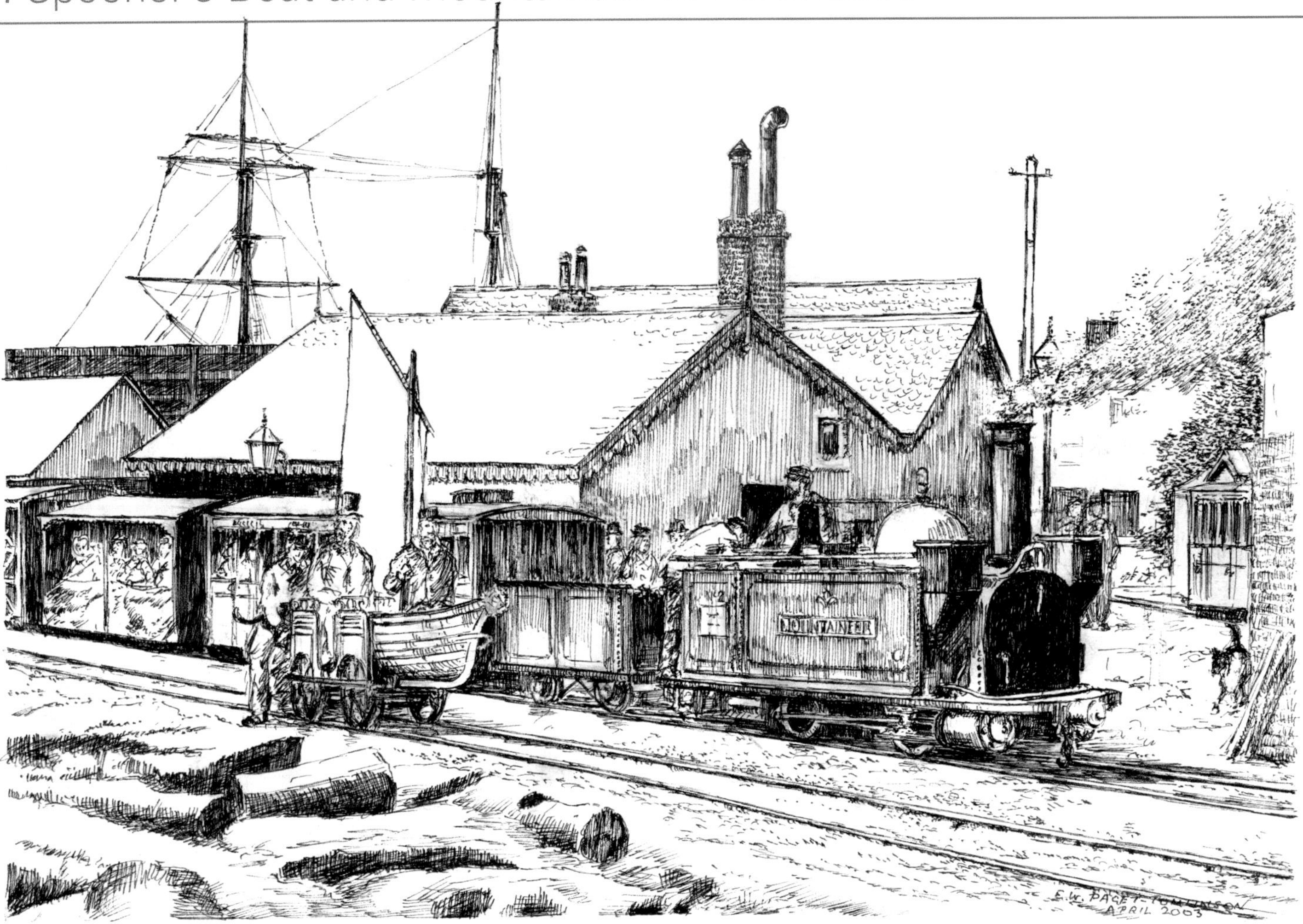

17. New arrivals at Boston Lodge locomotive shed

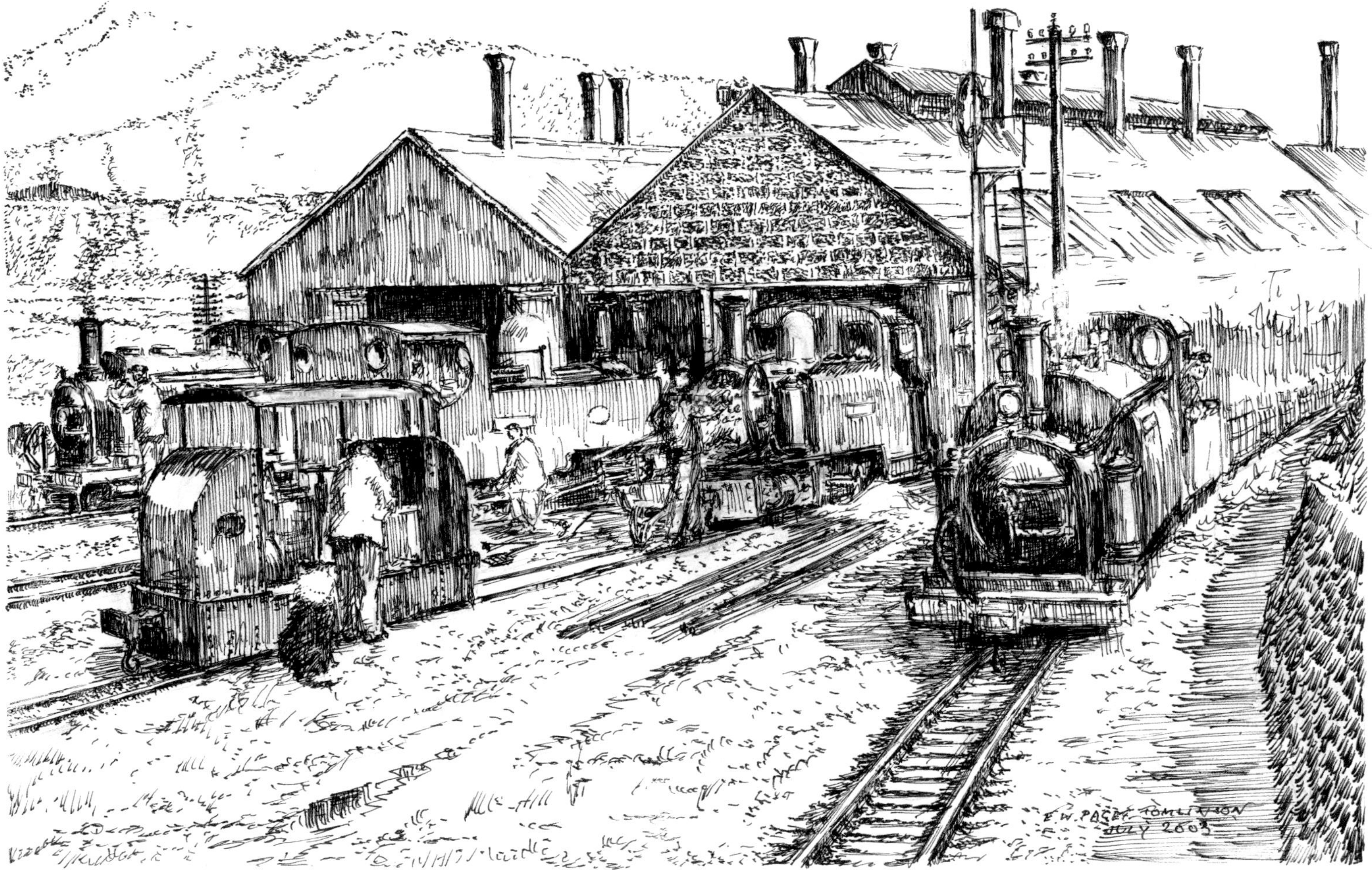

18. Gravity train and dogs

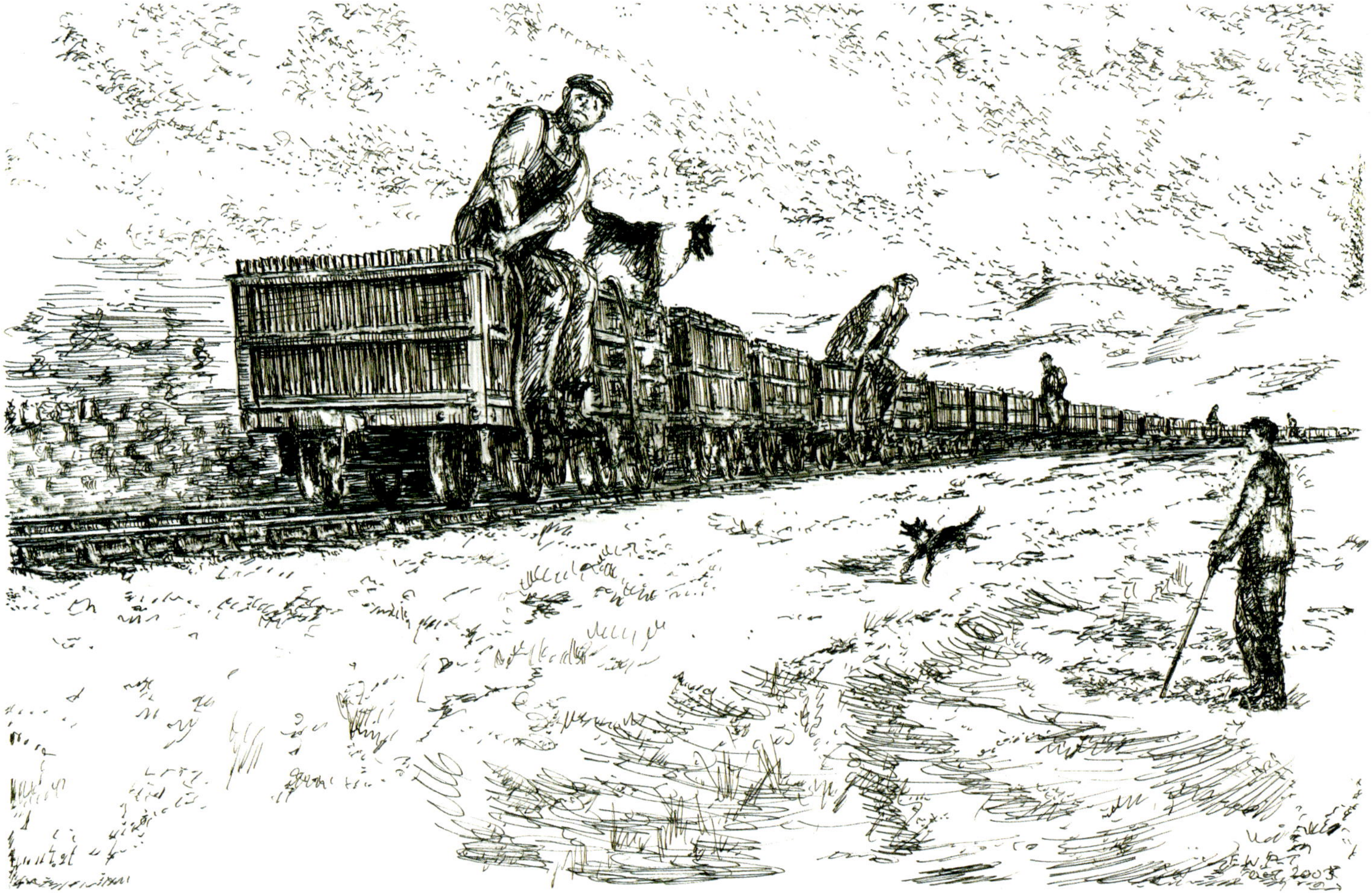

Epilogue

At the time of Edward's death in November 2003, three final paintings were planned to bring the total to forty and the agreed conclusion of the Project. As with all the paintings, there is a story behind these three commissions.

The first of the three paintings was to have been another in the preservation era, depicting a huge Scammell Constructor towing a trailer loaded with equipment for the new pump storage power station at Tanygrisiau. The author's son Chris has restored Pickfords Scammell Constructor ballast tractor PUC 475, one of a number that were used to transport equipment to both Tanygrisiau and Trawsfynydd power stations. Edward was enthusiastic about this commission and wrote in typical fashion in a letter at the end of October 2003, just prior to entering hospital – "You did send a picture of Chris's Scammell under restoration and if I have details of the site and the train, I can cope, as I can find pictures of a Scammell hauling a transformer in my own collection. A preliminary sketch will be submitted as usual." The location would have been on the new road, which cut the Ffestiniog line at the east end of the former Exchange LNWR Station. This was constructed in 1956 to improve access to the power station, the year after the Scammell was built. The Ffestiniog train would have been the Simplex petrol tractor, which made a number of trips to Blaenau Ffestiniog in the mid-1950s to recover slate wagons and redundant equipment. These trips ceased soon after, when the Ffestiniog was again severed, this time between Tanygrisiau Station and the Moelwyn Tunnel where the route was flooded by the power station's lake.

Next was to have been a painting suggested by David Newham, a Ffestiniog volunteer from the early years and much involved latterly on research and restoration of the heritage carriage fleet. David was also involved in the project to build the replica of Spooner's Boat and his commission was to have been of the day in 1886 when, legend has it, the Boat was destroyed in a head-on collision with Double Fairlie James Spooner just outside the north end of the Moelwyn Tunnel. David had done a rough sketch of what he had in mind, with members of the Spooner family leaping from the Boat just prior to impact. Needless to say, the idea greatly appealed to Edward. Sadly, David died in October 2004.

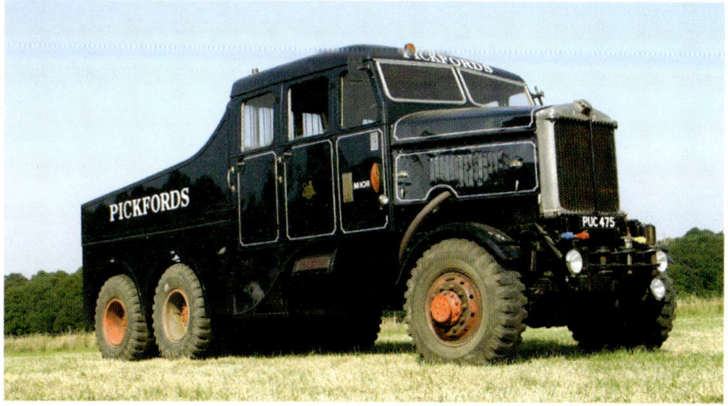

Scammell Constructor PUC 475. Photo: Nick Corley Collection

The fortieth and final painting was to have been commissioned by the author and was a scene he and Edward had been keen to do earlier in the Project, but deferred to allow other paintings to be undertaken. The author lives right beside the Railway just above Penrhyn Station and his garden runs alongside the line as it approaches the level crossing over the main road. Here from 1865 to 1879 was the original station, but no photographs exist showing it and there is little evidence of how it might have looked, although plans show a siding and even today a recess in the wall remains where the point lever was once located. The scene would have been 1863, with one of the first two George England locomotives, either Mountaineer or The Princess, on a trial run and in original condition as delivered, without a dome. They proved unsatisfactory and domes were fitted almost immediately. In the siding would have been a couple of wagons being loaded from a horse-drawn wagon from Croesor Quarry, an arrangement that ceased early in 1864 when the Croesor Tramway opened to Porthmadog.

Thus the story of the Heritage Paintings Project concluded.

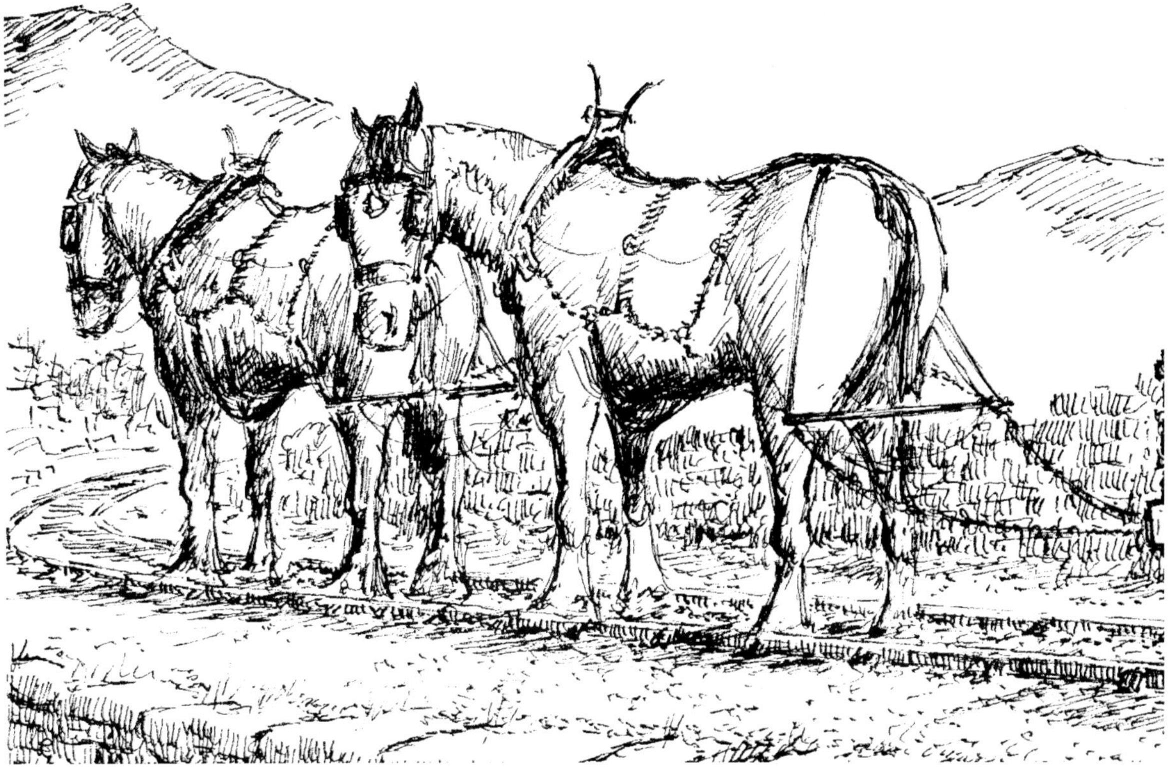